T0344945

Get the eBook FREE!

(PDF, ePub, Kindle, and liveBook all included)

We believe that once you buy a book from us, you should be able to read it in any format we have available. To get electronic versions of this book at no additional cost to you, purchase and then register this book at the Manning website.

Go to https://www.manning.com/freebook and follow the instructions to complete your pBook registration.

That's it!
Thanks from Manning!

Succeeding with AI

Succeeding with AI

How to Make AI Work for Your Business

VELJKO KRUNIC

MANNING
SHELTER ISLAND

For online information and ordering of this and other Manning books, please visit
www.manning.com. The publisher offers discounts on this book when ordered in quantity.
For more information, please contact

> Special Sales Department
> Manning Publications Co.
> 20 Baldwin Road
> PO Box 761
> Shelter Island, NY 11964
> Email: orders@manning.com

Manning Publications Co.	Acquisitions editor:	Mike Stephens
20 Baldwin Road	Development editor:	Marina Michaels
PO Box 761		and Jennifer Stout
Shelter Island, NY 11964	Technical development editor:	Al Krinker
	Review editor:	Ivan Martinović
	Production editor:	Anthony Calcara
	Copy editor:	Carl Quesnel
	ESL editor:	Frances Buran
	Proofreader:	Keri Hales
	Typesetter and cover designer:	Marija Tudor

ISBN 9781617296932
Printed in the United States of America

brief contents

contents

preface

Many AI projects are in progress today, and many of them will fail. This book will help you avoid starting an AI project that's doomed to failure and will guide you toward the projects that can succeed.

I wrote this book to help you get concrete business results, and to help you influence how AI is used in industry today. Current discussions about AI focus on algorithms and case studies of successful applications. What's lost in this discussion is the human element of AI. We see algorithms, and we know what large organizations have done with them, but what we don't hear about is the leadership needed for an AI project to achieve business success and the principles applicable to our own organizations for leading AI projects. That causes us to have unrealistic expectations of what AI can do, and when paired with only a vague understanding of the actions leaders must take for their AI projects to succeed, the result is that many of the AI projects we have in progress will fail.

This book addresses what differentiates the AI projects that will succeed from the ones that will fail. In one word, it is *agency*—a capacity that AI lacks. Conventional wisdom tells us that the determinant of success or failure of an AI project is the project team's in-depth knowledge of AI technology. Believing that success with AI is determined solely by technical prowess confounds *an enabler* with *a capability*. Although you do need to have technical skills on your team for your AI project to succeed technically, to implement AI in your business, you also need to link technical success with business results.

The very definition of *high tech* is that it refers to a newly emerging technology. As a corollary, the best practices of that technology are only developed later, once the experiences and early application of technology are understood and systematized.

This book introduces the best practices for using AI. It guides you through the treacherous waters of running an AI project in 2020 and beyond.

This book shows you how to lead an AI project toward business success, measure technical progress in business terms, and run your projects economically. You'll learn how to determine which AI projects are likely to give you actionable results, and how to get those results. Finally, this book teaches you how to analyze your technical solutions to help you find the investment opportunities with the greatest business impact.

acknowledgments

I want to thank my wife, Helen Stella, for love, support, patience, advice, and encouragement during the process of writing this book. You're there when I'm winning, and you're there while there are still challenges I have yet to conquer. Helen, I am lucky to have you in my life!

I'd also like to thank Dr. Jeffrey Luftig, from whom I learned that the key to business success is bringing together business competence and strong technical proficiency in scientific methods you're using. His work and teaching had a profound impact on my thinking (for example, his book with Steve Ouellette [1], his paper "TOTAL Asset Utilization" [2], and his course content [3]). Jeff taught me how to align business and technology, and I learned from him how to apply Peter Drucker's dictum that it's more important to be effective (do the right things) than to be efficient (to do things right) [4].[1]

I would also like to thank Steve Ouellette. Several years ago, I started writing a book quite different from this one, and Steve reviewed my early writing. This is, for all practical purposes, a very different book. Nevertheless, Steve's thoughts on my previous writing helped me write a better book.

Most importantly, I would like to thank all the early adopters of AI and other novel technologies. You're willing to take chances on the latest technologies, whose potential you have the vision to see, as opposed to playing it safe and opting for "what everyone else is using." Without people like you, software, high tech, and progress in general can't exist. You're the unsung heroes of technology revolutions.

---

[1] Peter Drucker, from "Managing for Business Effectiveness" [4]: "It is fundamentally the confusion between effectiveness and efficiency that stands between doing the right things and doing things right. There is surely nothing quite so useless as doing with great efficiency what should not be done at all."

xv

No book is the product of the author alone, and I would like to thank the Manning team. Associate Publisher Michael Stephens had the vision to understand what this book could become. All he had to work with at that time was a proposal for a book approaching AI projects from a different angle than any other book on the market. His ongoing help and guidance made this book possible. My copy editor Carl Quesnel has supplied a lot of invaluable suggestions regarding the style and the flow of the writing in this book, and the book is much better for his involvement. I would also like to thank my technical development editor, Al Krinker, for his technical review of this book and for pointing out many technical details to include in the text. In addition, I would like to thank my ESL editor, Frances Buran, who had the job of proofreading my initial drafts and correcting many spelling, grammatical, and typographical errors in them.

I would also like to thank the reviewers of this book. Our whole community owes gratitude to people like them. These reviewers are presented with texts and ideas still in draft form. They donate their considerable knowledge and experience to read and evaluate writing full of rough edges and then help authors to revise their rough ideas so that the whole community can benefit. I'm embarrassed to realize how rarely I think about the work of reviewers when I'm a reader of the finished book. As an author, I came to appreciate their role, help, and guidance, and I did my best to incorporate their advice in this book. Those reviewers were Andrea Paciolla; Ayon Roy; Craig Henderson; David Goldfarb; David Paccoud; Eric Cantuba; Ishan Khurana; James J. Byleckie, PhD; Jason Rendel; Jousef Murad; Madhavan Ramani; Manjula Iyer; Miguel Eduardo Gil Biraud; Nikos Kanakaris; Sara Khan; Simona Russo; Sune Lomholt; Teresa Fontanella De Santis; and Zarak Mahmud.

Although the whole team did their best to help me write a flawless book, I'm afraid that any published book will still have some errors and typos. My name is on the cover, and the buck stops with me. While I'm grateful to share the credit for many things that went well with this book, I invite readers to assign full credit for all errors, typos, and imperfections in this book to me.

about this book

The purpose for writing *Succeeding with AI: How to Make AI Work for Your Business* was to help you lead an AI project toward business success. This book starts by showing you how to select AI projects that can become a business success, and then how to run those projects in a way that will achieve it.

Who should read this book

I wrote this book for the business leader who's tasked with delivering results with AI and views technology as a vehicle to deliver those results. I've also written it for the leadership team that is working with and advising such a business leader.

As a prerequisite, the reader of this book should have experience on the leadership team of a successful software project and should understand the business basics of their organization. Although an engineering background or deep knowledge about AI isn't required, an open mind and a willingness to facilitate conversations between people with technical and business backgrounds are.

I also wrote this book for leadership-focused and business-focused data scientists and data scientists who want to learn more about the business applications of AI methods. I purposely don't focus on specific technologies in AI, so if you're interested solely in the technical side of AI, this is not the book for you.

How this book is organized

This book is organized into eight chapters:

- Chapter 1 is an introduction to the AI project landscape today. It introduces you to the critical versus nice-to-have elements of a successful AI project and helps you understand business actions you can take based on AI project results.

It also provides a high-level overview of the process that a successful AI project should use.

- Chapter 2 introduces you to topics project leaders must know about AI. It helps you find which business problems benefit from the use of AI and match AI capabilities with the business problems you need to solve. It also helps you uncover any data science skill gaps on your team that might affect your project.

- Chapter 3 helps you select your first AI project and formulate a research question directed at your business problem. It also presents pitfalls to avoid when selecting AI projects, as well as best practices of such projects.

- Chapter 4 shows you how to link business and technology metrics and how to measure technical progress in business terms. It also shows you how to overcome organizational obstacles that you will typically encounter at the start of your first AI project.

- Chapter 5 helps you understand an ML pipeline and how it would evolve throughout the project life cycle. It shows you how to balance attention between business questions you are asking, the data you need, and AI algorithms you should use.

- Chapter 6 shows you how to determine if you're using the right ML pipeline for your AI project. It introduces you to the technique called MinMax analysis and shows you how to both perform it and interpret its results.

- Chapter 7 shows you how to correctly choose the right parts of your ML pipeline to improve for optimal business results. It also introduces the technique of sensitivity analysis and demonstrates how to interpret its results, as well as how to account for the passage of time in a long-running AI project.

- Chapter 8 focuses on trends in AI and how they'll affect you. This chapter introduces you to trends such as AutoML (automation of the work that data scientists do in AI) and explores how AI relates to causality and Internet of Things (IoT) systems. It also contrasts AI system errors with the typical errors humans make and shows you how to account for those differences in your project.

Some further comments about the organization of the book:

- The material in this book is multidisciplinary and requires a combination of both theory and practice to understand. Each chapter in this book combines the use of concrete examples illustrating general concepts and a detailed explanation of those concepts. The exercises at the end of each chapter will help you apply what you've learned in the chapter in the context of new business problems.

- Executives should make sure they read and understand both the content and details of the first four chapters and the last chapter. The business-focused exercises in those chapters will help every reader, up to and including the level of business-focused executives. Even if you prefer to skip the exercises, I recommend you still carefully review the answers provided in appendix B, "Exercise solutions." Business-focused readers should understand chapters 5, 6, and 7 broadly, while technically-focused readers should understand those chapters in detail.

- Some concepts discussed in this book are complicated. Instead of overwhelming you with every part and particle related to a concept the very first time you encounter it, I start with a high-level description of the idea. After you've mastered the basics of a concept, later chapters refer to the concept you already know and explore the finer points of its applications. If you ever wonder "Hey, didn't you already cover that concept in a previous chapter?" I certainly did, and now we're applying that concept in a brand-new context.

- Speaking of examples, I use examples from many different business verticals. I encourage you to scrutinize even more the examples of verticals with which you are not familiar. They're chosen to be small, self-contained, and described so that you can easily understand them in a business sense. I then show you how to apply the technical concepts you're learning in this book to these business examples. This is the position in which you will find yourself when applying AI to a new problem in your own business. No two business problems are identical, so you should already be used to comprehending the simple business concepts that come with new problems, even when they're in an unfamiliar business domain.

- The methods described in this book are independent from any underlying technical infrastructure. That infrastructure is evolving rapidly and consists of cloud or on-premise big data systems, development frameworks, and programming languages. I focus this book on the mechanisms of how to tie AI and business together, and I hope that the material in this book will serve you well years from now. I stay technology-neutral and leave it for other books to discuss the characteristics and tradeoffs of various infrastructure products marketed today.

- As in any other business book, the audience and readers for this book come from diverse backgrounds. Business and AI are broad topics, but most leaders of AI projects are already familiar with most of the terms I'm using. If you find a term you're not familiar with, please consult appendix A, "Glossary of terms," which contains the definitions of these terms.

- This book covers a wide range of topics and builds on the work of many other people. You will find many citations of other works, such as "[4]." The citation style used is Vancouver style notation, and [4] is an example of a citation. You can find the reference corresponding to [4] in appendix C, "Bibliography." In addition to giving credit where credit is due, the references cited direct you to where you can find more in-depth information about topics discussed in this book. Those references range from popular texts intended for a wider audience, to books focused toward practicing management professionals, to academic business publications, to technical and academic references requiring an in-depth knowledge of theoretical aspects of data science. I hope that the reference list will be of interest to everyone on your team.

liveBook discussion forum

Purchase of *Succeeding with AI: How to Make AI Work for Your Business* includes free access to a private web forum run by Manning Publications where you can make comments about the book, ask technical questions, and receive help from the author and from other users. To access the forum, go to https://livebook.manning.com/#!/book/succeeding-with-AI/discussion. You can also learn more about Manning's forums and the rules of conduct at https://livebook.manning.com/#!/discussion.

Manning's commitment to our readers is to provide a venue where a meaningful dialogue between individual readers and between readers and the author can take place. It is not a commitment to any specific amount of participation on the part of the author, whose contribution to the forum remains voluntary (and unpaid). We suggest you try asking the author some challenging questions lest his interest stray! The forum and the archives of previous discussions will be accessible from the publisher's website as long as the book is in print.

about the author

 VELJKO KRUNIC is an independent consultant and trainer specializing in data science, big data, and helping his clients get actionable business results from AI.

He holds a PhD in computer science from the University of Colorado at Boulder and an additional MS in engineering management from the same institution. His MS degree in engineering management focused on applied statistics, strategic planning, and the use of advanced statistical methods to improve organizational efficiency. He is also a Six Sigma Master Black Belt.

Veljko has consulted with or taught courses for five of the Fortune 10 companies (as listed in September 2019), many of the Fortune 500 companies, and a number of smaller companies, in the areas of enterprise computing, data science, AI, and big data. Before consulting independently, he worked in the professional services organizations (PSOs) of Hortonworks, the SpringSource division of VMware, and the JBoss division of Red Hat. In those positions, he was the main technical consultant on highly visible projects for the top clients of those PSOs.

about the cover illustration

The figure on the cover of *Succeeding with AI: How to Make AI Work for Your Business* is captioned "le Gouv d'Enfans de Vienne." The illustration is taken from a collection of dress costumes from various countries by Jacques Grasset de Saint-Sauveur (1757–1810), titled *Costumes Civils Actuels de Tous les Peuples Connus,* published in France in 1788. Each illustration is finely drawn and colored by hand. The rich variety of Grasset de Saint-Sauveur's collection reminds us vividly of how culturally apart the world's towns and regions were just 200 years ago. Isolated from each other, people spoke different dialects and languages. In the streets or in the countryside, it was easy to identify where they lived and what their trade or station in life was just by their dress.

The way we dress has changed since then, and the diversity by region, so rich at the time, has faded away. It is now hard to tell apart the inhabitants of different continents, let alone different towns, regions, or countries. Perhaps we have traded cultural diversity for a more varied personal life—certainly for a more varied and fast-paced technological life.

At a time when it's hard to tell one computer book from another, Manning celebrates the inventiveness and initiative of the computer business with book covers based on the rich diversity of regional life of two centuries ago, brought back to life by Grasset de Saint-Sauveur's pictures.

Introduction

Today, the topic of AI comes up quite often, not only in the technical and business communities but also in the news intended for nontechnical audiences. Discussions of AI are even entering the domain of public policy. It's likely that your own organization is considering the impact of AI and big data on its business, and that will lead to projects that use AI. I've written this book to help organizational leaders succeed with those AI projects.

As a consultant and trainer, I've been privileged to work with a large number of clients since topics like big data, AI, and data science have been taking off. Those clients have ranged from startups to Fortune 100 companies. Between projects, I've witnessed an emerging picture of the state of the industry. That picture includes many positive elements, with many millions of dollars made on successful projects. It also includes less talked-about projects. Those projects were managed in a way that doomed them from the start. But before they met their doom, those projects sent millions of dollars circling down the drain. The goal of this book is to help your project avoid becoming one of those doomed projects.

You might have heard of an AI platform called IBM Watson. The University of Texas MD Anderson Cancer Center partnered with IBM to create an advisory tool for oncologists. It was reported that Watson was canceled after $62 million was spent on it [5]! This example shows that even a high-profile project supported by a famous company with highly visible technology isn't a guaranteed success.

In this book, you'll see that the successful use of AI requires significant human involvement and insight. AI on its own isn't a substitute for business knowledge, nor can it improve your business by solely looking at the data and making recommendations.

> **WARNING** The fastest way to fail with AI is for the executive and business leaders to think, "AI can solve our problems; we don't need to do anything except hire the right tech geeks and unleash them on our data," or for the whole data science team to think, "Businesspeople take care of the business; we focus on technology." Business and technology must work together for success.

Initially, this situation may seem disappointing, but on closer examination, it's good news for a project leader. If AI could figure out your business, it would quickly put you out of a job. It can't, so your job is safe for the foreseeable future. But to intelligently apply AI, you need special skills and knowledge to enable you to combine your business domain with it.

> **WARNING** Technical knowledge regarding AI algorithms isn't sufficient to get business results using AI.

This book teaches you what you need to know to run and get good results from an AI-based project. It's assumed that you can run a general technical project.

The methods and techniques I teach are process neutral; you can use them in organizations of all sizes. To help you successfully run AI projects in such a wide range of organizations, this book focuses on the principles and skills that you must apply to your project, as opposed to providing rigid checklists and sequences of steps that you must perform in only one way. By learning these principles and skills, you can apply the techniques that are critical for the success of your project to any environment and process. But before we talk about how to get results with AI, let's first review the skills you need to have to get the most out of this book.

1.1   Whom is this book for?

If you feel that insufficient information has been published on how to deliver business results with AI, this book is for you. You'll find many books on the technical side of AI, data science, and big data, and some universities recently have started to add data science and AI programs. The result is that a lot of data scientists (and academics) know a lot about AI technology; however, they know far less about the business applications of AI.

I wrote this book for the business leader who is tasked with delivering results with AI and views technology as a vehicle to deliver those results. I also wrote it for the leadership team that's working with and advising such a business leader. This section provides an overview of the skills these leaders need to follow the book.

To get the most value out of this book, you'll need the following qualifications:

- You've been part of the leadership team of a successful software project. It doesn't matter whether the project used Agile or some other software development methodology. It doesn't matter whether the project used Java, Python, or some other programming language. What matters is that this isn't your first software project and that you're confident you can deliver a successful software project with the technologies you've used before.
- Whatever software development methodology you're using (Agile or not), you must understand how your organization manages software development. This includes managing the requirements, deliverables, resources, and reporting mechanisms used to track progress in a timely fashion.
- You understand the basics of the business your organization is in, on a level commensurate with your position in the organization. This means that you understand your organization's day-to-day business and what it involves, what business actions are possible for your organization, the main sources of income for your organization, and the basics of its budgeting process.
- If you're a leader with profit and loss (P&L) responsibility, it's also assumed that you understand how your business generates profit, as well as how to succeed in your business.
- You have experience with using business metrics to score the success of a business initiative. You know why metrics are important, how to measure the value of metrics, and how to recognize a metric that's inappropriate for your business. Data science and AI are quantitative fields, and the data sizes used make it difficult to get an intuitive feel for how well a project is progressing based on a few examples.
- Although an engineering background or previous deep knowledge about AI isn't required, an open mind and a willingness to facilitate conversations between people with technical and business backgrounds is.

With regards to the prior technical knowledge you'll want to have, the due diligence you already did before you decided to join the AI project should suffice. You need to have a basic understanding of what terms such as AI and big data mean. You need to know that you'll need data scientists on your AI team. And you need to know that before you can use an AI algorithm, you must collect the necessary data and train that AI algorithm. As long as you meet these qualifications, your official title doesn't matter. Your position in an organization might range from executive or senior vice president to product manager. You may also be a software architect or a business-focused data scientist in one of the teams working as part of a much bigger project. Your team may be working on a big data infrastructure or may be analyzing data using various techniques from the fields of data science, machine learning, artificial intelligence, and statistics.

I also expect that the organization you're working in already has a team with some basic technical knowledge of data science or can hire some specialists in the area, or at the very least has enthusiastic engineers willing to learn. You already know that you can't hope to manage successful web projects unless you have people on your team who know something about web development. AI is no different. As long as your organization meets this basic requirement, you can use techniques in this book whether you're in a large or small organization.

> **WARNING**   A team that pays attention to how to link technology with the business problem will beat a team that consists of (slightly) better specialists in a limited area of technology or business. If you aren't taking a genuine interest in what the other side does, this book isn't for you.

If your interest in business is limited, and your main interest is in AI methods and algorithms (or if your interest is mainly academic), this is *not* the book for you. My focus in covering any AI methods isn't on the technology but on what those methods mean in the context of the overall business.

> **NOTE**   If you're a data scientist, this book will be of value to you, as long as you're interested in how to achieve business results with AI. This book expects the reader who has a business background to be willing to learn the basics of how AI works. Similarly, if you're a leadership-focused data scientist, you're expected to be willing to learn about the business side of the equation.

If you're interested solely in the technical side of the AI, you'll be better off with books that focus on the technical side of AI. If you're just getting familiar with AI, some good places to start for some current trends are *Practical Data Science with R* [6], as well as *Deep Learning with Python* [7] or *Deep Learning with R* [8] (depending on your programming language preference).

1.2   *AI and the Age of Implementation*

Organizations new to AI have a lot of confusion regarding how to best organize projects around it. The root cause of that confusion is that the ways AI is best used in academia and industry are different. This section highlights the differences and advises you on what aspects of AI are most applicable to the typical project in business and industry.

When you hear terms like *data science* or things like "we should use the methods described in this scientific paper," it's easy to imagine academic disciplines and diligent scientists trying to discover new scientific principles. That's certainly happening, as plenty of recent and widely publicized research has been going on in the AI field.

WARNING   Successfully applying AI to business problems is *not* research in the traditional academic sense. Unless you're a researcher at a university (or in an industry-supported basic R&D effort) who's getting paid for conducting research itself, additional research results are difficult to monetize. You need the best practices for *implementing* AI projects, and those practices are the focus of this book.

If you're working in a typical corporation, you shouldn't organize your AI efforts in the mold of traditional scientific research. There are debates as to whether business success in the AI field as a whole is even contingent on the need for new AI discoveries. Influential voices [9] in the AI community believe that, as far as AI is concerned, we are entering the Age of Implementation of our existing knowledge.

Kai-Fu Lee, in *AI Superpowers* [9], uses the terms *Age of Implementation* and *Age of Discovery* to describe the state of AI today. He states that AI could be considered to be in the Age of Implementation in the sense that, in such an age, a scientific discovery (for example, the steam engine or electricity) that's already known needs to be widely disseminated throughout different areas of business and society. This is contrasted to the Age of Discovery, in which progress is driven by regular new discoveries of new scientific principles (for example, the second law of thermodynamics or the existence of X-rays). His argument that we are in the Age of Implementation is founded on the fact that many of the basic technical principles behind the current AI explosion have been known to the research community for a long time.[1] What we're doing today is *applying* known principles of AI to concrete business problems. For example, we know that AI excels in recognizing what's in an image, and we're now using that ability to recognize what is in that picture in a *business* context.

    TIP   If we're in the Age of Implementation, what we need most are practices for the best application of AI to new areas of the business. This book describes such practices.

Kai-Fu Lee is not alone. Andrew Ng, another prominent AI pioneer, believes that we need wider applications of already-known AI techniques to problems in business and industry, as opposed to more academic publications describing research results [10].

    At the time of this writing, it isn't clear whether AI's long-term progress is more representative of the Age of Implementation or the Age of Discovery. While this may not be clear on the level of AI as a field of endeavor and its influence on broader society, *in the context of an AI project you start in business and industry today,* that question is settled. For the duration of such a project, you're working in the Age of Implementation mindset. This book, therefore, focuses on applying what's already known, so let's start talking about how to succeed with AI in the context of your business.

---

[1]   For that matter, the argument could be made that a lot of the recently published papers are more focused on how to apply deep learning on the new problem domain rather than on investigating new fundamental principles of AI.

WARNING   In almost all industry projects, it's dangerous for both your project and your career to depend on the need to make new scientific discoveries to be able to deliver the project.

1.3   *How do you make money with AI?*

There's often a perception that using AI makes it possible for you to make a lot of money (or, in the case of nonprofits, help some cause). This section highlights the relationship between AI and making money.

What you may have heard is

$$Data + AI = \$$$

This is partially true. Actually, in at least one situation, it's completely true: if $\$$ stands for cost, you can rest assured that, most certainly, those systems (and people operating them) would come with a significant cost. But if you want $\$$ to stand for profit, the equation looks somewhat different:

$$Data + AI + \textbf{\textit{CLUE}} = Profit$$

This book is about the **CLUE** part of the equation. I define CLUE in more detail in section 1.10; briefly, what I mean here is that you need to *think* (have a clue) about how to make a profit.

Often, people hope that data and technology will pave the way forward. That hope may tempt you to proceed with a significant investment without being sure of how to monetize the results of your data science project.

TIP   The main insight to remember is that *using AI to analyze data doesn't make money; properly reacting to the results of the correct analysis does.*

If you don't have any idea how you'd react to the results of a data project before those results are delivered, chances are you won't have a clue about what to do with the results once you receive them. People who make money correctly tie technology to the business problem. *The right time to figure out how to tie technology and business is at the start of the project, not once the analysis is already complete.* Both now and in the foreseeable future, that tie-in would have to be conceived, engineered, and executed by people, not AI.

It's not always about money!

Not all organizations are interested just in making profit. If you're working for a charity or non-governmental nonprofit organization (NGO), you have nonmonetary goals, such as the number of people you help. These are worthy goals, and the methods in this book are fully applicable in nonprofit environments.

For the purpose of brevity, I'll often use phrases such as "the way to make money with AI is to do X . . . ." In all those examples, the techniques described aren't limited to just making money. I don't think that the for-profit sector is more important than the nonprofit sector. I'm just using "money" as a convenient shortcut.

If you're a nonprofit devoted to helping people, then substitute an appropriate, *quantifiable* metric for the word "money." How many people did you help? To what degree did you help them?

1.4 *What matters for your project to succeed?*

Before we talk about what matters most in an AI project, let's talk about best practices of time and project management. Not every technology you'd use on your project is equally important for success. Nor is every part of your project equally important. Your time should be focused on those parts of your project that matter the most for success.

An AI project's leadership has to make many choices, and it's easy to get lost in them. Those choices are in many different technical areas—areas like what infrastructure to use, how to handle big data, whether to use cloud or on-premise solutions, and which AI algorithms to use. Within each one of those categories are many additional choices you'd have to make.

Here are some concrete examples of some of those further choices:

- If you're using the cloud, is it AWS [11], Google Cloud Platform [12], Microsoft Azure [13], or something else?
- Do you need a big data solution? If you do, do you use Apache Spark [14], Apache Hadoop [15], or Apache Flink [16]?
- What monitoring and security infrastructure do you need?

It's understandable that with so many choices to make, the temptation is to put the early focus of management's attention on making the choices I've listed. If you see that happening, you should stop the discussion. You're getting pulled into the details and should refocus the conversation back on the business problems you're trying to solve.

> **TIP** Think about the following analogy. There is a similarity between going on a sailing vacation and running an AI project. If you're sailing for the first time and have an experienced captain with you, your main expectations are that *the sailboat is a seaworthy vessel that will sail and that it won't sink*. It's of little relevance whether the sailboat is capable of a speed of 9 knots or is limited to 8 knots. Just as the first question for your sailing vacation should be *where you intend to sail*, the first question for your AI project is how to properly react to results of the analysis.

Although you must choose your infrastructure correctly (on a *do not sink* level), the primary determinant of the AI project's success lies in how well you connect the answer to your research question with a specific business action. Once you're confident in that connection, *then* you can focus your attention on infrastructure and making good infrastructural choices.

> **TIP** When embarking on an AI project, the highest priority for management attention must be on linking a research question to specific business action.

Speaking of infrastructure, it's easy to assume that you need to start by building infrastructure that's capable of supporting any conceivable AI project. You have plenty of choices in the space of big data and AI frameworks. But always remember that those frameworks are just *enablers*. As a project leader, you must be careful that you don't intermix the *enabler* with the *value* you're building. Your primary focus should be on value. You should never allow yourself to be in the situation in which you're discussing infrastructure but have no concrete idea of what specific business questions you intend to use AI to answer.

> **TIP**   Vendors make the fair point that if you have many AI projects using different and incompatible infrastructural stacks, you're risking a significant amount of chaos in the infrastructure space. I also agree that infrastructure is an important consideration, as there are real and substantial differences between the technology stacks of different vendors. I encourage you to pay attention to infrastructure, but not at the expense of losing focus on the business value you're creating.

Starting with technology stack considerations as your main focus can lead you into the trap of overconcentrating on the infrastructure, and you can lose focus on the sequence of data science use cases that you should implement. Remember, your attention is a finite resource too.

> **TIP**   Let's embrace the analogy that *data is the new oil*. If you need a new oilfield, you'd put your greatest focus into finding oil and understanding what an oilfield looks like. You most certainly wouldn't start by buying the best oil drilling equipment in the world, with the drilling location as an afterthought. The same thing applies to data—concentrate on finding oil, not on the drilling equipment.

There is one exception to the "Don't start with the infrastructure" rule. If your enterprise is large and has already made the decision to adopt data science across the board, you may need an infrastructure that supports as wide a range as possible of technologies used in AI today. Only the largest companies with the biggest data science departments are in this position, and, for them, my advice is that they build infrastructure in *parallel* with the definition and development of data science use cases that need to be supported.

Finally, because this field is rapidly evolving, in this book I don't discuss any of the individual frameworks available today. Some are better than others, but I want this book to outlast the current generation of frameworks.

1.5   *Machine learning from 10,000 feet*

For the successful application of AI to business problems, close human involvement, with the application of engineering and business skills, is essential. This section explains the roles that humans will need to fill for a project using AI to succeed.

AI and machine learning (ML) are closely related. ML allows computers to learn an underlying pattern in data on their own, without being programmed with the prior knowledge of those data [17]. Today, in business and industry, most AI projects use algorithms that are (strictly speaking) part of ML.[2] There's a lot of confusion among the wider public about what ML can do, so if you aren't an expert in ML, it's easy to imagine that ML is some magical box that's given data and *somehow* produces an impressive result.

Let's clarify just how that *somehow* happens. ML uses various algorithms—a sequence of predefined steps—that produce an answer. An ML algorithm guarantees that if you provide it data in a particular format with some metric related to its output, it will generate some mathematical transformation that reveals the optimal value of the metric that you provided. ML isn't a genius that discovers what you missed. It's an idiot savant that performs complex math on the numbers you feed it, but it has no comprehension of the meaning of those numbers. The only goal an ML algorithm has is to find an optimal value of a given evaluation metric, *all the while not knowing or caring about why it's optimizing that particular metric.* Figure 1.1 shows what an ML algorithm is actually doing.

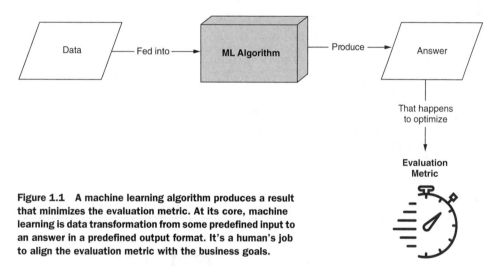

Figure 1.1 **A machine learning algorithm produces a result that minimizes the evaluation metric. At its core, machine learning is data transformation from some predefined input to an answer in a predefined output format. It's a human's job to align the evaluation metric with the business goals.**

> **TIP** Informally, ML is the application of some mathematical algorithm that requires data input in a certain format, produces an answer in a predefined output format, and doesn't provide any other guarantee except that it will minimize some number that we call the *evaluation metric.*

When you look at the definition provided in the TIP, ML certainly doesn't sound magical, nor is there some genius lurking around in the algorithm. The trick of using ML isn't so much in what ML algorithms do, but in *how you use them.*

---

[2] Exceptions are in the field of robotics, which can use algorithms that are traditionally not part of ML but are part of AI as a broader field. The broader field of AI includes not only ML, but also fields of robotics and machine perception [18]. To address the broadest category of projects used in the industry today, the early chapters in this book primarily concentrate on projects using ML.

Let's expand on how data scientists use ML. Who defines the format of the data, the answer, and the metrics? To understand how to apply ML algorithms, it helps if you think about ML in the form given in the paper "A Few Useful Things to Know About Machine Learning" [19]:

Machine Learning = Formulation + Optimization + Evaluation

Those terms are defined as follows:

- *Formulation*—Finding a clever way to describe a business problem so that it relates to the input and output data that your ML algorithm knows how to process. This means you package data related to your business problem in the format an ML algorithm expects as its input and find a way to interpret the answer provided by that ML algorithm in your business context.
- *Optimization*—What the ML algorithm does internally. It's the process of applying math to get an optimal solution. How is that optimal solution defined? It's defined according to an *evaluation metric*.
- *Evaluation*—The application of the aforementioned evaluation metric to measure the success of the optimization.

It's up to you as the user of the algorithm to understand which evaluation metric is best and what the best format is for your data. Figure 1.2 shows the roles that humans and computers play in ML.

Wait—what do all these concepts in figure 1.2 even mean? What do they have to do with your business? As far as ML or AI is concerned, *it doesn't care at all about your business.* That's your job.

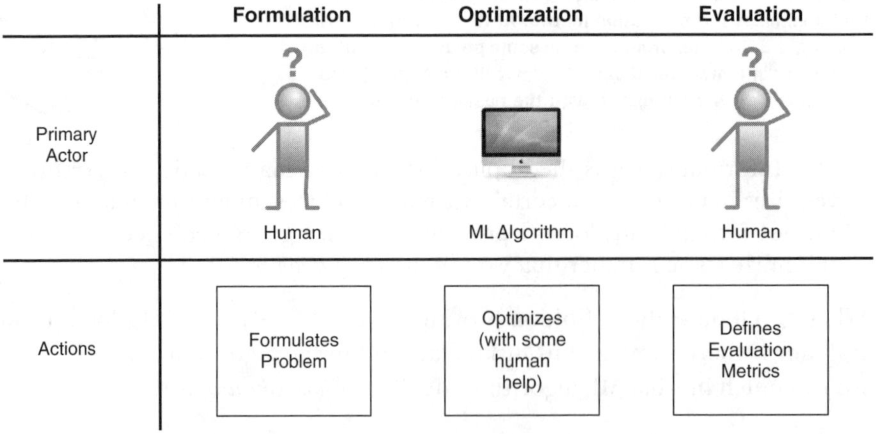

	Formulation	Optimization	Evaluation
Primary Actor	? Human	ML Algorithm	? Human
Actions	Formulates Problem	Optimizes (with some human help)	Defines Evaluation Metrics

Figure 1.2 Machine learning is a combination of formulation, optimization, and evaluation. The only part that the computer can do (mostly) on its own is optimization.

TIP If you're an executive, one way to think about ML is as a black box that operates on numbers. Who then is responsible for bringing intelligence to that ignorant black box? Humans, through the proper *formulation* (that's the job of data scientists) and application of the appropriate *evaluation metric* that measures something relevant to your business (that's your job as an executive, in cooperation with the data scientist).

If you're a data scientist, you're aware of what ML is. But here's a detail that's easy to miss: because the only guarantee provided by the algorithm is that it will optimize the evaluation metrics, *those metrics must have a business meaning.* Those metrics can't just be something you've seen in an academic paper, and certainly not something you don't know how to relate to anything concrete in your business.

When a data science team is choosing the evaluation metrics, they must do so in close cooperation with the executive team. Here's the scary thing—a lot of ML projects use evaluation metrics that aren't clearly tied to business results. Evaluation metrics have their roots in ML theory and history, as opposed to in business. At best, most of the technical evaluation metrics are merely *correlated with but not identical to the business result you're trying to get.* At worst, those evaluation metrics that your data scientist can't even explain in business terms are in the *will not help your business* category.

TIP If you're an executive, a good habit for you to form is to speak up when you see an acronym in a business presentation that you don't know (for example, RMSE).[3] Similarly, with ML, demand an explanation in the form of, "Don't tell me the mathematical definition of that metric; tell me how to relate the value of that metric to something in my business."

If your evaluation metric isn't tied to your business result, you're using a black box (the ML algorithm) to generate a random number (a value of the evaluation metric) and then trying to figure out how to run your business based on that random number. Good luck!

1.6 Start by understanding the possible business actions

Focused human involvement and attention makes or breaks an AI project. This section discusses the first questions you should ask in the context of every AI project, as well as the most important ideas to keep in mind during any AI project.

You don't make money simply by knowing the answer to a business question—you make money when you take action. And that action is constrained by what you can and can't do in the physical world (for example, the number of possible management decisions). A business action can require approval from your boss(es), the creation of external partnerships, and getting the whole team to buy in on that decision—that's the real world we're talking about.

---

[3] RMSE stands for *root mean square error* metric, defined with a mathematical formula whose terms aren't inherently related to any business concept. Chapter 4 shows you how you can express the RMSE using metrics related to business.

TIP   The number of *good, effective actions you can take to affect the physical world is relatively small.* Many analyses you can perform will yield results that are not actionable.

The limits to business actions you can take can come in many forms. They may be limits of knowledge and know-how in your organization, or the limits of your budget. They may be imposed by the organization's internal politics and what you're able to rally people around, or they can be the result of which battles you're willing to fight. Whatever has summoned these limits into being, you're stuck with them.

You can spend a lot of time on analysis, get some results, and then say, "Well, there's nothing I can do to change this." The time and money spent on such analysis is wasted, and it is a *preventable* waste.

TIP   Don't ask a question if you can't imagine what you'd do with the answer. You should start an AI project by asking, "What actions can I take, and what analysis do I need to do to inform those actions?"

Once you know the business actions you can take, you should use these actions to drive the analysis, not vice versa. Figure 1.3 illustrates the relationship between the business actions you can take and the possible analyses you can perform.

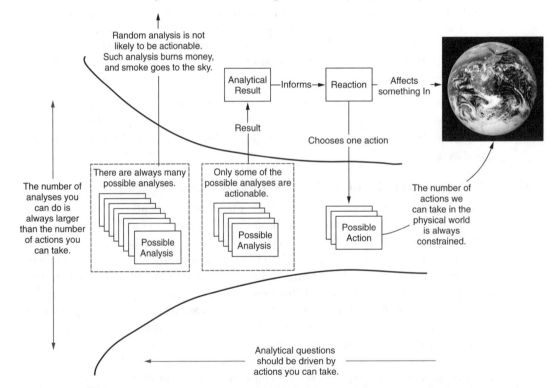

Figure 1.3   You can perform many more analyses than there are business actions you can take. Don't spend a ton of time and money on an analysis just to figure out it was never an actionable one. (Earth image is from Wikipedia [20].)

There's always something in the data, and it's possible to conduct hours of analysis on only a few hundred numbers.[4] Often, you'll find some interesting properties in even a small dataset. The problem is that the large majority of those analyses fall into the category of *that's interesting, but not really relevant to the business.* If you're focused primarily on analysis, you can spend a lot of money and time on interesting analysis and then not have any idea of how to execute on the results.

What about EDA?

There's a limited exception to the rule of "consider first what you'll do with results before you perform analysis." This exception is Exploratory Data Analysis (EDA), which helps data scientists understand the structure and basic properties of datasets. If an EDA effort is small (compared to the total project budget), it may be worth doing EDA just to better understand the datasets.

But to claim to be an exception to the rule, EDA and all preparatory work necessary for it (such as any cleaning of the data) must be a *small* effort that's part of the larger project.

If the effort needed to perform EDA is instead a significant part of your project, you'll need to justify the collection of those datasets, decide which datasets you'll perform EDA on, and explain why you think there's some value in looking at that data.

In every AI project, these are the two most important ideas to remember:

1   *Action is where you make profit; analysis without action is just cost.* You make money when you perform an *appropriate business action*, not when some analysis is completed. Analysis can be an enabler of making profits, but from an accounting perspective, analysis is a cost. Analysis stops being a cost and becomes an investment only when it can help you take good business actions.

2   *To succeed, focus on the whole system, not on its individual parts.* Your customers will never see the individual parts of the system. For instance, they don't care about the ML algorithms that you're using. They care only about the result, and that result depends on how well the system works as a whole.

1.7　*Don't fish for "something in the data"*

Teams that fail to start a project by focusing on which business actions they can take will routinely encounter two failure modes. They typically start by copying something that "worked for another organization," or use AI to look for "something in the data." This section explains why neither of those approaches works well in practice.

---

[4]   Improving business with data is not new. There's a long history of projects that were done in the factory and business process improvement space prior to the rise of big data. Those projects were done on small datasets but often used complex statistical analyses that required high technical proficiency with statistics and significant time to perform. Many such projects would fall under the umbrella of Six Sigma—see [21] and [22] for details.

Copying parts of a system that worked for someone else doesn't work, because that copying then confines you to the decisions someone else made for their context, whereas your project should deliver a *whole system customized to solve your business problem.* When you copy someone else's solution, you have no way of knowing if that system will be useful in the context of your problem and your organization. You may then learn too late that it's too difficult to modify the copied system to solve your business problem.

Nor does it work to collect a lot of data and then throw various AI methods at it hoping that one of them will reveal an action you've never considered. Suppose it does. What's the chance that you'd actually be able to execute on some random action that the analysis just divined? How much money do you want to spend on the off chance of getting *an idea* unrelated to your day-to-day business operations?[5]

Sometimes you can execute on an unexpected insight. Your batting average will be much higher if the studies you perform are related to areas of your business where it's obvious that you can take action based on the possible results of your study. For example, one of those famous anecdotes you might have heard is that analysis has shown that in supermarkets, beer and diapers are often bought together [23].[6] What happened next? Supermarkets supposedly put diapers next to beer and saw an increase in beer sales. *The ability to react on the analytical result was already there,* which is why the association study was done in the first place.

Profit of $10 million per unit

Imagine that your data scientist comes to your office with the following proposal:

Data Scientist: I have great news! I looked at that dataset you gave me, and I think I have a fantastic way to make money.

You: Great! Tell me more! [thinking to yourself] *Just in the nick of time. We've spent a ton of money on that project so far, and we badly need success.*

Data Scientist: I found a way to make a profit of $10 million per unit.

You [thinking to yourself]: *Sounds too good to be true.*

You: Any risks that could sink us?

Data Scientist: None that I can see. There are no competitors. We're able to serve at least 100 units. It'd be easy to execute.

You [thinking to yourself]: *Wow, that's a billion dollars!*

Data Scientist: I even checked with the organizations that take the welfare of the units into account. They love the idea. Consultants also say that the governments and populations of the countries involved would like the idea too.

---

[5] One extreme case of this question is "How much would you pay for just an idea of a totally new business that you can undertake, without any associated execution of that idea?" All venture capitalists have encountered this situation, and the usual answer from that community is "I wouldn't pay anything."

[6] This popular story has many details wrong or changed in the retelling, but, for the sake of argument, let's go with it in the form it's most often told.

[You start thinking about talking to the Board about the plan.]

You: Excellent! So what are those units?

Data Scientist: Elephants!

You [dumbfounded]: Elephants?!

Data Scientist: Yes, you see, elephants from region X will be much better off and will be safer if we move them to region Y. It's great for the ecosystem. Also, as I said, the governments and populations in X and Y will love it. Elephants would enjoy it too, and they'd be safer in region Y. Charities that worry about the well-being of elephants love it as well. We can get a profit of $10 million from the government of Y by . . .

[You aren't sure what to say next . . . . No, you shouldn't act on your first instinct . . . . Take a deep breath now and speak like a leader . . . .]

Then, you wake up from your nightmare and say, "Thank goodness it was just a dream. I don't think it was looking plausible anyway." But you can't go back to sleep. You still need to find a good business case. You wonder what your data scientist might find in that data.

There's always something in the data. It might be unexpected, insightful, and even potentially wildly profitable. The elephant in the room is that something being "unexpected, insightful, and even wildly profitable" doesn't mean it is *actionable*. It might be difficult to transform your current business into an elephant hauling business.[a]

---

[a] No animals were hurt during the construction of this elephant example, and I don't advocate elephant relocation or profiting from elephants in the real world—this is just a hypothetical example. If you're in any way offended by the idea of hauling elephants, feel free to use hamsters (or stone marbles) in the example instead.

1.8 AI finds correlations, not causes!

One word of warning, which I'll cover in more detail in chapter 8, regards a common misunderstanding that I want you to be aware of early on. AI as practiced in business and industry today finds *correlations*, not *causes*. This is important to recognize because newcomers to AI, after seeing AI answer a complicated question, sometimes anthropomorphize AI and attribute to it the ability to *know the reason behind the answer* when it's often just *guessing*.

Humans are causal model driven. Even if they don't know how a given system works, they usually have a theory, a *model,* of how that system works. The models built make it possible for humans to reason about cause and effect. Because that's how we work, we have the tendency to assume that AI works that way too. That's not correct.

When a human sees A and B going together, the human would easily give you some theory (very often, not a correct theory) of why A and B are causally related. AI wouldn't be able to give you any causal theory (much less ensure that the theory is correct), it would just say, "I think that A and B go together." You as a human can reason about causes, but AI as practiced today can't establish causal relationships on its own.

NOTE   If your neighbors look distant every time they see you, you might assume that they don't like you or that something is troubling them. You've just assumed a *model* of why people behave in certain ways. AI might predict that your neighbors will appear distant the next time you see them, but few AI algorithms would impute any cause: *they don't say* why *it is, just* that *it is.*

When you're thinking about what you need AI to do for your business, keep in mind the differences between the human use of causal models and how AIs work:

- The expectation that AI can automatically find *causes* (as opposed to *patterns*) isn't realistic in most cases.
- If you're required to explain why an AI algorithm made some decision, you must carefully consider how to translate the algorithm's behavior in a way that you and your audience can understand.
- Most AI algorithms used today, especially in the big data domain, have a limited ability to guide change. That ability is limited to situations in which you have data for both where you are now and where you want to go. Because AI recognizes *patterns*, if you have no data (or lack the ability to collect new data) on how the world will look after a change occurs, AI can't do much to guide you.

Always tread carefully when you think about using AI to impute causes or to guide change.

Most industry AI projects don't address causality

If you're interested in causality, several sources in appendix C [24–27] summarize the state of the field. Causality is an area of active academic research and isn't addressed by most AI projects in industry today.

Obstacles to the wider use of causality include the scarcity of experts in the field (especially among industry practitioners) and the need for more mature software support. There are also significant limits to what is known even in academic settings about inferring causality in complex scenarios.

1.9   *Business results must be measurable!*

For an AI project to succeed, you need to be able to measure the results of the data science project in the context of its business impact. That measurement needs to be quantifiable. AI and ML algorithms can't use *gut feeling* metrics as feedback on how well the project is doing, so someone needs to define a quantitative metric. This section discusses important considerations and pitfalls of the business metric used in the context of AI projects.

Before you can measure how your data scientists would impact your business, you need to be able to measure your business as it is today. As a business leader, you should have a way to measure how well your business is doing based on some numerical metrics directly tied to the business. Some examples of such metrics are revenue, number of customer purchases, and internal rate of return (IRR). Once you have those business metrics, you should have a way to tie those metrics to the *technical* evaluation metric that the ML algorithm uses. Chapter 4 describes in detail how to make that connection.

Depending on the methodology you're using to run your business, business metrics could be readily available, or you might have to develop them yourself. Various methodologies are available for running a business and measuring its results. If you're looking for a starting point, the Lean Startup methodology described in Ries's book [28] is popular in startup and IT settings. I also recommend reviewing the Business Performance Excellence (BPE) model described in Luftig and Ouellette's book [1].

> **NOTE** You may not have a direct business metric at your department level to which you can direct your data science project. If that's the case and you don't already have a metric to use, define one yourself.

Although I could provide examples of business metrics you could use, defining appropriate business metrics isn't a simple operation; there are many considerations to take into account to do it right. If you define the wrong metrics for the business problem you're trying to solve, your employees may work toward maximizing metrics as opposed to solving the business problem. At a minimum, the methodology you're using should ensure that the metric correctly measures whether the business goal is achieved and that the metrics on the department level help you align individual departments toward a common goal. A number of resources are available to you [1,2,29–33], and you may want to review some of them for a few guidelines.

The complexity associated with recognizing and defining good business metrics is exactly why I recommend that you develop a thorough understanding of the operations of your business. You need to recognize the appropriate metric to run your business with, versus which metrics might sound reasonable but will actually not measure what's really important for your business success. For example, it's your job to understand if it's better to direct your business in the next six months based on preferring to increase revenue growth or to increase total number of users.[7]

> **NOTE** A good business metric yields a number that's directly related to some business result. Such a metric is actionable. In the case of a recommendation engine, a good business metric could be expected increase in profit. Any technical metric that has no clear meaning in the context of business is obviously not a good business metric. In the absence of quantitative business metrics, you're running a project based on gut feeling.

What if you can't measure business results in a numerical way and can only use gut feelings? Then you're at a severe competitive disadvantage, at least as far as AI projects are concerned. Businesses that can't systematically measure business results aren't well suited for running AI projects. If the project's progress is measured based on the gut

---

[7] Quite often, early stage startups are looking for high growth. Such startups prefer to increase users in the short term, before they reach profitability.

feeling of a business leader, then measuring that progress takes considerable time and involvement of that leader. Even if a business leader's gut feeling is 100% accurate, due to the limited amount of times the data science team can consult the business leader, they will only get one or two data points on how well their AI project is doing. It's difficult (and often impossible) for data scientists to optimize their approach based on so few data points.

Without a business metric to measure progress, you're asking your data science team to use mathematics to produce something you already told them can't be quantified. To me, if a business result can't be quantified (at least approximately) with a metric, there's no reason to believe that math-based tools can help. And make no mistake—AI algorithms are a math-based tool.

Does having a lot of data guarantee results?

Think about your next-door neighbors. What do you know about them? Please take a moment to think about your neighbors before proceeding.

Great—welcome back to reading! You might know a significant amount about your neighbors: the size of the family, pets, cars they drive, and so forth. If you've ever talked with them or invited them to lunch/dinner, you might have learned even more: where they work, hobbies, their dietary preferences, and so on. Now ask yourself:

How much money did I make off my neighbors last year?

If your answer was, "I didn't make any money off my neighbors," welcome to the club. Almost without exception, everyone asked has the same response.

I've asked quite a few executives the same question. As you can imagine, many of them live in well-to-do neighborhoods. Their neighbors often have high net worth and command large budgets. And most of those executives have never made *any* money off their neighbors. *Even successful executives aren't particularly successful in monetizing random knowledge.*

A common assumption that organizations make is that the more you know about someone (client, customer, competitor, employee), the more money you'll make. That's true only if you have no idea what kind of data you need, so you think *more is better* because you hope that by some random chance there'll be something useful in all that data. Having a good idea of what to do with your data in the first place helps much more.

To make money doing business with your neighbors, you don't need a lot of random data about them. You need to know how they make purchasing decisions in a business area in which you (or your company) have an ability to sell to them. Not all data is created equal, and some data are just superfluous.

Finally, just in the case you were wondering, the second most common answer to the question posed in this example isn't "I made $X," it's "I don't socialize in my neighborhood, so I don't know much about my neighbors."

1.10 What is CLUE?

Many data science projects today are taking a haphazard approach, which doesn't amount to much more than "Let's look at the data and test the hypothesis that comes to our team members' minds, hoping we'll find the right one." The elephant in the room is that few things you find in data are actionable. The end result is likely to be a long, unpredictable research project that leaves you uncertain about its ability to ever turn a profit.

In the absence of a systematic process for generating and evaluating hypotheses, and then cost effectively managing that, you're missing *a clue.* Figure 1.4 shows you elements of the CLUE.

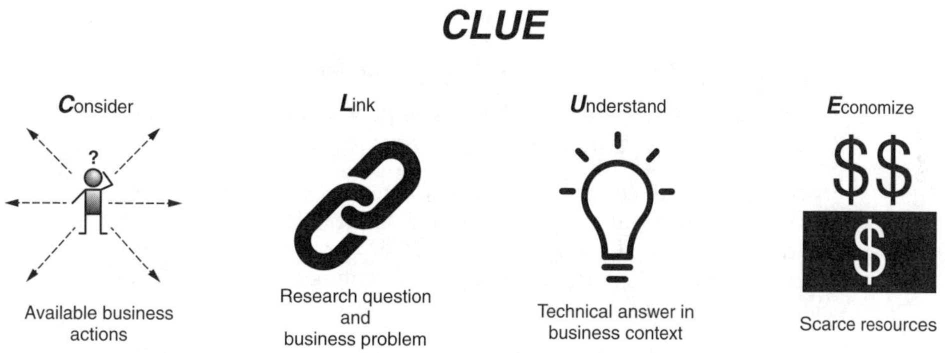

CLUE

| **C**onsider | **L**ink | **U**nderstand | **E**conomize |
| Available business actions | Research question and business problem | Technical answer in business context | Scarce resources |

Figure 1.4   Elements of CLUE. AI projects that don't have good answers for all elements of CLUE experience difficulties.

CLUE is an acronym for

- *Consider (available business actions)*—What business actions are possible for you to take? What business decisions can you make? What are some possible options for those decisions? How can you best choose among those options?

   Once you know what business actions you can take, the obvious question is, "Why haven't you taken that action?" Clearly, you have some doubt, some question that needs to be answered before you can take that action. That's good news! You now have a business question that should be answered with AI.

- *Link (research question and business problem)*—The information you need to make a choice among available business options leads you to research questions that your data science should answer. You need to ask that research question in the form that a typical data science project can answer. You'll need to link the business problem, the business action to be taken, and the research question with each other.

- *Understand (the answer)*—How will you know what the answer means when your chosen data science method produces it? How can you translate some technical metrics produced by the data science method (for example, a metric like RMSE) to your business domain? For that matter, how many people in your average business meetings know what RMSE means? If they don't know it, then why is a result presented using that metric?

- *Economize (resources)*—Your resources are scarce. Run your data science project in the way that provides you the highest expected payoff for resources invested.

Although subsequent chapters elaborate on each one of these elements, let's just quickly expand on why these steps are important.

You need to start contemplating your options from the business side. You can find a lot of the non-actionable things in the data. Conversely, there are much fewer actions you can execute on. You should start from the few things you can execute on.

Technical metrics are not business metrics

Suppose you're running a small sporting goods store. One business action you can take is choosing between stocking snowboards or mountain bikes.

Once you know which business action you have, two questions arise: why haven't you taken it yet, and what are you concerned about? Well, you might be concerned about the demand in the next three months. So now you have the question, "Based on historical trends and expected average temperatures, how many bikes or snowboards will I sell in the next three months?"

Your data scientists operate with mathematical formulas, computers, and software. They'll define some evaluation metrics to be used with their ML algorithms, but the project leader needs to work with the business domain specialists to understand how the values that those evaluation metrics yield map to business.

If your data scientists are off by three bicycles/week, how much would having three extra bicycles cost? How much would it cost if you lost the sale of three bicycles that you didn't have in inventory?[a] That's what the **U** in CLUE means. Would you rather hear in a business presentation that RMSE is 2.83 or that you expect that a wrong prediction would cost you between $7K and $12K a month?

---

[a] This is the reason why you need a business domain expert here. What's your cost of inventory? What's your profit margin?

NOTE If you've never encountered RMSE and are wondering what it is and what it has to do with your business, you're not alone. *Just throwing a technical metric at business users is confusing.* What units is 2.83 in—dollars, meters, points? Depending on the business problem, that RMSE can be all of the previous units—or none of them. If you are a data scientist, always use business metrics in presentations to the business user. You're better positioned to translate technical metrics to business terms, and you should do so before a meeting. If for any reason you can't do it, how can you possibly expect a much less mathematically inclined business user to do it, in real time, *during the presentation and* *using only mental math*?! Chapters 3 and 4 discuss the process of linking technical and business metrics, and appendix A has an explanation of RMSE.

Once you know what business actions are available, you can start an AI project that will help you choose between those actions. Every project has finite resources, so you should be a good steward of those resources. The foundations of the project you establish (for example, the architecture of the software or the business relationships you need to form to get data and execute on the project) need to be right the first time, because it will cost you a fortune to change them. The *E* in CLUE (economize) is about how you combine project management and data science best practices so that you can assign resources optimally in your project.

An overarching theme here is that a properly organized AI project can be managed with the management tools that successful executives are already familiar with. CLUE is the glue between the existing management practices you know and those specific to data science projects.

1.11 Overview of how to select and run AI projects

Throughout the rest of this book, I construct a process for getting concrete business results with AI. Let's briefly review the process here (figure 1.5).

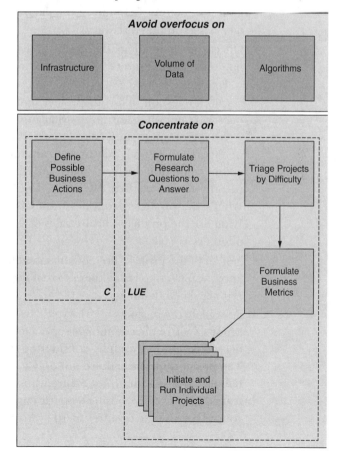

Figure 1.5 High-level overview of the process that a successful AI project should use. This workflow shows you how to make sure that all elements of CLUE are part of your project.

This process should be understood as a group of considerations that must be addressed in a successful AI project, not as a sequence of steps that always must be executed in the same order. If some part of your existing process already addresses the given considerations, you don't necessarily have to modify it.

For your process for running an AI project to be successful, you must do the following:

- Distinguish between what's most important to get right for success (having a CLUE) versus what's nice to get right—that which is mostly supporting your project.

  In the sailing example I gave earlier, the most important question was, "Where do you want to sail?" not "What is the max speed of the boat you're on?" Similarly, in the AI project, having a CLUE matters more than the infrastructure you're using, the collection of volumes of data, or the knowledge of the exotic, recently published AI algorithms.

- Start your analysis with the business actions you can take. If you instead start by saying, "Let me try some AI algorithms on data I already have," chances are that even if something is found in the data, you won't know what business action to take based on that discovery.

- Once you understand the business actions you can take, consider why you haven't taken them yet.

  You typically have a question or uncertainty there, and that's how you find a research question that your project should answer. On the business level, it's a question that, when answered, will cause you to take some business action.

  It's important to understand that a single business question can require from one to many research questions to answer. For example, you can break an overarching question such as "What inventory mix should I hold?" into several research questions like: "What are the best-selling items I have in inventory? What's the predicted supplier's availability of the items I have in inventory? What are the predicted future sales of these items?" You might be able to think of others as well.

- Not all of the projects are equally valuable or equally easy to do. As you already know, you need to triage them so that the easiest to implement, high-value projects are scheduled first.

- Formulate the business metrics you'll use to measure the results of your business actions. One of the common errors facing AI projects is that they make technical decisions without carefully considering the business impact of those decisions. The business metric is there not only to help your executives run the business, but also as a quantitative measure whose importance both the AI and business teams agree on. This business metric could be specific to each research question you ask, or a single business metric can apply to multiple research questions.

- Initiate individual efforts that will answer your research questions. It isn't necessary to initiate one project per research question, and the exact number of research questions that a project should answer depends on the research questions, team expertise, and the difficulty of answering the questions (or obtaining data for them).

At the end of this process, you'll have a set of AI projects that are in advantageous positions to succeed and make a difference. You'll know how difficult the implementation of those projects will be. You'll know that there's an implementable business action that you can take once AI provides you with an answer, and you have a way to measure how beneficial that action will be for your business.

Is CLUE limited to large companies?

CLUE is focused on highlighting the questions that you need to answer for your AI project to be successful. Those questions are derived from how AI functions, not from the size of your organization. As such, CLUE is applicable to AI projects in organizations of all sizes.

Larger organizations typically will need to coordinate larger teams and may have people specifically assigned to managing that communication or some parts of the CLUE process. They also would typically have to follow additional organizational processes compared to smaller organizations. Early startups with fewer employees may address all components of CLUE in a more informal way and may even have a single employee managing the whole CLUE process in parallel with many other duties.

If anything, it's more important in a smaller company to use CLUE or an equivalent process. Such a process is what prevents you from spending a lot of money on answering analytical questions that weren't actionable to start with. Well-funded projects in a Fortune 10 company could recover from the kind of error that causes a 10-person team to be wandering for six months in the wrong direction. Can a 10-person startup survive a comparable error?

1.12 Exercises

I strongly encourage you to complete these exercises to get a better understanding of the material covered in this chapter. This book's exercises highlight and reinforce the best practices in, and common pitfalls of, AI projects in business. If you elect to skip the exercises, I still recommend reading the answers to the questions.

These exercises may introduce some new concepts that aren't discussed in the chapters, but they should be already familiar to you or, if not, well within your ability to grasp. This is intentional and will help you practice the *application* of the skills and concepts you learned in this chapter to new business situations.

Solutions to the exercises are in appendix B at the end of this book.

1.12.1 *True/False questions*

Answer the following questions with True or False.

Question 1: You always need a lot of data to make significant money with AI.

Question 2: The first step when starting an AI project is to select the right technology tools to use.

Question 3: Sometimes, simple AI algorithms can produce large business results.

Question 4: Some tools can significantly automate AI projects. Just by using those tools, you can ensure a significant and lasting advantage over your competitors.

Question 5: Making money with AI requires a PhD in math, physics, or computer science.

Question 6: Every AI PhD is guaranteed to know how to make money with AI.

Question 7: All AI tools are created equal.

Question 8: You're a project executive, and you leave the definition of the evaluation metrics to your data science team. Unfortunately, your data science team doesn't have strong business domain knowledge, and they provide you with a metric that you don't understand—let's call it the Gini coefficient. If they do well on that metric, the project will help your business.

1.12.2 *Longer exercises: Identify the problem*

A short narrative description of a hypothetical project or actions taken during the individual projects follows. What's your opinion of the situation described?

Question 1: A friend who works in the IT department of an organization somewhat similar to yours uses tool X and approach Y with great success. Should you use that tool and approach because your friend was successful with them?

Question 2: X, a Fortune 100 company, begins their AI efforts by creating an infrastructure holding petabytes of data and buying an array of tools capable of solving a broad spectrum of AI problems. They've also created a department responsible for using and maintaining all those tools. Should you buy the same set of tools?

Question 3: You want to start your AI efforts with the use cases that other people successfully employed. Can you ask consultants with AI experience for an example of AI use cases often seen in your industry?

Question 4: What's wrong with the following approach? You're seeing that AI is getting better in video recognition. You plan to start an AI project that would apply AI to recognizing and scoring Olympic skating. By using such an AI, you can show the viewers what the predicted scores would be as soon as the skaters are done, without needing to wait for the judges. Your AI solution must be ready before the next Olympics.

Question 5: Is the following a good idea? You're in a heavily regulated industry that delivers products to end consumers. You have to run all your changes by a regulator, and changes are evaluated (almost exclusively) based on legal compliance, with a typical change taking five years to be approved. You plan to use AI to understand online customer feedback and your customers' satisfaction. The technical term for this process is sentiment analysis.

Question 6: What are some problems with the following proposal? We'll use this AI and feed it patterns of our customer behavior, and it will reveal to us the causes of our customers' decisions.

Question 7: You're working in a domain in which it isn't easy to define business metrics that you can use to measure the business result. Someone has proposed to use AI and make business decisions based only on technical metrics. Is this a good idea?

Summary

- Machine learning (ML) is a combination of problem formulation, optimization, and result evaluation. The only part of ML that artificial intelligence (AI) can (mostly) do on its own is optimization—a human has to do everything else.
- Profit isn't made when AI provides an answer to a research question; it's made when you take a business action. Always start by asking, "What business actions can I take?"
- AI is mostly about finding correlative patterns: *A is often present in vicinity of B*. AI has significant limitations in its ability to impute cause or operate in the changing world.
- Succeeding with AI requires a CLUE, the acronym for *C*onsider the business actions available, *L*ink a research question to the available business action, *U*nderstand the answer to the research question in the business context, and *E*conomize scarce resources. Total absence of any of these elements is usually enough to doom the AI project.
- You should use a standardized workflow in every AI project. That workflow consists of triaging the possible business actions, defining research questions, defining business metrics to track, and estimating project difficulty and expense.

How to use AI
in your business

2

This chapter covers

- What project leaders must know about AI
- Finding which business problems benefit from the use of AI
- Matching AI capabilities with the business problems you're solving
- Finding the gap between the skills the data science team has and the ones your AI project needs

You can spend years learning about AI, but because of the fast evolution of this field, even fully proficient data scientists need to spend a significant portion of their time on continuous and ongoing learning. The market of AI books and papers is dominated by technical information about AI. With all that wealth of knowledge, it's difficult to distinguish between what you need to know to manage AI and the knowledge necessary to have if you're an engineer building an AI system.

This chapter talks about aspects of AI and ML that are necessary to understand to lead an AI project. It also teaches you how to find business problems that benefit from the application of AI. It provides examples of how to make AI insights actionable by linking AI capabilities with the business actions you already know you can take.

I've chosen the examples given in this and subsequent chapters from different business domains. It's possible that some of the examples will come from a business domain unfamiliar to you. This is a good opportunity to practice one of the primary skills in successfully applying AI: adapting AI capabilities to business situations that you encounter for the first time.

2.1 What do you need to know about AI?

AI projects are very complex, combining business, computer science, mathematics, statistics, and machine learning. This section explains why technical knowledge about AI isn't the primary knowledge needed for managing AI projects. If you're an AI project leader who doesn't have an analytical background, it's understandable if you feel that you need to grasp all of those concepts to be able to make the best decisions.

The situation could be even worse: not only are the data scientists talking about concepts with which you're unfamiliar, but those concepts might look like something *you're supposed to know* but can't fully recall. The jargon they use is often rooted in (or related to) statistical terminology. You might have taken a statistics class or two during your MBA program, and you might not have paid particular attention to all the topics covered. Don't worry. The most important decisions for project success don't require or even necessarily benefit from an extensive knowledge of statistics or the details of AI algorithms.

What you do need to know to manage AI projects is the same as with any other project: how to define metrics and processes that allow you to properly comprehend and monitor the direction and success of the project. Once you understand that, managing AI projects is similar to running those projects you've overseen before.

Managing an AI project is another application of management science

To use an analogy from a well-understood domain, if you were managing a factory, you wouldn't think that you'd need to become as good a worker as your foreman to run it. For that matter, it's a safe bet that quite a few executives who successfully manage factories aren't remotely handy.

The same principles apply for IT projects. Do you really need to know your database as well as your database administrator (DBA)? Do you feel you need to become a DBA to manage a database project?[a] You manage database projects by separating the

---

[a] In case someone wants to argue that AI isn't a factory, no, it isn't, but then neither is a database project. We've learned how to manage database projects without executives needing to become DBAs. Management as a profession is based on some universal principles for running organizations and projects, and that body of knowledge applies to AI too.

(continued)

business and architectural aspects of such projects from the skills needed to maintain RDBMS systems.

Just like a factory manager benefits from knowing how a factory works, having technical knowledge about AI doesn't hurt the project leader. However, the factory manager can't focus on the details of their foreman's job as a substitute for *knowing how to manage a factory and actively managing it*. Likewise, an AI project leader must focus on *management considerations*.

Still, there's often a feeling that managing AI projects requires significant focus on the details of how AI works internally, while comparable focus on details isn't necessary when managing factories or database projects. To the extent that this is true, it isn't so much because AI is different from other fields, but because AI is simply *a much younger field*.[b] In the case of factories, we've had enough time to develop management theory to understand that management knowledge isn't the same as domain-level knowledge about manufacturing. Having more time has allowed us to build methods and systems that allow us to compartmentalize skillsets: those needed to run a factory versus those needed to build a product. The goal of this book is to help you to do the same with AI.

---

[b] Yes, finding good data scientists is difficult, and, currently, they're rare. Today, some of them might object to being compared to a foreman. But do you think that a shift foreman for a railroad was a common skillset when early railroads were built? Or that the DBA skillset was common when databases were introduced? That's what I mean when I say AI is a young profession.

Most AI concepts that are relevant to making executive decisions could be explained to businesspeople in business terms. Ideally, your data scientists should be able to do that. If they can't, you should supplement your project team with people who have expertise in both AI and business to help with communications.

> **NOTE** If you're feeling that you need to better comprehend analytics to make business decisions, what you have isn't a knowledge deficiency but rather a communications problem.

What you need to know to manage an AI project is how to relate AI concepts to business. Namely, you need to be able to answer the following questions:

- What can AI do, and how can I use that in my business?
- What type of AI project should I start with first?
- How will I measure how successful AI is in helping my business?
- How should I manage an AI project?
- What resources are scarce, and how should I best assign them?

The rest of this book shows you how to organize a data science project in such a way that you can apply the management skills you already possess with minimal modifications to run AI projects.

2.2 *How is AI used?*

You make money when you perform an *appropriate business action.* That leads us to where AI plays into any system it's using—AI *directs you in which action to take.* This section explains how AI does that.

While AI, ML, and data science are perceived as new, the role that they play in making businesses successful isn't new. There are quite a few professions that have historically used some form of data analysis to make money. Some examples of those professions include actuaries and quantitative analysts. Experts in the application of statistical methods to process engineering and quality improvement science also have a long history of using data analytics to improve business results. AI doesn't change the way analytics and business relate, it just changes the methods for doing the analysis and the capabilities (and cost) of the analysis. There are significant parallels between how AI fits in with business today (and in the future) and traditional uses of data analysis in business.

To understand how to identify an opportunity to apply AI to a business problem, you first need to understand how a successful application of AI to a business problem has to look at a high level. In any problem in which data is used to inform further actions, there's a common pattern describing that process. We collect data, analyze it, and then react to it. This is simply an age-old control loop, and it's important to understand the elements of this loop. AI just adds new capabilities in the analytical part of that loop. Figure 2.1 shows how these elements interact.

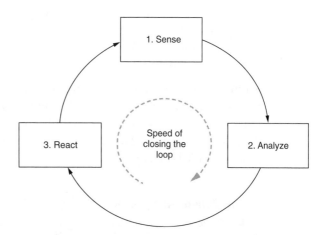

Figure 2.1 The Sense/Analyze/ React loop. Any successful analytical project must have all three elements of this loop.

Elements of figure 2.1 are as follows:

- *Sense*—The sensor part of the loop is where you get the data that the analysis looks for. For the majority of enterprise systems in the pre-big data age, data was in disparate databases. For big data systems, it's common to store data in a data lake.

- *Analyze*—That's the box in which you now apply AI to your dataset. Before AI, we used simpler algorithms (for example, a PID controller [34]) or human intervention (for example, a manual loan approval in the context of a bank). Although the introduction of AI to help with analysis is perceived as a recent development, it isn't—AI research started in 1956 [35]. We've been using computerized systems to perform analysis for decades. What's new is that today, with modern AI techniques, computerized analysis is much more powerful!
- *React*—Reactor/effector is the part responsible for the action in the real world. That reaction might be performed by a human or by a machine. Examples of manual reaction include many decision-support scenarios in which a management decision is made based on the results of the analysis. Examples of automatic reaction include robotics systems, smart thermometers [36,37], and automated vehicles [38].

The speed of closing the loop is the time between the moment some event occurs and the time when a reaction is performed. How much the speed of closing the loop matters depends on the domain. In a high-frequency trading system, there may be a strong requirement for completing a loop with the utmost speed. In other situations (for example, if you're performing data analysis in the context of archeological research), timing requirements may be much more relaxed. Sometimes the ability to guarantee that you'll meet time-critical deadlines matters too; an autonomous vehicle may require that your AI analytics *never* take longer than a specified time.

NOTE   The speed of closing the loop also depends on how often data is ingested into the system. Sometimes it's acceptable that data is periodically ingested into your system. In other cases, data must be analyzed in real time as it's arriving into the system. (This is called *streaming analytics*.)

An important consideration in the application of a Sense/Analyze/React loop is the question of *who or what is reacting*. It could be the system itself in some automated fashion. (That's what a self-driving car [38] does.) Or, based on the results of the analysis, it could be a human. The latter case is much more common today within an enterprise use of data science.

The Sense/Analyze/React loop is widely applicable

The Sense/Analyze/React loop is applicable across many scales. It could be applied on the level of a single device (as in the case of smart thermometers like Nest [36] and ecobee [37]), a business process, multiple departments, the whole enterprise, a smart city, or an even larger geographical area. I believe that the Sense/Analyze/React pattern loop will, in the future, be applied to the level of whole societies, in systems such as disaster relief and the tracking and prevention of epidemics.

The Sense/Analyze/React pattern isn't limited to the domain of big data and data science. That pattern applies to the domain of development and organizational processes too. You might be aware of various forms of the control loops that management sciences define and use. Examples of those loops are concepts like PDCA [39,40], OODA [41,42], and CRISP-DM [43], which have commonalities with and are further elaborations of this pattern. The Sense/Analyze/React pattern even applies to biology (for example, how octopuses and other animals behave [44]). In some domains, people might call the React part of the loop the *Effector* instead [45].

Automation of any business process is just an application of the Sense/Analyze/React loop. Using AI allows the application of that loop to some problem domain in which an automated reaction wasn't previously possible.

Automated data analysis is a recent development?

Even uses of fully automated and rapid Sense/Analyze/React loops using complicated and computerized analysis are nothing new. Capital markets, especially combined with algorithmic trading, implement this pattern on a large scale. With the further advancement of the Internet of Things [46] and robotics, these large-scale, fully automated, closed control loops will become much more prevalent within the physical world.

2.3   *What's new with AI?*

The advance of AI broadened the applicability of the Sense/Analyze/React loop, because AI brought to the table new analytical capabilities. This section explains those new capabilities.

What's new with AI and big data is that automated analysis has become cheaper, faster, better, and (using big data systems) capable of operating on much larger datasets. Analysis that used to require human involvement is now possible to do with computers in areas like image and speech recognition. Thanks to this new AI-powered capability, whole Sense/Analyze/React loops became viable in these contexts, when it wasn't economical to apply them before.

Examples of AI making automation viable

The following are some examples where an introduction of AI makes it possible to automate tasks that previously required a human to perform them:

- *Automated translations from one language to another*—Language translation is nothing new and is something that humans have done since the beginning of time. What's new is that AI has reached a level at which automated translations are now viable and, as such, a translation web service becomes practical.[a]

---

[a] Note that the actual control loop in a real translation system typically requires that at least two control loops are present. One loop translates from one language to another, while another loop makes money for this service. That second loop may also work by collecting information about what translations you need, analyzing them, and performing some action that makes money for the provider of the translation service.

(continued)

- *Autonomous cars*—We've had some form of the automobile for the last 250ish years, always requiring a human operator.[b] What's new with AI is that we may be on the verge of being able to construct a car that doesn't need a human driver.
- *Ability to diagnose eye diseases*—We've all read letters at a distance for ophthalmologists and optometrists and stared into the bright light on command. What's new is the ability of AI to detect diabetic retinopathy from simple retinal images [49].
- *Ability to read comments posted on the web*—If you read enough material in the comments section of a website, you can surmise whether people are enthusiastic or skeptical with regards to some topic. Now AI can do it too. AI can read a much larger number of comments faster and cheaper than a human ever could, and then tell you whether the audience is predominantly enthusiastic or skeptical. We call this capability *sentiment analysis*.[c]
- *Product recommendations*—Each one of us has friends that recommend books, movies, and products we might like. When AI does that (for example, on the Amazon website), it's called a *recommendation engine*.

Historically, when the size of datasets was small, humans were able to perform the same analysis that was done by AI. In some cases, what AI does is worse than what humans can do looking at the same dataset. But AI is more economical in the long run, and it can operate on datasets that are too big for humans to look at.

---

[b] The first self-propelled vehicle with wheels was invented in 1769 [47], with the first gasoline-powered cars appearing in 1870 [48].
[c] At the time of this writing, AI isn't nearly as good a reader of web content as a human is, and it's struggling with cynicism and subtle messages in text—it often misses even the basic thesis of the message. However, for the purpose of answering the question, "Has sentiment about the product improved in the last three months?" AI is good enough and can provide an answer much more cheaply than you or I can.

What's *not* new or different with AI is that analysis still can't make money all by itself. Note that in none of the use cases given in the previous examples did I talk about how to make money. While some of those use cases are clearly straightforward to monetize (for example, an autonomous vehicle that drives better than humans), in others it may not be clear how to monetize AI.

AI can't help you with a poor business case

Sometimes you won't be able to make a profit *regardless of how good your AI-powered analysis is*. Suppose that an ill-advised manufacturer of traffic signs decides to do sentiment analysis of the public opinion of those signs. The manufacturer would likely lose money on this analysis. It's not clear that drivers' feelings have a significant practical influence on the selection of traffic sign vendors (or for that matter, that sentiment about the sign would be determined by the choice of vendor as opposed to where the sign is placed).

When you perform an analysis, you incur the cost of that analysis. Profit may happen when you react based on the results of analysis. If there's no business action you can take after getting the results of analysis, such an analysis is always a loss.

2.4   *Making money with AI*

If AI allows for improved analytics with the Sense/Analyze/React loop, how do you make money with AI? By finding a situation in which AI allows you to apply Sense/Analyze/React loops so that one of the business actions available to you could be automated using that loop. This section shows you how. Figure 2.2 presents the general process of making money with AI.

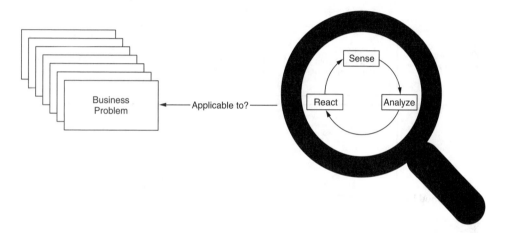

Figure 2.2   Making money with AI is based on finding a business problem in which you can apply the Sense/Analyze/React loop to one of the actions you can take.

You can apply this control loop in a new context because of the capabilities of AI. But to successfully apply the Sense/Analyze/React loop, you must make sure that all components of the loop are technically possible:

- On the Sense side, you must have the ability to collect the data that AI-supported analysis will need. Chapter 3 addresses how to ensure you've collected the appropriate data for your chosen AI method.
- On the Analysis side, you must make sure that you stay within the boundaries of what's possible with the available AI technology.
- On the React side, you must link the results of the analysis with one of the actions that you can actually implement in your business. You'll make a list of the possible business actions that you can take, and ask, "Is there an AI analysis that I can perform that will better inform this business action?"

Once you know that the Sense/Analyze/React loop is applicable to your business problem, you know that you have the ability to solve that business problem using AI. Let's start with an example.

2.4.1 AI applied to medical diagnosis

Suppose you're part of a software development team in a large hospital. Your team's goal is to apply AI to clinical and diagnostic procedures in the hospital. This section shows you how to find a use case in which AI can help.

To keep this example small and manageable, I'll concentrate on a single diagnostic workflow: a patient getting an eye exam. An image of a patient's retina is taken to check if there are any diseases. Assume that this procedure consists of the steps shown in figure 2.3.[1]

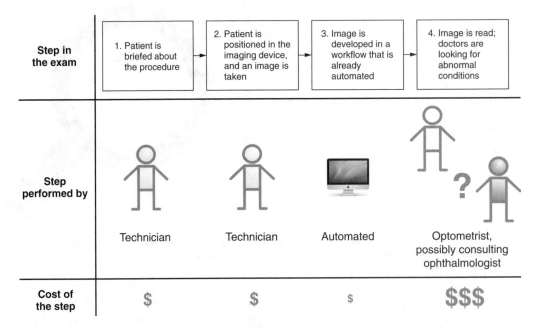

Figure 2.3   A workflow of a routine optometry exam. We'll apply AI to automate part of this workflow.

The workflow shown in figure 2.3 consists of the following steps:

1 Patient is briefed about the procedure. This step could be performed by a technician with minimal involvement of the optometrist.

2 Patient is positioned in the imaging device, and an image is taken. This step is also performed by the technician.

---

[1] An actual optometry/ophthalmology exam is more complicated and is simplified here for the sake of illustration.

3 Image is developed in a workflow that's already automated.

4 Image is read by the optometrist, looking for abnormal conditions. If necessary, additional doctors would be consulted.

Now you'd find a place where AI can help. In this workflow, you have three steps to which you could apply AI: two interactions with the patient and the final reading of the eye image.

Never start by thinking which analysis to do!

To illustrate why you don't start by asking, "What analysis can I perform?" let's construct a scenario in which you start with an analysis based on knowing that AI can do something for you.

You might be aware of voice assistants like Apple Siri [50] and know that their voice recognition is getting better. What if you combine a voice assistant/voice recognition with the chatbot so the patient can be briefed by a machine? You're lucky to have a good data science team that's happy to work with this cool technology. This looks like a good application of AI, doesn't it? Let's build a quick prototype!

Unfortunately, any time you spend on such a prototype will be wasted. Replacing a technician has limited value—the cost of the time a technician spends on briefing the patient is relatively small. More importantly, you're serving a diverse patient population, including multiple languages, disabilities, ages, and comfort with interacting with the machine. Human technicians are good at dealing with this population; today's AI isn't, if for no other reason than some segments of the population aren't used to talking with a voice assistant.

The idea you had was based on an interesting technology. The use case is inherently interesting and straight from sci-fi—many sci-fi stories feature patients talking with an AI doctor. The problem is that you've tried to apply AI to a situation in which a business action isn't profitable from the start, due to factors beyond your control.

This is a common trap. Everyone who works with AI in a business setting claims that they have a good business case, but often the business case was an afterthought, and the team's initial excitement about the project was caused by the opportunity to work with interesting AI technology.

In the worst case scenario, it might be impossible to monetize the project from the start, even if its technical portion was successful. Good AI implementation can't bail out a poor business case.

Let's use a systematic approach to better apply AI to this optometric exam. You start by enumerating the domain actions that you can perform and then see if you can apply the Sense/Analyze/React loop to those actions.

TIP Start by asking, "What are my viable domain actions?" As the number of domain actions that you can take is limited, you need to consider only a small number of use cases.

In this workflow, you have the two interactions of a technician with the patient, and you have the ophthalmologist/optometrist reading eye images to check for the presence of eye diseases. The interactions with the patient consist of an initial briefing and then positioning the patient in the imaging device so that a good image can be taken. You saw a moment ago why you can't automate the briefing. What about positioning the patient? That requires robotics expertise, and your executives are adamant that you're a software development company and not a robotics company. In your case, no action in the domain of direct patient interaction is viable.

What about interpreting the images? It turns out that interpreting images for certain eye diseases is complicated and that, in some cases, optometrists may miss important conditions. Professional interpretation is also costly and something that your hospital would save money on if you could make an alternate system that's helpful when diagnosing eye diseases. This use case is worth further investigation.

Further research from your data science team shows that there has been significant progress in the application of computer vision to medical diagnosis. You find that Google's team created an AI capable of diagnosing cases of moderate to severe diabetic retinopathy [49]. You have enough data from past optometry exams that you can train AI on that data. To make sure the Sense/Analyze/React loop is applicable in this use case, you need to cover only the *Sense* part. That proves to be easy; you already have an image of the retina of the patient, and you can send that image to your AI system.

2.4.2 *General principles for monetizing AI*

The previous example showed you how to find an opportunity for using AI in one business scenario. This section shows you what general principles you can extract from this example. Figure 2.4 shows those principles for applying AI.

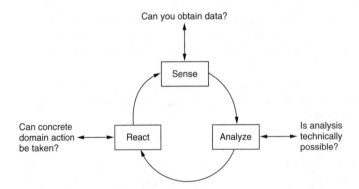

Figure 2.4   General principles for applying AI to a business problem. The basic idea is to make sure that you'll be able to implement all parts of the Sense/Analyze/React loop.

The approach shown in figure 2.4 covers each part of the Sense/Analyze/React loop:

- *Sense*—Can you collect the data you need? How much does it cost to collect that data?
- *Analyze*—Can AI do that analysis under ideal circumstances, or has anyone ever succeeded in doing something similar with AI? Is it well known that AI has such a capability? Does your team have expertise in applying those AI methods? How difficult is it to apply them?
- *React*—Find a domain action that would be of value and possible for AI. What is the economic value of that action? This information lets you judge if automating that action with AI is economically viable.

Chapters 3 and 4 will discuss how to use business metrics to cover the economic aspects and the application of the Sense/Analyze/React loop. For the time being, lets concentrate on how to cover the React and Analyze parts of the loop. You need to answer the following two questions:

1 Is there a systematic way to think about your business that helps to find domain actions that can benefit from AI?
2 What are the high-level capabilities of AI?

Once you know the answer to these two questions, you can perform an analysis like the one shown in section 2.4.1 to find viable use cases for AI.

Making money with AI isn't based on AI being smarter than humans

Examples in this chapter (and chapter 1) show why, to achieve success with AI, linking AI with business is much more important than specific algorithms and technology. AI isn't bringing superhuman intelligence to the table; it possesses humanlike capabilities in limited domains, such as image recognition. It can also apply those capabilities economically and operate with larger datasets than any human can. But you still need to figure out how AI's capabilities translate into improving your business.

AI can sometimes find insights that escape human intelligence because of its ability to process large datasets. However, when operating in complicated domains, AI still lags behind humans. By itself, AI can't figure out how to make money.

Peter Drucker believed that it's more important to do the right thing than to do things right.[a] AI's job is to help you do better analyses, and it could help you do things right, but only you can ensure that AI is applied to the right problem.

---

[a] From the article "Managing for Business Effectiveness" [4]: "It is fundamentally the confusion between effectiveness and efficiency that stands between doing the right things and doing things right. There is surely nothing quite so useless as doing with great efficiency what should not be done at all."

2.5   *Finding domain actions*

Now that you understand that the application of AI is simply a matter of applying the Sense/Analyze/React loop to some domain action, the next question is how you can systematically find domain actions that you can take. This section shows you how to find them.

There's a limited set of high-level roles that AI can play in your business. Figure 2.5 shows those roles.

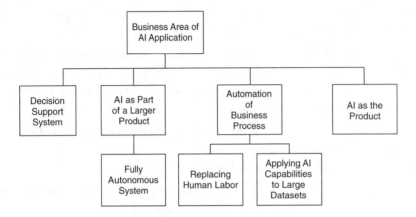

Figure 2.5   AI taxonomy based on the high-level role it plays in business. You could use this taxonomy to guide you in eliciting available business actions you can help with AI.

You can use AI as a part of the following:

- *Decision support system*—AI helps an employee or manager of your organization to make better decisions. Uses of such systems range from helping management make decisions affecting the whole organization to helping line employees in their day-to-day tasks.
- *Larger product*—AI could be just part of a larger product. Such a product has capabilities that AI may enable but that aren't purely AI capabilities. An example here would be house cleaning robots (like Roomba [51]) or smart thermostats (like ecobee [37] and Nest [36]). In the case of a fully autonomous system, AI guides the system's operation and makes its decisions without needing human involvement.
- *Automation of the business process*—AI automates some steps in the business process. Sometimes this is done to replace human labor; other times, it's done to process datasets that are so large that humans can't possibly handle them.
- *AI as the product*—You can package AI tools as a product and sell them to other organizations. An example is an AI product capable of recognizing images on traffic signs that will be sold to manufacturers of autonomous vehicles.

The rest of this section provides discussion of each of these bullet points.

2.5.1   *AI as part of the decision support system*

One of the most common scenarios for the use of data science in the enterprise today is the one in which AI is used as a decision support system. This section shows you how to use AI as a part of such a system to find domain actions.

AI as a part of the decision support system is the easiest scenario for elicitation of domain actions. In any decision support system, you're already focused on the options you need to decide on. When using AI as a part of the decision support system, you should consider the user (or management team) whose decisions you're supporting. Then you enumerate a spectrum of the decisions they can make. Finally, you ask yourself this question: "What information is needed to choose between these possible options?" The project is then organized around providing that information.

> ### AI helps the management team
>
> Suppose you're supporting a large manufacturing operation. The operation has multiple large suppliers that ship thousands of components to it every day. A big cost concern for your organization is that if a certain percentage of the supplier's components are faulty, the organization will spend a lot of time in the manufacturing process on troubleshooting problems. Such troubleshooting is costly. Even worse, the quality of the manufacturer's own end product could suffer.
>
> Although individual suppliers are a big part of your business, this sector is dominated by a few large suppliers, and your ability to force suppliers to improve the quality of their product is limited. How can AI help the management team for your manufacturing operation?
>
> Start by enumerating the options regarding what the management team can implement and which ones are viable. Because your organization has little leverage on an individual supplier, the only viable business action your organization can take is to change suppliers.
>
> What questions do you need to answer to change the supplier? Here we concentrate on one possible answer:
>
> > *Ideally, you want to be proactive and switch suppliers before their quality deteriorates—by then, our manufacturing operation has already incurred costs. It's difficult to decide to terminate the relationship with the supplier, because you don't know what the cost of staying with the supplier will be. Ideally, you want to act proactively, based on where the trend of the supplier's quality is heading. You don't want to cut a supplier whose trend in quality is improving. Nor do you want to wait to switch suppliers if the trend is diving.*
>
> Based on management response, you now know that if you could use AI to analyze the historical trend of quality and to predict a trend in future quality, you'd have a system that would be useful to management. This is an example of using AI as a part of the decision support system.
>
> This example also illustrates why customizing AI's use to your own business case is better than applying AI solutions that worked for someone else. If you were a much

> **(continued)**
>
> larger customer to those suppliers, your management team might be able to negotiate the terms of the relationship, as opposed to just switching suppliers. Examples of adjusting such relationships might include escalating problems to the supplier's management or asking for monetary compensation for defective parts.
>
> While those might be viable actions for customers of your suppliers that are much bigger than your organization is, they aren't viable actions for your organization. Generic AI solutions tailored to much bigger organizations might focus on actions you can't take.

One final question in this scenario: Supposing that you're a large organization with many departments, on which level of granularity should you request that business actions be supported by the decision support system? You should consider the options that are directly within the scope of responsibility and execution of the team that's performing the analysis.

> **WARNING**   It's critical that you choose the right level of organization to look for possible actions you can take. If you finish with a list that enumerates 20 or more different options that you believe you can take, the granularity level on which you performed analysis was wrong.

When discussing the use of AI as a part of a decision support system, the danger lies in diving in too deep. If you're applying AI as part of a decision support system for the team of senior managers, then you should analyze the actions that senior managers take, not the actions that each individual worker working in their organization can take. Don't analyze the actions an intern can take on their first day.

> **TIP**   The decision maker doesn't have to be a high-level manager. Imagine an AI that recommends to your sales force which customers to approach and displays a dashboard with the further information about each customer. However, that AI leaves the final choice to the individual sales professional. Such an AI is a decision support system.

2.5.2   *AI as a part of a larger product*

Another common situation occurs when AI capabilities are part of a larger product. In this situation, a key characteristic is that the end customer isn't buying the AI itself; they pay for some capability that the larger product wouldn't have without using AI. This section shows you how to use AI in the context of a larger product.

AI as a part of the product itself is already extremely important. Examples include products that range from smart speakers (Amazon Alexa [52], Google Home [53,54], and Apple HomePod [55]) to autonomous vehicles [38]. Although you can think of AI as a way to differentiate products, you're generally better off thinking about it as an *enabler* of your value proposition to the customer.

TIP Few people would buy a product specifically because it uses AI. The key question is, "What value is the product providing for your customers?"

There might have been a time when saying "We use AI" was a viable marketing/fundraising technique, but that time is over. Over time, AI will play the same role in autonomous products as an engine plays in a car today: you can't go anywhere without it. However, most car buyers don't care about a particular engine, but rather its ability to move the car from point A to point B.

AI as a part of the product

An example of an AI product that also loops in humans is a home security company that uses an AI-powered device as a part of the security system. What are the relevant actions that such a system can take? For one, it can sound an alarm if it believes there's an intruder.

For various cost and liability reasons, management will probably require that the final action of sounding the alarm or calling the police must always be initiated by a trained, live operator in a monitoring center. Management could also decide how many operators will be assigned to monitor the properties. This business would be much more profitable if a single person could monitor multiple secured properties.

AI could be leveraged in such a system to help the operator seated in the monitoring center. If AI can recognize faces, it can also sound an alert when humans are in the house who are not part of the family that lives in the home. The AI can then notify the operator so that a check can be made and, if necessary, the operator can raise an alarm.

When AI functions as part of a larger product, that product operates somewhere within the physical world. Because the customer is paying for some capability the product has, not for the fact that the product is using AI, start with how the product functions. Which potential actions could the system carry out? Once you know the set of possible actions, the next question is, "When should the system take each one of those actions?"

NOTE When AI is part of a larger product, the product itself could be fully autonomous, or it could be a hybrid product that performs some functions automatically, while depending on humans for other tasks.

AI in the fully autonomous product

An example of a fully autonomous system would be a vacuum cleaning robot like the Roomba [51]. In this case, the vacuum needs to clean the whole room. The relevant domain action is, "Where should I go, and what areas should I avoid?"

AI can be used to provide navigation capabilities for the device in its environment. Note that such an AI could range from a sophisticated navigation system to relatively

(continued)

simple operations. A robotic vacuum can use AI to learn the layout of your rooms and recognize changes in that layout. You can also trade sophisticated mappings of the room for a bigger battery, allowing obstacle avoidance using a time-intensive trial-and-error approach.

That bigger battery is another example of the whole system being more important than the choice of AI algorithms. A few years back, it was simpler (and cheaper) to add a larger battery to increase run time than to spend a lot of time and money on significantly improved AI navigation.

In the context of a fully autonomous product, you also need to consider not only what actions the product can take, but that some actions and outcomes are neither desirable nor permissible. You don't want to watch an expensive robotic vacuum such as the Roomba crashing down the stairs.

How would capabilities of your product evolve?

It's important when using AI as a part of a larger product to consider not only the capabilities you're planning to add in the initial product, but also the whole roadmap of product capabilities that you plan to add later.

Often, your product is a physical system shipped to the customer. For example, in the case of the AI-powered autonomous vehicle [38], you'd ship the vehicle itself. Once the vehicle is delivered, an additional capability could be added to it as a software upgrade. But you're stuck with the sensors and effectors (engine, brakes, steering mechanisms, horn, signal lights, headlights, and so forth) that are shipped with the car. Once you distribute physical systems to your customers/users, it's often impossible (or expensive) to add the capacity to perform new actions that you didn't envision at design time. Whatever autonomous cars we have in the future, it's a safe bet that some of their capabilities will be fixed at the time the car is manufactured and will be difficult to change later.

2.5.3   *Using AI to automate part of the business process*

One of the uses of AI that's getting increasing attention in both industry and the popular press is the use of AI to perform actions that previously required humans. This section shows you how to apply AI to optimize existing business processes.

AI automating part of the workflow

Suppose you have a facility that's using CCTV cameras and security guards to monitor it. Looking at the screens is part of the workflow of the security guards. AI could be used to make this part of the security guard's workflow more efficient by monitoring the video streams and highlighting unusual situations.

When you're looking at using AI to automate part of the business process, start by sketching out that process and then ask, "Can any of these steps be made more efficient or eliminated using AI?" This is using AI to perform a one-to-one task replacement: the task that used to be done by humans is now done by AI.

As the capabilities of AI and humans differ, a one-to-one replacement of tasks performed by people with performing them using AI is complicated and expensive. In most workflows, a few tasks are essential, and they prove to be difficult to automate, even if the most time-consuming function of the job is automatable!

In practice, it's usually necessary not only to apply AI to steps in an existing process, but also to re-engineer business processes. Re-engineering should separate out operations that are easy to automate with current technology into a separate step of the workflow. Then you assign AI to only those parts of the process that are easy for AI but time-consuming or error-laden for people.

Creating new jobs with AI

The use of AI for automation is a controversial topic. If AI replaces a human in performing some action, and that action is the primary purpose of that person's job, that job can now be in jeopardy.

There are significant costs that should be considered when eliminating jobs. Foremost are the costs to the people whose jobs disappear. There are also costs to your company, not just monetary, but also in the goodwill of both the public and your remaining employees. It's important to keep that human perspective in mind when you talk about automation of your processes, and to understand that this scenario is often a zero-sum game.

If you're limiting yourself when thinking about AI only to scenarios in which you're replacing jobs with AI, then you're actually missing an opportunity. AI can allow you to create new businesses that weren't possible or economical before. This scenario generates new jobs—not only jobs building and supporting that AI system, but also all other jobs that come with such a business.

Take, for example, using AI to monitor the behavior of pets when owners are at work. At the moment, no one is doing this, because such monitoring isn't economically viable as a service if it has to be done by humans. An AI that's capable of monitoring the behavior of pets and entertaining them requires people in the loop to handle some rare situations that AI can't (for example, situations in which the pet appears to have a medical issue). Such an AI creates jobs for the people monitoring those pets. These jobs weren't economically viable at all when 100% of the work had to be done by humans. Such jobs become viable once an AI handles most of the monitoring and humans handle the exceptions.

2.5.4 AI as the product

Sometimes you have an AI solution, or an infrastructure solution supporting AI, that you believe to be applicable to many business contexts and many different customers. When that happens, such an AI solution is valuable in and of itself and could be packaged and sold as a standalone product. This section talks about some special considerations that apply when you're intending to sell an AI solution as a complete product.

You have a complete product when you have customers who are willing to pay for the AI capability that you can develop. There's a long history of companies offering various analytical products (such as SAS [56] or IBM's SPSS [57]), and AI-based products could be considered a continuation of this tradition, wherein complicated analytical capability is packaged in a format that customers can use.

> **TIP** You're selling a product. The key question is whether you can find customers that are willing to purchase this product. With regards to the sales cycle, the fact that the product itself is based on AI is secondary to all other sales considerations.

But there's a specific consideration that you must address when you base your product on AI. You must correctly assess the capabilities of your organization and your team regarding their knowledge of AI. There's a vast difference between developing an unprecedented AI solution and applying known AI capabilities in a new and specific context.

Developing new AI solutions and capabilities is a different ballgame that requires significant prior expertise in the field. When you're selling AI as a product, you must assess not only the ability to deliver an initial version of the product, but also your ability to out-innovate the competition.

> **WARNING** Unless you have a team of experts in AI research working for you, stick to applying an existing AI capability to a new context. Avoid AI products that require you to develop new AI capabilities that no one else has demonstrated yet, because they're unpredictable, difficult, and risky to develop.

On the other hand, if you understand a general AI capability, then there is much less risk in applying that capability to a product in some new field. For example, it's known that AI is getting very good at recognizing the context of an image—that's a general capability. If you can apply that capability to a specific area, you might have a viable product. One example would be software that's able to recognize defects on a factory line. This could be invaluable, provided you know to whom you would sell it.

Is my AI product widely applicable?

Some AI products are general frameworks that are (clearly) widely applicable, but others are specific to one category of problems.

If your AI solves one category of problems, it can stand alone as a product if you can find multiple examples where the use of your AI solution makes new business actions viable. If, instead, you find only a single example of AI producing a new business action, then you're better off thinking about what you have as an example of AI being part of a larger product.

When trying to figure out what new business actions AI makes viable, you'll be applying the techniques in sections 2.5.1, 2.5.2, and 2.5.3. However, instead of applying them to your own business, you'll apply them to your potential customer's business.

2.6 Overview of AI capabilities

Section 2.5 showed you how to find a business question on which you can act if you can pair it with the appropriate AI capabilities. This section presents the taxonomy of AI capabilities that helps you answer the question, "Is there a broad area of AI capabilities that could address my business problem?" Figure 2.6 presents such a taxonomy of AI methods.

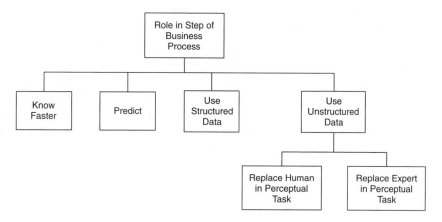

Figure 2.6 Taxonomy based on AI capabilities. This framework groups broad areas of AI capabilities so that you can quickly check if any of them are applicable to the business problem you're addressing.

This taxonomy is a modification of the taxonomy originally presented in Bill Schmarzo's books [58,59] with the "Use of unstructured data" category expanded to highlight the use of AI in perceptual tasks. The main goal of this taxonomy is to guide a discussion between the AI expert and the business expert. Categories in this taxonomy follow:

- *Know results faster.* Here, AI helps you discover a result more quickly, and that has a business value in many scenarios [58,59]. Suppose that you run a car manufacturing plant and you're assembling cars from parts that are made in one area of your factory. If you know that some car part is defective as soon as it's made, you can discard it at once and never install it in the car. This is much better than learning that the part was defective after you've already installed it in the car and shipped that car to the customer.

- *Predict some event that occurs in the future, based on current trends.* You saw this technique used in section 2.5.1 when predicting the future quality of the supplier based on historical trends.
- *Use structured data.* Sometimes you can find the answer you're looking for in one of the relational databases that you already have, especially if you have a large volume of data [58,59]. There are also AI methods that work well with data that's already in tabular format.[2]
- *Use unstructured data.* AI methods can also help you process and comprehend a large quantity of unstructured data, such as text, images, video, and audio [58,59]. In this case, you can use AI methods to recognize the context of the image, video, or audio recording.
- *Replace humans in perceptual tasks.* This subcategory of unstructured data use is based on the fact that, in recent years, AI has matched and even exceeded human abilities on many simple recognition tasks, such as image recognition [62,63]. You can think about this category of AI as having the ability to perform simple perceptual tasks that humans easily and instinctually perform. An example of such a task is recognizing objects in a photographic image.
- *Replace experts in perceptual tasks.* This subcategory of AI capability also comprehends unstructured data, but here AI performs perceptual tasks that otherwise require a high-level human expert. Such an expert uses skills that, after years of training, have become instinctual. An example of this would be using AI to interpret medical imaging. In recent years, AI has demonstrated an ability to interpret medical images on a level that in some cases rivals human experts [64,65].

Now you see how we've found AI solutions applicable to the business problems presented in section 2.5. In all those examples, you start by finding an actionable business problem and then the domain actions that could be taken. You ask the question, "Can we apply any of the six categories of AI capabilities shown in figure 2.6 to this business problem?"

Can you enumerate all the individual AI methods out there?

There's no way to describe all the capabilities that AI has in any single book, including this one. AI is a rapidly developing area, and AI capabilities transform daily with the development of novel methods and applications. If you're interested in the details of individual AI methods, you need an experienced data scientist or consultant to guide you through the details of the latest capabilities of AI.

The taxonomy presented in this section isn't a substitute for AI expertise, but it's a systematic way to frame a discussion between a business expert and an AI expert.

---

[2] An example of such a method is *gradient boosting.* If you're interested in the technical details of this method, see the discussions on Wikipedia [60] and the Kaggle website [61].

> It provides common terminology and concepts in a way that's easy to comprehend for the business users. If you're an expert in AI, you can use the taxonomy presented in this chapter as a quick checklist for a class of methods and algorithms that should be checked for applicability to business questions.

2.7   *Introducing unicorns*

This chapter has shown you how to determine which business problems can benefit from AI techniques, but does your particular development team have the knowledge necessary to implement the solution you just proposed? This section helps you answer that question.

    The skills we're using on AI projects are still new (and rare), and there's still some amount of confusion in the industry about the skillsets that data scientists and data engineers should possess. Because of the rarity of those skills, there's a joke that such experts are *unicorns*. In this section, I'll start by describing the skills that are often *attributed* to unicorns. Then I'll explain why most real-world teams will never have all those skills. Finally, I'll show you how to make sure your team possesses all the skills that the specific AI project you're running requires.

2.7.1   *Data science unicorns*

Data science could be considered an umbrella term that covers many skills. A survey performed in 2013 lists 22 different areas that are part of data science [66]. Examples of those areas include topics like statistics, operational research, Bayesian statistics, programming, and many others. It gets worse! Today, there are new areas that would certainly be considered important (for example, deep learning).

> **NOTE** Clearly, a data science unicorn should be a world-class expert in each one of those areas, right? No, these are individually very complex areas. Many distinguished professors in leading universities spend the totality of their time and effort to be an expert in just one of those areas. Most likely, no one in the world has expertise (defined as being on a level comparable to the skills of the aforementioned professors) in all those disciplines. Even if such a unicorn exists, which AI projects would have the budget for one?

Why are so many different skillsets part of data science? Because different practical problems benefit from different skills. No single ML method beats out all other methods across all possible datasets.[3] Each of these methods emerged because when the AI community tackled real, practical problems, some of them worked better than others. After many years, we use a combination of many methods from different disciplines.

---

[3] This is also known as the *No Free Lunch Theorem* [67].

> **How to grow unicorns**
>
> Did the leading data scientists start by learning all the methods that they know today? To be an accomplished data scientist, must you first build a skillset that emulates the skillset of a famous data scientist? No. Often, the skills of two accomplished data scientists don't match. Even among accomplished data scientists, it's virtually guaranteed that one will have expertise in at least one area with which the other is unfamiliar.
>
> The skillset of accomplished data scientists is often acquired by working through problems that benefited from specific types of AI methods. They had to learn those particular AI methods *because they were necessary to solve a concrete problem in the domain in which they worked*. Each new project brings them new skills, sometimes in new areas that weren't previously part of their core domain of expertise. For example, in 2011, few people in the world, in business or academia, were working on what today is known as deep learning.
>
> If you want to become a unicorn, work on problems worth solving. You'll acquire a strong skillset along the way.

As a manager, you should look for two things when hiring data scientists for your team. You should look for a candidate who has skills in the core domain that your initial AI project is likely to use, but you also need them to have a demonstrated ability to learn new skills. Chances are good that, along the way, your data scientist will need to learn many new methods. When hiring senior data science team members, don't just look for a strong background in one set of AI methods. Senior data scientists should have a history of solving concrete problems using a diverse set of methods.

> **TIP**   Data science is a team sport. To completely cover all of the knowledge that's part of data science, you need a whole team, so you must assemble a team with complementary skillsets.

How should you assemble your initial data science team? Your team needs both enough business expertise to understand your business problem and enough proficiency in AI methods to perform an initial analysis and determine if AI can address your problem. Keep in mind that on the way to delivering a full AI solution, the team will have to learn some new skills.

2.7.2 *What about data engineers?*

When we discuss AI, we often talk about operating with some datasets so large that they don't fit on a single machine and require a big data framework to manage. While data scientists are proficient with the use of big data frameworks, they're rarely experts in the details of those frameworks. As a result, you'll need specialists who are primarily focused on the use of the big data frameworks themselves. We call them *data engineers*.

Just like data science, big data is a large area. Let's take the example of just one popular product in the big data space—the Apache Hadoop framework [15]. A few years back, the distribution of one of the leading Hadoop vendors consisted of 23 separate components, each one of which was large enough that a separate book could be (and often has been) written about it [68].

The body of knowledge that falls under the umbrella of data engineering is much larger than any single big data framework. Data engineers often need to be able to operate in both an on-premise and cloud environment. Cloud services like Amazon AWS [11], Microsoft Azure [13], and Google Cloud Platform [12] have different platforms with significant differences between them. That means that in addition to the specialist skills in big data frameworks, data engineers you hire may also need to have a skillset in the cloud platform of your choice.

Clearly, the same limits that apply to data scientists also apply to the data engineers: they're also humans and can't know everything. Data engineers are characteristically experts in a few of the components of the leading big data frameworks.

2.7.3 So where are the unicorns?

I hate to break this to you, but it's highly unlikely that you'll find any single human that has a strong expertise in each one of the methods, products, and technologies that are part of data science and data engineering. At best, you could hope to find a couple of senior people who have strong experience in individual data science and data engineering topics and who have enough familiarity with other related subjects to talk with specialists in areas in which they themselves aren't experts.

Although universities have started offering programs and degrees in data science and data engineering topics in recent years, it's not likely that this problem is solvable through better education. The field of knowledge is simply too large, so you should have a realistic expectation of what these institutions can teach their students.

> **WARNING** As a project leader, you must differentiate between the skillsets that your team possesses and skillsets that you need for your project. You should identify and close skill gaps. Don't assume that your senior data scientists and architects know everything in their fields, and don't impose expectations on them that they should. Such expectations only make people less likely to acknowledge skill gaps.

Project leaders must know where the knowledge gaps are in the team. Piloting an AI project that requires skills your team doesn't already possess means that you need to close these knowledge gaps. You do that by applying *gap analysis* [69]. An example of a gap analysis between the skillset a team presently has and the skillsets that are needed is shown in figure 2.7.

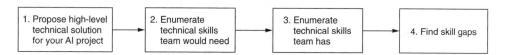

Figure 2.7 Gap analysis between skills the team has and the ones needed. This analysis allows you to create a plan for how to address missing skills.

You perform gap analysis by applying the following steps:

1 You first work with your technical team to sketch a high-level technical solution. Match the time spent on this technical solution with the likelihood that you'll implement it. If you're just considering the project, then the solution should be a high-level one. If you're planning to initiate the project soon, then your initial technical solution needs significant detail.

2 Based on the solution, take an inventory of the technical skills you expect the project will need to address your identified use cases. This summary of skills should be made by people who both are familiar with the business problem you're trying to solve and have enough technical expertise to quickly identify a high-level technical approach to solving it.

3 Which skills do your team members already have? Ask your team about their skillsets and avoid assumptions in this area—AI and data engineering are highly technical fields, and it's easy to have unfounded assumptions.

4 Find any gaps between the needed and current skillsets. These gaps are useful in estimating the project's difficulty level for your team. Keep this list. If you decide to proceed with a project that addresses this business question, you'll need to make a plan for how to close the gap. (You close knowledge gaps by training your team, hiring new team members, or hiring consultants.)

Understand that gap analysis is always performed based on the current situation. If you're just thinking about an AI project as a possibility, you should perform this gap analysis on a coarse level with just an outline of a technical solution. For projects that are in progress, you need a much more detailed solution as a starting point. That means that throughout the project life cycle, you'll typically perform gap analysis multiple times.

Beware how you ask

When you ask about gaps in technical skills, you're asking your technical staff to admit to areas in which they personally don't have expertise. If poorly handled, they might rightly consider it a landmine. Put some thought into this before you ask; it's your job as a leader to make sure that you create an atmosphere in which it's easy for team members to admit that they don't possess some technical skills.

One preferred technique to create such an atmosphere is based on building trust among team members so that they can talk about issues like this. Other techniques you might find useful are asking for the skillset in private, creating an anonymous survey, or asking a trusted intermediary to approach the subject with your team members.

2.8 Exercises

The goal of this book is to help you develop practical skills you can use when running your project. To help you with that, the exercises in this section ask you to apply skills learned in this chapter to new business scenarios.

2.8.1 *Short answer questions*

Please provide brief answers to the following questions:

Question 1: Think about a failed project in your enterprise. Would that project have failed in the exact same way if it also had a component based on AI?

Question 2: Do you personally have enough knowledge of data science and data engineering to understand the gap between the technical skills that your team has and the skills that they need for this project?

Question 3: Do you have a good enough relationship with your team members that they're comfortable admitting the limitations of their skillset to you?

2.8.2 *Scenario-based questions*

Answer the following questions based on the scenarios described:

Question 1: One of the important skills in applying a Sense/Analyze/React loop is to identify who will execute on the React part of the pattern. For the following scenarios, answer this question: Who or what will carry out the action and fulfill the React part of the Sense/Analyze/React loop?

- **Scenario 1:** You're making an automated car, and the AI that you're using will allow fully autonomous driving under all conditions (so-called Level 5 autonomy [38], in which there are no available controls for the driver).
- **Scenario 2:** You're writing a recommendation engine in which products are suggested to the customer.
- **Scenario 3:** You're writing an AI program to regulate a smart thermostat that controls the temperature in your home.

Question 2: Use AI to create a new job. Find an example of an AI capability that would let you offer a new service that your organization doesn't yet provide. (For the job to count as a solution to this exercise, it must be a job that's so unrelated to the software development team that's building the AI, that the person hired for the job is unlikely to ever meet that team.)

Question 3: Suppose you're using an AI algorithm in the context of a medical facility—let's say a radiology department of a large hospital. You're lucky to have on the team the best AI expert in the field of image classification, who has you covered on the AI side. While you're confident that expert will be able to develop an AI algorithm to classify medical images as either normal or abnormal, that expert has never worked in a healthcare setting before. What other considerations do you need to address to develop a working AI product applicable to healthcare?

Question 4: Apply the previous example from a hospital setting to a classification problem in your industry. What are the new considerations that exist in your industry as compared to the healthcare industry?

Question 5: Provide an example of an AI that has replaced a human role but doesn't provide as good of an experience as a human would.

Question 6: You're a manufacturer of security cameras, and you've developed an AI algorithm that can detect a person in a picture. Regarding the taxonomy of its role in your business, how would you classify this use of AI?

Question 7: You're an insurance company, and you've developed an AI program that, based on static images from an accident site, could recognize which parts of the car are damaged in a wreck. Can this replace an insurance adjuster?

Summary

- Managing AI projects doesn't require expertise in the details of AI algorithms. Instead, you need to know how to explain the benefits of an AI project in business terms. What business problem is being solved? What business benefit does AI provide? How is that benefit measured?
- You can discover business actions you can take and those that may benefit from AI using a systematic process. Apply the taxonomy described in figure 2.5 to your organization.
- AI capabilities are based on being able to know sooner, predict, process structured and unstructured data, and perform perceptual tasks.
- AI can help your business by performing analysis that informs some concrete business action. AI opportunities arise when you can apply a Sense/Analyze/React loop, with the Analyze part based on AI capability and the React part based on concrete business actions you can take.
- No individual is an expert on all topics of AI, data science, and data engineering. Project leaders must identify and close any relevant gaps in the knowledge and capabilities a team has.

Choosing your first AI project

This chapter covers

- Selecting AI projects that are matched to your organization's AI capabilities
- Prioritizing your AI projects and choosing which AI project to run first
- Formulating a research question that's related to a business problem
- Pitfalls to avoid when selecting AI projects, and best practices of such projects

To develop a sustainable analytical organization, you shouldn't start with an AI project that involves complex technical challenges. Instead, you should choose your initial project so it provides clear and actionable results quickly. Your whole process should be organized to optimize *time to success*.

This chapter shows you how to select your first AI project. It also teaches you how to check if the research question that your AI project uses correctly reflects the business concerns it's supposed to address. Finally, it presents a list of common pitfalls that young AI teams might fall into.

3.1   Choosing the right projects for a young AI team

I assume that your long-range goal is to build an AI team that will help the success of your parent organization by delivering a series of successful AI-related projects. To achieve that, you need to understand the journey that a successful AI team will take. This section explains that journey.

> **TIP**   If you're after a one-off AI project, you might be better off buying an off-the-shelf solution or contracting with an outside partner to do it for you.

One of the most crucial decisions that you as a leader need to make is how you want to prioritize the order of the initial AI projects that your team must undertake. Before you're ready to make that decision, you need to understand its impact. To understand how AI teams succeed or fail, you first need to understand what success and failure look like.

3.1.1   The look of success

Leo Tolstoy wrote in *Anna Karenina* [70]:

> *All happy families are alike; each unhappy family is unhappy in its own way.*

Likewise, all successful AI teams are alike: your AI team is growing in expertise (and possibly headcount) and is solving more and more complicated problems. Unsuccessful AI projects result from an assortment of errors (many of which are described in section 3.4), and they may take your whole AI team down with them. This section explains why you should start with projects that are quick to deliver but still provide significant value for your business.

If you're initiating AI efforts in your organization (or even if you're part of an established analytical organization), you're subject to three forces:

1 *Plentiful opportunities*—You're operating with technologies (AI and big data) that weren't present in business and industry historically, and you're the first to apply them to the many datasets your organization has.
2 *Limited time and resources*—You have limited resources to devote to analysis. Chances are, you don't have enough qualified people to run AI projects you're thinking about.
3 *Success makes you stronger*—If you make money for your business, your analytical resources will increase over time. Management invests in teams with a good track record of providing value. Additional data scientists will want to join projects with a history of success. Solve some easy problems first, and you'll get the resources you need to address larger problems.

How do you succeed in an environment like this? Does it make sense to first concentrate on large wins regardless of how difficult they are (for example, projects that provide significant monetary value)? Clearly not. What's difficult today will be easier tomorrow, so start with a project that has significant monetary value and can be delivered quickly.

> **TIP** The key is a fast turnaround on initial projects so that you can learn quickly. You're the first one in your company that has applied AI to your data and business problems, and there are plenty of opportunities to succeed with AI. Frankly, if you can't find an easy win in such a setting, then AI simply can't help your business.

Let's use another analogy here. The position your team is in (with respect to the opportunities) would be similar to a hunter that finds a rich hunting ground. If opportunities to make money were animals, and you were a prehistoric hunter, you'd be operating in a target-rich environment (see figure 3.1).

Figure 3.1 You're in a rich hunting ground—plenty of rabbits and a big mammoth are in sight. Which animal should you try to catch first?

Building a successful analytics organization is similar to surviving and prospering as a hunter. Now, ask yourself, "If I were in that position, would I aim for the biggest animal in the field first?"

The answer is probably no, if for no other reason than that you're at the end of a long and distinguished line of ancestors that have succeeded in passing their genes to the next generation. They had the common sense and the skills to survive. You don't initially have the hunting skills that bring you success if you go after the mammoth first! If you're like me, the author, chances are that by the time that mammoth turned around, you'd deep-six it, run far away, and convert to vegetarianism for the rest of your life. But I'd like to believe that even I can be successful snaring a rabbit. All successful hunters should be able to catch rabbits (see figure 3.2), right?

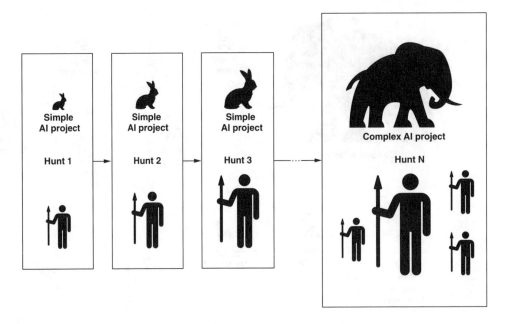

Figure 3.2   Start with easy projects. Success with those projects enhances your skills and reputation within the rest of the company, allowing you to attempt more difficult hunts later.

You don't want to start with a technically difficult project that requires a long time to deliver, even if that project is perceived to have a high business value. If your team is the hunter, the easier projects are the rabbits of the project world.

> **TIP**   Once you're known as a good hunter, the rest of the tribe is going to be more willing to help you with hunting mammoths. As your AI team learns and builds a solid reputation with the executive team, you'll get more resources. That's the time to take on difficult AI projects.

Start simple and build from there: An example

A large and established engineering company building heavy machinery was interested in using AI. The initial project was relatively simple, and the AI technologies used were something that you'd find in almost every machine learning (ML) introductory textbook. Analysis consisted of the basic clustering of problems encountered with the equipment and a basic trend prediction. But the volume of data about equipment failure was large, so that type of analysis wasn't something that could be performed manually across the complete line of equipment manufactured by this company. The details of the business case were specific to that operation, but a monetization case was simple and straightforward. The higher level management agreed that it was a good idea to start that project and agreed to take business actions based on what AI advised. The business action to be taken (based on analysis) was changing the allocation of resources for future equipment maintenance.

A small team finished the technical side of the project quickly. It was simple to persuade managers to immediately adapt the results. A strong business case had helped the AI team leader to navigate the many organizational constraints and bureaucratic obstacles, which are a fact of life in any large organization. (And the AI team learned how to avoid many of those obstacles the next time around.)

The solution provided high visibility to the AI team and an excellent relationship with the executive team. The AI team now had access to all the resources it needed and was able to hire new people and take on more difficult projects. Regardless, the next project selected was again relatively simple technically and, again, had large business consequences. This is a virtuous cycle: the AI team becomes more highly respected and has access to even more resources. Today, as you can imagine, the team is much larger and works on some of the most complicated AI projects in its industry.

3.1.2 *The look of failure*

What must you avoid to prevent a massive failure? Yes, there are many ways in which individual small AI projects can fail, but there's only one general way in which a whole AI team fails. Total team failure occurs when the AI team places all their bets on a single AI project that subsequently fails.

Let's extend our previous analogy of the hunter. How does the hunter fail? At the end of the day, a successful hunter has something to eat, and an unsuccessful one doesn't. Why do unsuccessful hunters starve in a target-rich environment?

In a target-rich environment, you don't starve because your hunt for the biggest animal failed. You starve because you spent too much time chasing the biggest animal, overlooking smaller ones that would have been an easy dinner. The time to hunt big animals is when you've honed your skills on the smaller ones and have a full belly.

NOTE When you're just starting your AI efforts, you'll have a hard time assembling a large enough team that's capable of tackling your biggest, toughest opportunity. The dangerous approach, "Let's go for the big opportunities first," too often becomes a risky bet that can destroy your team.

Choosing to start with the technically challenging projects, even if they have a higher perceived value, is dangerous. If your project is complicated, your analytics team might not have enough resources to run any other significant projects. All of your eggs are in one basket.

Medical diagnostics is a difficult problem

Suppose you're part of a hospital team that's interested in AI, and you try for the biggest *moonshot*—using AI to help in the oncology department. You form a large project team to build a decision support system for the oncology department. But cancer is a complicated illness, and in hospitals, within clinical guidelines, doctors have the last word in how things get done.

So now you're working on a complicated project requiring millions of dollars of investment, and you're trying to address an overly broad problem. You also didn't build trust incrementally with your end user (the oncologists), so they're skeptical of the results of your AI system. Even worse, they're right to be skeptical! Early system prototypes working on a different problem provided poor results. You're stuck in a vicious cycle, with no alternative but to double down on the project into which you've already invested millions of dollars.

Your team might have done much better if they'd concentrated on a simpler problem and built good relations with the doctors first. To start with, cancer isn't a single disease, but a large group of illnesses. Significant advances have recently occurred in AI's use in medical imaging [64], allowing for a good diagnosis of heart arrhythmia, for example. Why not build a good relationship with some cardiologists and take on more difficult projects later? It certainly won't hurt your chances of success if the head of cardiology is willing to recommend your expertise to their colleagues in other departments.

Figure 3.3 shows what can happen if you take on a project that's too hard for the initial skills of your team.

Sometimes, if you start with a complicated project, you might get lucky. Perhaps you'd be able to keep management's trust for long enough to be able to deliver a successful project, and success can help when tackling larger efforts later. But is betting

Complex AI project

Figure 3.3   You've cornered the mammoth on your first hunt. What are you going to do now?

on that kind of support wise, or is it a huge risk in which your most precious resource (your team's time) is spread thin on one large attempt? Furthermore, remember that this type of success will also set high expectations for future accomplishments. Even if your first project succeeds, now you have to find another large and risky project. How long will it be before your luck runs out?

When running a data science team, the real dangers lie in taking on a complex project, persisting too long on the wrong track, monopolizing your scarce resources, and having nothing to show for your efforts. All the while, you're incurring significant costs. Also, you're putting management in the position that they have to continue supporting an expensive project that doesn't deliver any result quickly. What if they decide that pulling the plug is the rational thing to do?

> **WARNING** When you're building an AI project that will be used as a decision support system, your business organization needs time *to learn how to implement* the results of your AI-powered analytics. If your management team gets nervous before the technical part of the project is completed, your project is dead on arrival.

3.2 Prioritizing AI projects

How do you choose the right first AI project? Simple: it must be, from a business standpoint, viable, valuable, and simple. That means each project must be able to deliver a result that's actionable for your business. It must have a significant business value, and you must be able to estimate how difficult it is to deliver. This section shows you how to create a list of projects that meet that criteria. Figure 3.4 describes the process that you should use to create a list of projects.

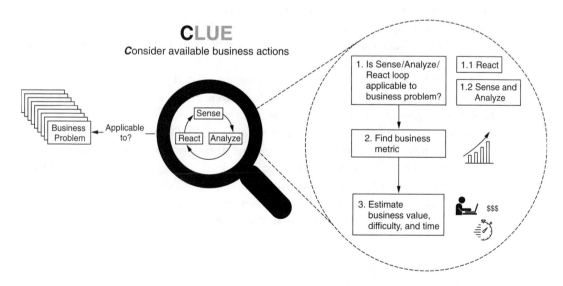

Figure 3.4 The *C* part of the CLUE allows you to create a list of viable AI projects and estimate their complexity.

Figure 3.4 shows these elements:

1. Start by looking at all the business areas your team is responsible for.
2. In which of those areas is it possible to apply AI and make sure you cover all elements in the Sense/Analyze/React loop? (A good reference for this step is figure 2.4 in chapter 2.)
    - Start with React, by finding the available actions that can be taken. (See section 3.2.1 for details.)
    - Then make sure that you can cover the Sense and Analyze side of the loop. (See section 3.2.2 for details.)
3. Determine which business metric you'll use to measure how much your AI project is helping you to achieve the business goal. (See section 3.2.3 for details.)
4. Estimate the business value of the given AI project.
5. Estimate the difficulty of implementing this business case and how long it will take to implement (section 3.2.4).

I'll assume you're able to estimate the business value (step 4) of the AI project on your own, as I don't know your organization or your business as well as you do. The rest of this section shows you how to implement the other steps in this workflow.

3.2.1   *React: Finding business questions for AI to answer*

After reading chapter 2, you're already aware of AI taxonomy based on the role AI plays in business. Using that taxonomy is a good way to elicit business actions that can be used in the React loop. This section shows you how to apply that taxonomy.

You find the appropriate React part of the Sense/Analyze/React loop by using a process of elimination. First, look at all the areas of your business. Then determine which of those areas will benefit from AI by applying an AI taxonomy at a high level (as described in figure 2.5 in chapter 2). Figure 3.5 shows you how to use that taxonomy to help facilitate discussions to discover the domain actions that cover the React part of the loop.

Figure 3.5 simply applies the existing business-related taxonomy of AI and asks a question designed to find a business problem that needs to be answered by AI. I'll show you an example of how you can use it.

Imagine you're working with a retailer that's nominally independent but part of a bigger franchise. Any process changes require the franchise owner's approval, and store management isn't willing to ask for that until you've shown them that AI can improve the bottom line. Consequently, the retailer's management isn't willing to change or automate their business processes yet, but it can change the *product mix* (how many products of which type are in the store).

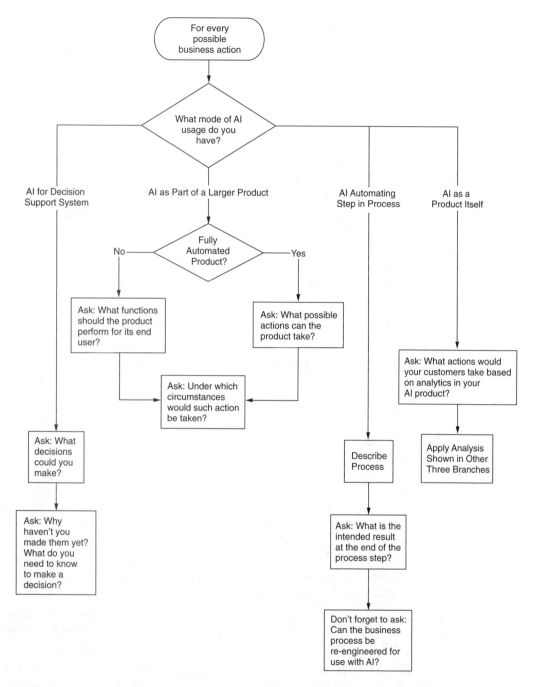

Figure 3.5 The React part of the Sense/Analyze/React loop: finding business problems that AI can react to. Once you've identified the role AI plays in your business, ask the questions provided here.

TIP Management's skepticism toward an AI-based solution is an issue that often needs to be addressed in the real world. Technologists often take AI capability for granted, but businesspeople can be skeptical. You need to earn their trust before larger and more effective AI projects can be adopted. Put yourself in the shoes of the retailer's management. How would you feel about going to the franchise owner and opening up with, "Can we change the processes that impact all the stores in the franchise? I want to try something called AI in my store, but I don't know how it will work out."

In this example, the only use of AI you can make is helping the store management itself. This is clearly an example of creating a decision support system. Look at figure 3.5 in the branch AI for Decision Support System. Questions applicable to this branch are which decisions can management make and why haven't they made them yet? That's where you learn that all your management team can do right now is change the product mix—you can put different products on different shelves. This is the React part of the Sense/Analyze/React loop.

The business question you're answering is, "What is the most profitable product mix in my store, based on historical sales?" Now you can move to the Sense/Analyze part of the loop.

Don't stop as soon as you find the first business problem

Before we proceed, let's see if there are other options for using AI in this retail store. Look again at figure 3.5. Is there any way to use the AI as Part of a Larger Product branch? Well, there's already a video surveillance system in the store. Can you use that video surveillance system with AI? If management wants to optimize the store's product mix, what function of AI combined with video surveillance can you perform for management? This is how you find additional actionable business questions:

- Did a customer look at the product and walk away? Is that product more expensive than the competition's?
- Did a customer look for a product that's out of stock? (They approached the area where that product is displayed, saw that you're out of the product, and walked away from the store.)

If you can use AI to answer these questions, you may have found a viable use case that can help you with the product mix optimization. When using figure 3.5, remember that each area of the business can generate multiple use cases.

But before you spend too much time on using AI for video stream analysis, be aware that this isn't an easy problem to solve, and it will take time to implement such an AI project.

Before you start the prototype, you decide to ask the retailer's management how they feel about the use case you've found. Good that you asked! Management tells you that they're worried about legal and public relation aspects of this use of AI in their store. They aren't interested in using video analysis. You've just saved the company the cost of implementing an AI solution that wouldn't be used even if it was successful.

3.2.2   *Sense/Analyze: AI methods and data*

Once you've established the React part of the loop, you must decide which AI algorithms you'll use, and make sure that you have sufficient data to use them. This section talks about the relationships between AI methods and data.

This is one area where, if you aren't proficient in AI yourself, you need an expert with a strong command of a broad range of AI and ML algorithms to help you. The field of AI is simply too large and changing too fast for any single book to teach you enough to replace that expert. Still, the taxonomies presented in figure 2.6 in chapter 2 can be useful to frame the discussion and remind you of high-level AI capabilities that you can apply to the business questions you want to address.

Once you have an idea of the type of AI methods you'll use, you need to be aware of the relationship between those methods and data, as shown in figure 3.6.

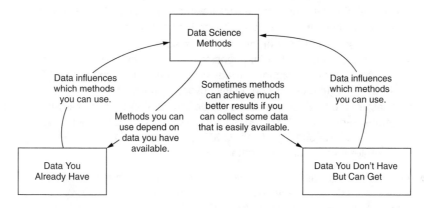

Figure 3.6   Data science methods and data are interconnected and influence each other. Never discuss a method without asking where you can get the data needed to train it.

You must always consider the data and AI methods that you're planning to use together. You can divide data into two groups: data that your team has and data that your team can collect.

> **TIP**   Data you can collect isn't only data that you have somewhere in your organization but that isn't immediately available to your team. It can also be data you can acquire from sources external to your organization or data you can purchase from business partners. Getting access to such data often requires negotiation and signed contracts.

Considerations when collecting data

Data collection has many pitfalls, and you must carefully govern it. Ask at least the following questions:

- What does your chosen ML algorithm need to train on this data? What data format does it require? What volume of data does this algorithm need to be trained? What quality?
- What sources provide this data?
- Who owns the dataset?
- What is the cost of acquiring this dataset? How long would it take to acquire it? Is it necessary to negotiate (or even sign legal contracts) to get access to that data?
- How closely does this dataset conform to the data format that you'd obtain in a production system? Do you need to preprocess the training data before it can be used, and does the data need to be labeled?
- How big of a data infrastructure will you need to store the dataset?
- How can you collect new data after the initial dataset is constructed?
- Is it possible that your organization has some data, but that your team isn't able to access it? It often happens that you're not able to access some of the data that your organization already has. Data can be confidential for reasons of ethics, regulations, or company privacy policy.
- What are the legal and ethical considerations (copyright, privacy policy, expectations, and so forth)? You should always consider ethics, organizational policy, and regulations (with GDPR [71] and HIPAA [72,73] being some examples) when collecting data.

Once you go through this checklist, you'll notice that, in some cases, you're able to easily collect the data that your ML algorithms need. In other cases, you may find that the data is unavailable or too expensive to collect.

In the retail example given in the previous section, your data scientist assures you that you can use one ML method to predict sales trends and another to optimize product mix. The names of these algorithms and methods don't mean much to you; some terms like ARIMA, LSTM, and operational research might pop up. Those methods require data about past sales. Such data is available internally in your organization, and your project can access it immediately. You've now identified a use case for which all elements of the Sense/Analyze/React loop are covered—this is a viable use case for an AI project.

AI that recognizes your food

Another example of the relationship between data and the algorithm used can be seen when using AI to do image recognition of food. The context can be a food processing plant or a smart, internet-connected oven [74] that has a camera inside it and uses AI to automatically recognize the food you put into the oven.

To make such an oven, you need to use an AI algorithm that can recognize an image (at the time of this writing, usually some form of convolutional neural network), and you need data to train such an AI method. This data consists of pictures of various kinds of food.

When you're beginning a project, you won't have many pictures of food in-house. But there may be some external sources from which you can collect data. Such sources are websites that feature pictures of food, or even pictures of the foods that users of your oven are cooking. There are additional considerations when collecting pictures of food from these sources that are typical to data you don't have but can potentially collect. You need to make sure that copyright and privacy laws are respected.

Another interesting aspect of collecting data is that some data you collect is subtly different from the ideal data you'll want for training your AI. The position and type of the camera in the oven make the pictures of food it takes look a little different from pictures of food on a plate (which is what you'll typically find on the web). Also, ovens are greasy places, and grease on the glass may impact the image of the food in the oven. No picture of food on the web is shot through a greasy lens!

What if some of your business questions could have benefited from some AI technique that isn't known to the best data scientist you were able to find? If the best AI experts you can find aren't even remotely familiar with that particular AI technique, drop it from consideration, as it's unlikely that you can assemble a team that's strong enough to deliver using it.

Big data or small data?

Big data has a large mindshare, and most AI conversation occurs in the context of big datasets. Big data is certainly necessary: if you're going to store hundreds of pictures per person, at high resolution, taken by millions of people, you certainly need a large storage capacity.

But big data is just one type of data your AI algorithms can use, so you shouldn't think solely of big versus small data. Think instead about *all the data necessary to make decisions.* Sometimes you don't need (or can't get) big datasets. For example, quarterly results happen once per quarter. A drug study won't be able to recruit millions of patients. Car accidents are common, but (fortunately) aren't measured in trillions per year.

Some datasets may be small, but they still hold information about important outcomes. They also may be expensive to collect. Consider a reinsurance market like Lloyd's of London. When claims are measured in the hundreds of millions, the dataset is (hopefully) small but important and expensive to acquire.

3.2.3 Measuring AI project success with business metrics

By making sure that all parts of the Sense/Analyze/React loop are covered for a specific use case, you've verified that this case is technically possible and actionable. But how can you know how it affects the bottom line? This section shows you why you should use business domain metrics to measure the outcome of your AI project.

AI is metric driven, but you must use AI to satisfy a business goal. That goal should be represented by a business metric. That business metric should, in turn, indicate how valuable an answer to your question is when used to improve your business. The measured metric doesn't have to be a single, exact number like "Profit improved 10%." It can also be estimated, such as "Profit improved between 8% and 12%."

> **WARNING**   The business metric must be defined for every single AI project. AI methods are, by their nature, quantitative methods, in the sense that they operate only with hard data. Don't attempt to use AI if you're unable to define a business metric first that you can use to measure the project's result.

Being able to choose an appropriate business metric is a business skill that's anything but trivial. But the good news is that if your organization is using metrics correctly, you should already have a business metric defined for you—the same one that already measures business results in the area to which you're trying to apply AI. That metric should also measure how much AI improves your business.

Examples of possible business metrics

As a word of caution, the correct business metrics are always *specific* to your organization, not something you pick up from someone else just because it worked for them. The following metrics aren't exceptions to that rule—they're *examples* of what can work for some organizations.

- When choosing between different suppliers, one possible metric could be the *total cost of using their parts in your product*. Note that this is different from the *price* of their parts, as it includes other related costs you'll incur due to the use of those parts. This includes the cost of support or repair of your product when those parts break.
- If you're a book publisher debating how many new books to print, one good metric could be the *expected profit from the sales of physical books*. This is different from profit per book sold, as it includes factors such as the cumulative cost of the printed books, the cumulative cost of storing the books in the bookstore or some other storage facility, the schedule and price you expect to sell the books at, and the cost of capital.
- Suppose you're a retailer optimizing your product mix, as in the example given in section 3.2.1. One correct business metric for that retailer was *how much did the change in net income relate to all items in the product mix*? The net income is impacted not only by the sales volume of individual items in the mix, but also by the costs of changing that mix, storage, transportation, and many other expenses specific to each individual retailer.

A good business metric should be customized to your organization's needs and the concrete business outcome that you're measuring.

This book can't provide all the best practices for building good organizational metrics; that would be a book in itself (Luftig and Ouellette's book [1] and Ries's book [28] discuss the topic of business metrics). But I'd like to point out that a good business metric should be specific to your organization, quantifiable, measurable, relevant to the desired result, and free of unintended consequences.

> **TIP** Sometimes your organization is using a business metric, but you suspect that what it's measuring is wrong and isn't helpful for running your business. If you're in such a situation, fix the metric *before* you start an AI project, and use that fixed metric to measure the end results of your AI project. Otherwise, you'll optimize AI to produce the wrong business results.

Once you've selected a business metric that you can use to measure the business contribution of your AI project, you can define the threshold. This *threshold* represents the minimum value that AI directed action must accomplish for your project to be worthwhile. As an example, if the business metric you choose to use is "profit increase," your threshold might be that your profit must increase by at least $2M/year for the AI project to be worthwhile.

> ### Threshold for the retailer example
>
> Thresholds are always organization-specific, as they depend on your organization's cost and profit structure. You need to obtain them from the business team. The following is an example of you getting targets for the retailer example given in section 3.2.1.
>
> **You:** If the AI project provides an increase in *net income* of 1%, would you be willing to change the product mix?
>
> **Retailer's manager:** While I'm willing to change the product mix, signing on new suppliers is costly. I need to account for the costs of signing the supplier: not only monetary costs, but also management attention and the time required to sign them. Our metric should account for how many new suppliers I need to sign on. Specifically, I need my *net income to increase by 0.3%* to justify signing on a single new supplier. So I can't say across the board that 1% is enough to change the product mix—it's enough if I need to sign up to three new suppliers, but not if I need to sign 20 new suppliers.
>
> In this example, *net income* is the metric, and 0.3% for each new supplier is the threshold.

Now that you have the metrics that you intend to use with your project, you need to confirm that it's possible to measure the results of your AI project using those metrics. Present the business metrics to your AI expert, and request that they confirm that their team will be able to report the result of the AI project using those metrics. Your AI expert needs to establish a link between that business metric and one of the technical evaluation metrics (as in RMSE, for example) that they intend to use in the AI project. Chapter 4 shows you how to tie together business and technical metrics.

> **TIP** A business metric is appropriate for an AI project when it correctly measures the business result you want to achieve, and when technical experts know how to report their technical progress using that business metric.

What if you can't find an applicable business metric?

The inability to easily recognize business metrics by which an AI project should be measured raises a big red flag. If you can't quantify the business result you're hoping to achieve, you have to ask yourself and your colleagues, "Should we start an AI project in the first place?"

Without the ability to define your business metric, you also can't define any value threshold for your AI project. Without the threshold, you don't know if the results of your project are substantial enough to use in your business. Without a business metric and threshold, you also have no way to estimate the business value of your AI project, and you won't know if it's cost-efficient. In all cases, in the absence of a good business metric, management of the AI project will degenerate into a series of decisions made by gut feeling.

The inability to select a business metric for your AI project may be a sign of a poorly constructed business metric, creating a situation in which you may provide value to the business but can't measure it. It can also indicate that you're not able to provide a business value at all. Or it may indicate that the AI project is so disconnected from the core business that the business has no idea of what to do with the results. Such projects are risky at best.

Sometimes there is a clear business value, but management may perceive it as intangible and something that can't be measured. Examples of intangibles might be employee morale and brand value. This happens when management isn't aware that intangibles could be measured by using a *range* instead of a single number. See Hubbard's book [75] for many examples of the best practices for using ranges to measure so-called intangible quantities in business.

3.2.4 *Estimating AI project difficulty*

Now you've confirmed that the AI project you're considering is technically possible, and you have a way to measure its business impact and its business value. To determine if the AI project is viable, you need to know its cost, the difficulty of its implementation, and how long it will take. This section details considerations in estimating those quantities.

To estimate difficulty, you need to sketch an outline of the technical solution that will be used in the AI project. You need to have representatives from your data science and data engineering teams, plus your software architect, work together on this outline. Your goal is to provide a high-level outline of the solution, to compare a selection of possible AI projects.

Once you have this outline, use it to estimate the difficulty, cost, and length of time to deliver the project. These are, again, rough estimates intended for comparing different AI project options.

Considerations for estimating AI project difficulty

When estimating AI project difficulty, be aware of the following considerations:

- Account for the time required to collect the data you need.
- Do you have the infrastructure necessary for your data size? Do you even need a big data framework?
- If you're using large datasets, don't forget to account for the time necessary to process the data and train AI algorithms.
- Does your team have all the skills necessary to cover this use case? What are the gaps in their skillsets, if any? (As advised in chapter 2, a team leader should be aware of knowledge gaps in the team.)
- Is it certain that the project is even technically possible? Do you understand the proposed AI methods enough to be positive that your team can build it, or do you just know that area of AI enough to assume that the project is possible?

Once you can account for the specifics of the AI project, you can use any estimation methodology that you're familiar with in your organization to estimate other software projects.

TIP Remember that people aren't particularly good in estimations [75], are worse if the estimate is based on just a sketch of the solution, and are worse still if they must estimate in technical areas they know little about. Your estimate will be very rough by necessity. It's only intended to compare different AI project options, and you should make no strong commitments to management based on this estimate.

At this point, you have all the information you need to create a list of viable and actionable AI projects. You know how to determine whether the proposed project is actionable and technically possible. You know how to measure the business value of the AI project, and you can make a rough estimate of the cost, difficulty, and duration. Now it's time to select the first AI project to run. The next section guides you through the selection and preparation for running your first AI project.

3.3 *Your first project and first research question*

As discussed in section 3.1, if your goal is to build an AI team that's a long-term asset to your business organization, then initial projects should be simple and fast to deliver. The criteria for selecting your first AI project to run is therefore simple: choose the project that's fast to deliver and has significant business value. When you've chosen that project, you need to do the following:

- Define the research question that the project would answer (section 3.3.1).
- Organize the project so that if it fails, it fails fast (section 3.3.2).

The rest of this section shows you how to define the research question and explains what fail fast means.

3.3.1   Define the research question

You've chosen your first AI project. That project has a clear business question that needs to be answered, and that question is written in a form that a business decision maker will understand. Now that question needs to be translated into a format that AI can understand—the "research question." This section shows you how to ensure that your research question matches your business question.

Suppose you're a manufacturer, and your research question is, "Should I go with supplier A or supplier B based on the quality of their product?" You need AI to answer this question, but there's a problem: AI has no idea what the concept of *supplier* means.

AI DOESN'T UNDERSTAND BUSINESS CONCEPTS

People unfamiliar with AI capabilities are often under the impression that AI can find some novel business reaction that's escaping human capacity. With the current level of AI, that's rarely possible.

There's no AI algorithm that could look at a retailer and figure out how to improve profits. The reason is that AI doesn't know what the words *retailer, product*, and *profit* mean. AI has no idea what a supplier even is, much less what makes one supplier better than another. Those are business concepts. Nor does AI understand that there could be ethical, public relations, and legal considerations regarding the use of AI in analyzing surveillance video in the store.

Business concepts may be understandable to humans, but the data regarding those concepts must be packaged in a format that AI/ML algorithms expect. That's your data science team's job. To do that, they must first formulate a research question. You can view the research question as a translation of the business question into a form that AI can understand.

THE CONTRACTUAL LANGUAGE OF THE TECHNICAL DOMAIN

AI methods operate in a technical domain. Language used in that domain is contractual in nature and is of the form, "If you present me an input in format X, I guarantee that I'll provide answer Y." Those contracts are often convoluted and require an expert in the field to really understand their precise meaning, as well as all the implications of what is said.

Let's demonstrate this contractual language in some concrete examples:

- AI that's based on classical statistical methods will use the language of hypothesis testing: "Is there a statistically significant difference between part samples from supplier A and supplier B at $p = 0.05$?"
- AI that's based on image recognition will express in the language of ML: "If this is a picture of your part, I can tell you with 95% confidence that it's much more similar to the class of parts you labeled as defective, compared to other classes."

AI can also tell you that, overall, it reaches 98% accuracy in correctly classifying parts between classes.

- AI used in the publishing industry, to predict how many physical books should be printed in a second batch if the first batch sold in three months, might be based on a time series model. Depending on the model used, one research question can be, "Predict with a 95% confidence interval the book sales in the next three months, based on the sales in the previous three months."

If you aren't a data scientist, your head is probably spinning right now. What do those sentences even mean? Sounds geekish? That's because it is! AI methods are defined in an abstract format that's intended to be understood by computers and data scientists, not by business users. To solve business problems, you need to translate them into *AI language*. That's what I mean by *formulation* of the problem when I say that ML is a combination of formulation, optimization, and evaluation. Figure 3.7 shows this process.

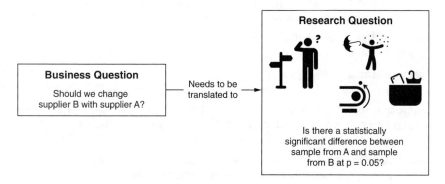

Figure 3.7 **The translation of a business question into a research question. AI doesn't understand business concepts. If you aren't familiar with statistics, a research question formulation might be difficult to understand.**

The job of your AI experts is to select the appropriate research question and translate it into a format the AI methods can answer without compromising its relationship to your business question.

> **WARNING** Projects often go awry when the business and data science teams don't communicate closely. Business questions can be incorrectly translated to poor research questions, causing you to get an answer to a question you didn't ask. The problem is compounded if you then use that answer to take the wrong business action.

It's important to understand that this translation is a highly complex activity requiring that your team share an understanding of both the business and AI domains. This translation isn't straightforward. It's almost impossible to devise a translation that evaluates all possible business actions. It's the job of the business leader to guard against misalignment between the business question and the research question.

> ## Misaligned business and research questions
>
> Here's an example of how business and research questions can get misaligned in a way that a business leader or a data scientist is unlikely to catch unless they talk directly.
>
> **Business leader:** Give me an example of one possible answer that you'd provide when you finish the analysis.
>
> **Data scientist:** We have enough statistical evidence to infer that there's only a 5% chance that we'd get the result we did if supplier A wasn't indeed better than supplier B.
>
> **Business leader:** So, you're telling me that supplier A is better than supplier B? I expect that, three months from now, we'll have a big project that we need a good supplier for. I plan to replace supplier B with supplier A. We'll increase orders from supplier A 100 times. Is your analysis sufficient to support such a business decision?
>
> **Data scientist:** Well, what we know is that on the sample we tested, A was likely to be better than B . . . .
>
> **Business leader** [thinking to himself]: *This is interesting. What does the technical jargon mean? This isn't a simple yes or no. Let's dig deeper . . . .*
>
> **Business leader:** Wait. How is that different than what I just said? Give me an example of a situation where you'd report that we have enough evidence to *interfere . . .* , and it would still be wrong to drop supplier B.
>
> **Data scientist:** Well . . . when I say we have enough statistical evidence to . . . um . . . *infer,* we cover only the sample that was given to us last week. We can't say that would still be the case in three months. We also can't say that supplier A could deliver the same level of quality if the order you make is 100 times the size of the sample we tested.
>
> **Business leader:** I see. What if it's important to me to consider trends of improvement in suppliers A and B? I need to know what's likely to happen in three months, if current trends continue. I'll place an order of 10,000 parts to be delivered by supplier A in three months. Does your analysis support these actions?
>
> **Data scientist:** No, it doesn't. We need to perform a different type of analysis . . . .

BEST PRACTICES FOR THE BUSINESS LEADER OF AN AI PROJECT

The "Misaligned business and research questions" sidebar shows an example of a project that could have gone horribly wrong, as the business leader and data scientist are talking about totally different questions. But until that conversation happens, you won't notice that you're not talking about the same thing. The following provides best practices for business leaders who are starting an AI project:

- Never sign a document that proposes a highly technical research question you don't understand. Instead, call a meeting with the data scientists. Ideally, someone who has a strong background in both business and AI should facilitate this meeting. If there's no such person in your organization, you should enlist a consultant to help you.

- Ask your data scientist to provide you with a couple of the possible answers that the proposed research question can produce.
- Play out a scenario analysis (as in the previous example). Take the answer to a research question and describe what you think it says. Then, state the exact business decisions you'd make, explaining all your assumptions.
- Always repeat how you interpret the answer that the data scientist gives you. Use simple, nontechnical terminology.
- Don't worry about looking stupid if you misunderstand something. Finding misunderstandings at this stage saves a ton of money later. You'd really look stupid if you waited until the wrong AI project was run.
- State clearly the business actions that you intend to take, based on their answers. Ask if those business actions are reasonable.
- If the data scientist responds to your planned business action with anything other than a simple yes or no, investigate in which circumstances it would be wrong for you to take such a business action, based solely on the results of the analysis.
- Don't be afraid to further explore your research question, together with your AI experts. Get educated about the details of what the research question means; by the same token, educate your data scientist on the details of your business.
- Understand that the mapping between a business question and a research question is never perfect. Research questions rarely correctly capture all aspects of the business problem. The question is, "Are those aspects important to you?"
- Beware of discussing business problems using highly technical terminology. Terminology that isn't shared between all meeting participants is an excellent vehicle to hide misalignment between technology and business. If a business doesn't have properly thorough discussions to ensure that research questions and business problems are aligned, they're in fact leaving it up to the technology team to fill in critical business details.
- Always make your business experts available to the technical team for consultation about clarification of important details. It isn't realistic to expect that the technical team will make optimal business decisions when the specification of the business problem is vague.

WARNING Always perform a scenario analysis of a research question *before* the AI team starts its work. The chance of a project succeeding if you ask the wrong research question is about zero.

A final point to remember when defining a research question is that correspondence between business questions is not "one research question per one business question." You might need multiple research questions to cover a single business question. It's also possible (although rare in practice) to have a single research question that can answer multiple business questions.

3.3.2   If you fail, fail fast

You're starting this first AI project with the assumption that it will be an easy project to deliver. However, your estimates were coarse; it's quite possible that the project, once you start it, will be more difficult to deliver than you initially calculated. This section explains how you should manage that initial AI project so that if the project is unexpectedly difficult, that becomes immediately obvious.

> **TIP** You should optimize your project delivery process for *speed to success*. When hunting in rich hunting grounds, the more you hunt, the more you catch. In the early days of your AI efforts, you shouldn't persist on projects that looked easy early on, but on closer examination were difficult. Instead, stop them early and use the remaining project's time to start an easier project instead.

Your project should start with a proof of concept that builds a quick prototype. That prototype serves four purposes:

1. It demonstrates to you that the engineering team has the technical expertise needed to deliver the project.
2. It gives you a concrete AI implementation, which is the Analyze in the Sense/Analyze/React loop you identified. Now you can test the React part of the loop (for example, you can test how difficult it would be to implement the required business action).
3. The prototype can be analyzed to determine how your proposed system solution behaves when exposed to either more data or different ML algorithms. Chapters 6 and 7 of this book show you how this analysis is performed.
4. The prototype shows you how difficult it will be to implement your AI project. If the level of difficulty is much greater than you expected, that should be quickly obvious.

Until you have an experienced team that has passed through such processes many times, don't get stuck on projects that take a lot of time to implement. As a hunter, you won't starve because you failed to catch a single prey; you'll starve because you were trying to catch a single prey for way too long.

> **TIP** If your project is more difficult than expected, pause it and choose an easier one instead. *If you stumble upon the Gates of Hell, turn around and run!*

3.4   Pitfalls to avoid

When running an AI project, there are some common pitfalls that you should avoid. Some of the most important ones are as follows:

- Not communicating with the organizational actors that own the React part of the Sense/Analyze/React loop, or, even worse, not working with them at all until your AI project is well on its way
- Transplanting use cases (and metrics) from other projects or organizations
- Running fashionable AI projects that are likely to grab headlines

- Believing that you can buy a tool, any tool, that will give you a sustainable advantage
- Hoping that throwing random analysis at your data will produce results
- Selecting which project to run based on a "gut feeling" instead of the results of analysis

This section discusses each one of these pitfalls in more detail.

3.4.1 Failing to build a relationship with the business team

When using AI as a decision support system, it's never enough to just deliver a good analysis; you need to execute well on the specific business actions recommended by an AI-powered analysis. That means that executive attention must hone in on the link between the analytical result and the business action. This section highlights why the AI team must build good relationships with the department of your organization that will take business actions, based on your AI analysis.

> **TIP** Analytics is just like a speed gauge in a car. If the speedometer is telling you that you're going too fast, the driver must reduce the car's speed. Who's the equivalent of the driver in your project/organization?

A nonspecialist can misinterpret analytical results. A classic problem is that nonspecialists won't understand the limits of the analysis and when the assumptions basic to the analysis are violated. An example of that problem was shown in section 3.3.1, when the research question and business question were misaligned.

I've personally witnessed several organizations hand off an analysis report to separate business teams. These business teams proceeded to take business actions without the input of data scientists. This is always a mistake.

> **TIP** Analytical expertise should always be represented in any group that's discussing how to react to analytical results. You need to ensure that the business team understands your analytical results and prescriptions fully and correctly. The analysis result must be valid in the light of the intended business actions.

If you're the leader of an analytical project, your job isn't done when you deliver the results. Your job is done when the analyst's prescription is successfully implemented. You must build good working relationships with departments that will implement the analysis. If the analysis has prescribed a particular business action, don't underestimate the need for you to help and follow through with its execution.

3.4.2 Using transplants

People are often tempted to copy what worked for the people and organizations that surround them. As a result, you see what I call *transplant projects*. Here, an enterprise decides to form an AI team and embarks on some AI project they've heard other organizations similar to theirs performed. This section explains why transplants are a bad idea.

Examples of transplant projects abound. Some examples are projects like "let's have our own recommendation engine" or "let's do sentiment analysis of customer feedback." Sometimes these projects make sense in the context of the business, but all too often they're just vanilla use cases that you heard about from someone else and didn't analyze in the context of your own business.

> **NOTE** For some reason, people have more common sense when they're thinking about real transplants as opposed to business transplants. You'd never get a kidney transplant just because it worked well for your neighbor. Why should you behave differently in your business?

Instead of just blindly adapting a project that worked well for someone else, consider it to be just one of many possible AI projects. Use the analytical approach presented in this chapter to determine which AI project you should start first.

3.4.3 *Trying moonshots without the rockets*

Many of the world's largest technology companies have made fortunes based on the use of data. In the core, companies such as Google, Microsoft, and Baidu are heavily dependent on AI for their success. They have significant research capabilities and have a vested interest in ensuring that they won't miss the train of important AI advancements. This section explains why your organization shouldn't blindly follow those companies.

Imagine that you're a CEO

Suppose you're running a company that's making $30 billion a year, and you're in a business that's associated with AI. Let's go a step further and assume that there's a 1% chance that someone in the next 10 years might invent something approaching a strong, human-level AI—so called Artificial General Intelligence (AGI) [76]. If the search for AGI fails, there may still be an autonomous vehicle [38] as the consolation prize. Finally, you know that your competitors are investing heavily into AI.

Will you invest substantial money into AI and hire accomplished researchers to help you advance the frontiers of AI knowledge? Or will you opt not to invest in AI, and accept the risks that:

- Your competitors develop AGI or autonomous vehicle technology. Your company may have been better positioned, but you failed to even try!
- Your error will be taught in every business school for many years to come.

While the logic from the sidebar "Imagine that you're a CEO" applies to businesses such as Google, Baidu, or Microsoft, there's an unfortunate tendency for many enterprises to emulate these companies without understanding the rationale behind their actions. Yes, the biggest players make significant money with their AI efforts. They also invest a lot in AI research. Before you start emulating their AI research efforts, ask yourself, "Am I in the same business?"

If your company were to invent something important for strong AI/AGI [76], would you know how to monetize it? Suppose you're a large brick-and-mortar retailer. Could you take full advantage of that discovery? Probably not—the retailer's business is different from Google's.

Almost certainly, your company would benefit more from AI technology if you used it to solve your own concrete business problems. This means that instead of teams populated by the smartest researchers and processes oriented toward the acquisition of new AI knowledge, your organization needs people who know how to make money in your business domain *with existing AI technologies*.

Don't emulate organizations richer than yours without first understanding how you'd exploit success. For most organizations, the road to success isn't found in advancing the frontiers of AI knowledge, but in knowing *how to tie AI results into their business*. You need a data science team focused on applications, not research. That doesn't mean that you shouldn't hire bright PhDs, but that the leadership of your AI teams must primarily be experts in applying AI to the task of making money.

3.4.4 *It's about using advanced tools to look at the sea of data*

Another common pitfall is the belief that you can buy an AI or big data tool that will make it trivial to look at your data, find insights, and then monetize the insights found. Some organizations adopting AI might even take the attitude that the main focus of early AI efforts should be on finding the right tools. This section explains why this is a pitfall to avoid.

> **TIP** If monetization is trivial, so is explaining how it happens. Ask vendors detailed questions until you really understand the finest points of how to apply an out-of-the-box tool all the way from the point of purchase to the end-point where your organization makes profit as a result of use of that tool.

In most business verticals, it isn't trivial at all to monetize AI. And while many tools can help you get there, it's unlikely that these tools can solve monetization problems for you. Even if there are tools that let you monetize by just installing and running them, what you're dealing with is a commoditized use case. Heck, someone already has a product that does it!

> **TIP** The early focus for your business should be on finding AI projects that provide a concrete business value. Tools are enablers of those projects.

A salesman might advise you to "Build a large data lake and unleash your data scientists on it; there has to be something in all that data." You might even have been given an example of the unexpected insights that only analytics on a big dataset can provide. However, those situations are rare and unpredictable. Don't count on the tooth fairy. Don't start with the Analyze part of the Sense/Analyze/React loop. In our framework, always start with the React part.

> **WARNING**   It's always possible that there might be something special lurking deep within your data. With the proper analysis, it might give you some unexpected business idea that you can implement and with which you can make a ton of money. While *possible*, this is certainly not *guaranteed*, isn't *predictable*, and there's a big question of *is it likely enough to justify it as a main strategy you should adapt?* Worse, the lucrative bluefin tuna you hope to catch might turn out instead to be a slimy monster of the deep. Instead of going on a fishing expedition, organize your early AI projects for predictable success.

3.4.5   *Using your gut feeling instead of CLUE*

Often a decision about running an AI project is made in a haphazard way, as little more than a technical idea that excites the team. Running an AI project primarily because you want experience with the underlying technology is the tech equivalent of buying a sports car. This section explains why following your gut may result in poor business results.

> #### Video analysis of the behavior of retail customers
>
> Let's return to our retailer from section 3.2.1, for whom you're optimizing a product mix. There were two proposed approaches: one based on predicting sales trends and another one based on video recognition of customers' behavior.
>
> If I put my data scientist hat on, I'd have to admit that video recognition of customer behavior is a more technically interesting project for me. That project would excite a lot of the technology teams today. It uses cutting-edge AI video recognition abilities, whereas sales prediction may make do with older time series analytics methods.
>
> Sometimes that technical allure is all it takes for a team to decide to build a prototype, and the data scientist in me certainly understands this urge. However, this is a classic "gut" or "Oh, shiny!" approach to project selection.
>
> To see why this would be a mistake in this example, recall what happened in section 3.2.1. When you're talking with management, you may learn that your business isn't comfortable with the legal and public relations ramifications of doing video analysis of customers' behavior. Your effort is unlikely to be adopted even if it's technically successful. This doesn't take long to learn when you bother to talk with business leaders about your proposal before building a prototype.
>
> Also, even if you somehow persuade management to allow you to continue building your AI prototype, you failed to define a business metric for measuring success. Now you've created problems in managing your project. Suppose your project is in progress and has achieved some initial success. How would you know if it's good enough to release? How precisely does it need to recognize customer behavior? Can it make recognition mistakes, and, if so, under which circumstances? Which mistakes are most damaging?

Be extremely skeptical about counting on intuition to select which AI project to run first. Section 3.2 showed you the steps necessary to correctly determine which is the best project to run. When selecting a first project, there are simply too many moving parts to consider for gut feeling to provide the right answer. You need to verify that the project is actionable, technically possible, and business valuable. You need to know its cost, as well as the outline and difficulty of the proposed technical solution. It's highly unlikely that you can assess all those attributes of a proposed AI project by just thinking about the problem for a minute or two.

> **TIP** Above all, be on the lookout for any situation in which, during a well-attended and important company meeting, everyone immediately exclaims, "This looks like a great idea!" Such a social situation isn't exactly conducive to encouraging people to perform the careful analysis needed to disprove the group consensus. In short, beware of groupthink.

But we're using an MVP approach!

Some teams are Agile and/or use Lean Startup [28] methodologies for developing their software projects. In a Lean Startup methodology, the team is encouraged to dice projects into small chunks of work that can be presented to the customer for feedback. This chunk of work is called the *minimum viable product* (MVP). Part of the Lean Startup methodology is that if you find that your MVP isn't what the customer wants, you can then try something else—the so-called *pivot*.

Some will argue that because you're building an MVP, you should quickly select some initial AI idea, show it to the customer, and see what the customer says. *Don't do that!*

Using MVP has many advantages with real-world products, and CLUE can combine well with a Lean Startup strategy. However, MVPs taken alone aren't solving the same problems that CLUE is addressing; for example:

- If you choose an MVP based on a gut feeling, you've started a project before knowing if the business is willing and able to adopt your analytical solutions.
- Although MVP can show you that you're on the wrong track faster, you're on the wrong track, right from the beginning.
- If your gut feeling was to think about the analysis you can do (versus starting with the React part of the Sense/Analyze/React loop), you're playing *analysis roulette*. You're hoping and praying that the analysis you do will yield a result that your business can somehow implement.

MVPs aren't valid excuses to promote a gut feeling approach to selecting and running an AI project. MVPs reduce the cost of finding out that you're on the wrong track, but that's just *reducing the price of failure*. The ability to pivot isn't an excuse to run projects haphazardly, hoping that with enough random AI ideas you'll stumble on something that just happened to be actionable.

The CLUE approach can be integrated, and is compatible, with MVPs and Lean Startup. The *C* part of CLUE analysis is about selecting a first AI project, and such a project can be an MVP—an MVP that's based on analysis, not gut feeling.

The biggest cause of failure of AI projects today might be technical. But even among technically successful projects, there are far too many that aren't even used by the businesses that paid for them. Those AI projects shouldn't have been started at all and were usually started because a gut feeling about their value was wrong.

3.5   Exercises

The following questions each give a concrete business scenario and then ask follow-up questions about that scenario. Please answer the following questions:

Question 1: Suppose you're working in the publishing industry, and you're wondering if it's better to release printed, electronic, and audiobooks at the same time or one after another. Also, if delivery is staged so that printed books are released first, how long should you wait before releasing the other formats? Within this setting, answer the following question: "What business metrics should you use?"

Question 2: If you're a business leader, define a business question and an appropriate metric to measure it. Think about some hypothetical scenarios not directly applicable to your organization (for example, some scenarios related to philanthropy). Think about actions that you can take while running a nonprofit. Use the techniques introduced in chapter 3 to select your first hypothetical business question, as well as the metrics you'd use to measure success.

Question 3: Once you've identified your business question from the previous exercise, take your senior AI expert to lunch and talk about the business problem. Ask them how they'd formulate a research question. Use the process described in chapter 3 to check whether or not the answer supports the business action you intend to take. And, while you're having that lunch, talk about how you'd find a dataset to answer such a research question. Do you think you can acquire that dataset?

Summary

- AI, when introduced to new businesses, falls on rich hunting grounds. Don't start by chasing difficult projects that tie up all your resources and destroy you if they fail. Start instead with simple projects that have big business value and are quick to complete.
- Use CLUE to select and organize AI projects. The *C* part of CLUE (figure 3.4) allows you to create a list of actionable AI projects that you can implement and helps you estimate their size and value.
- The business question that AI needs to answer must be translated into a technical format by defining a research question. If that translation is incorrect, it can wreck the business outcomes. Before starting a project, check your research question using scenario-based testing.

- Use business metrics to measure the progress of your AI project. Business metrics should be customized for your project and organization. Don't start an AI project if you don't have the business metric for measuring its success.
- Organize your AI project so that if it fails, it fails fast.
- Start with the proof of concept. If the project happens to be more difficult than you thought, stop it and work on an easier project instead. The goal is to *optimize time to the next success.*
- There are common pitfalls to avoid when running AI projects. They include failure to build a relationship with relevant business leaders, transplanting use cases, adopting a "moonshot" project but missing the rockets, placing too much hope in random tools (or random analysis), and substituting a gut feeling for CLUE.

Linking business and technology

In chapter 3, you selected your first AI project to run. Now you have the research questions that project needs to answer. This chapter shows you how to properly organize that project by using metrics to link a business problem with the technical solution you're building. It also shows you how to understand what your technical progress means when translated into a business result. Finally, it shows you how to avoid typical organizational obstacles you might meet in your quest to link business and technology. But before we get to all that, I'll first explain what causes the average organization to fall into the trap of making AI project decisions based on intuition as opposed to data.

4.1   *A project can't be stopped midair*

Running any project is more like piloting a plane than driving a car. When you're piloting a plane, if something happens, you don't have the option of pulling onto the side of the road and sorting out the problems. The flight has to continue, and you have to sort things out while you're still flying. This section shows why such a situation could incentivize an organization to make many decisions based on instinct rather than data.

Once a project starts, you have people working on it and money and time being spent on it. That puts pressure on the team to *do something* because all team members want the project to succeed. And once the project starts, team members on all levels of the project devote themselves to working on what they're directed to work on. However, in the absence of directions, they'd most likely work on what they perceived to be the most important activity for the project's success. As every manager knows, team members working in isolation and without knowing what a project's priorities are often working on the wrong thing because they aren't aware of what should really happen first.

Managers are people too. In the absence of knowing what the best thing to do is, they still need to make management decisions, because there comes a point in the project when it's in flight, and decisions must be made. In the absence of guiding principles, managers would try to help a project the only way they know how. That's why *gut feeling* projects are so common in the industry.

How do you know what or how well your AI project is doing? The simple answer is that when you're getting good business results, it's doing well. But how do you know you're getting good business results? Let's look at one typical situation in which it's difficult to have an intuitive feel for what good results are for your AI project.

4.1.1   *What constitutes a good recommendation engine?*

You're in charge of the recommendation engine of a large retailer. The retailer is selling 200 K products, and it has a total of 80 million customers and close to 2 million products viewed every day. Your recommendation engine suggests to every customer additional products they might be interested in buying. You've just made an update to your recommendation engine. How do you know that the latest update is moving the system in the right direction?

You can look at a few products overall, but looking at a few products doesn't actually tell you if your latest change is doing well across all of your customers. Instead, you need to develop some metric that would *summarize* the behavior of the system as a whole. Such a metric should tell you how you're doing overall, across all products and customers.

In this situation, you have the following alternatives, all of which I've seen used in the context of Fortune 500 companies (even when they should have known better):

- Manually look at the recommendations given by the engine and see if they appear to make sense to a human. Clearly, one problem is what "makes sense" and how to ensure that two different testers have the same criteria. It's difficult to ensure reliable, repeatable, and correct scoring of the recommendations with this approach.

- Application of various metrics seen in the scientific papers (such as "Evaluating Recommendation Systems" [77]) on recommendation engines. An example of such a metric is novelty [78], which measures how many new items that the user didn't know about were recommended. What is often not clear is if such technical metrics positively impact any aspect of the business—I might not have known that the retailer stocks garden hoses, but do I care?

- Measure the sales increase from improved recommendations. This approach has clear business relevance and is unambiguous. You don't have to deploy your recommendation engine fully in production to test the sales increase. You can also perform a test on a limited subset of your customers to measure the progress of the recommendation engine.

The very nature of the AI project is that it's difficult to get a feel for the results by simply inspecting a few samples. By definition, if you're using AI, you're using it because the answer to the question of what is the best thing to do isn't self-evident, and/or the size of the data is too large for any single human to manually inspect.

> **NOTE**   This characteristic of an AI project makes managing such projects different from managing other software projects. It's much easier to say what good progress is for a web application than for a recommendation engine. Similar problems emerge when you're wondering what task the team should work on next.

Once a project is in flight, decisions need to be made. You're better off if those decisions are made in a systematic way. Figure 4.1 uses an analogy from another domain to contrast systematic decisions with making decisions based on *feel*.

Figure 4.1   Once a project starts, decisions have to be made. In which plane would you rather be?

4.1.2   What is gut feeling?

If you can't explain the reasons for the business decisions you make, *you're making those decisions based on gut feeling.* You can't be sure that you've explained something well when people present at the meeting nod their heads and say, "That makes sense!" People often nod their heads just to fit in with a group. You've explained something well when someone not present at the meeting looks at the same data and makes the same decision you did.

Making decisions based on gut feeling doesn't mean that you're making wrong decisions, but good gut-feeling decisions in the field of AI aren't easy. This means that even if it was the right call, it's improbable that anyone else would make the same decision, that anyone (including you) would always make the same decision in similar circumstances, or that an organization would learn from the decision. Such lack of consistency is a red flag for any project, even if a few decisions happen to work out.

Making your decisions based on business metrics ensures that they're explainable, repeatable, and predictable. It also makes it easy to train new team members on how to make good decisions and learn as an organization from your past decisions.

4.2   Linking business problems and research questions

So far in this book, I've shown you how to select actionable business problems to solve with AI and how to use business metrics to measure business results. You've also selected your first AI project to run. This section elaborates on how to run that AI project. Your first step is to link the research questions with the business questions.

> ### Act based on the information you have now!
>
> There's another similarity between managing a project and piloting a plane: you operate under a time limit. For example, what would you do if the plane's instruments suddenly showed that only one hour of fuel remained? Would you land as soon as possible, which could be unnecessary and somewhat costly? What if it's just a faulty fuel gauge? If you wait for an hour, you'd know for sure, but by then it would be too late. You'll have to act soon and make the best decision you can.
>
> When managing a project, you face a similar dichotomy between being able to make a better decision after you collect more data about a problem and the cost of obtaining that information. The right way to address that dichotomy is to compare the cost of waiting to obtain the information and the value of the decision you can make once you have that information, which is hopefully much higher. You should focus on the cost and value of information and understand the *expected value of better information* (or "expected value of perfect information" [75,79]).
>
> A consequence of time sensitivity is that most of the models we use to make a project management decision would develop iteratively. This is already something to which you're well accustomed. Modeling the cost of the project is a typical example. Initially, you'd start with rough estimates and decide if it's worthwhile to begin the project. As the project progresses, and you find new information, you're likely to refine the model's cost further.

To link a business problem with the research questions for your AI project, you must make sure that you have the right research questions and that you're using the correct business metrics. You do that by following the CLUE process, and it's time for the *L* part of CLUE.

4.2.1   Introducing the L part of CLUE

In section 1.10, I defined CLUE in detail. Now we'll talk about the *L* part of CLUE: *Link* the research question and the business problem. This is done by scrutinizing and further refining both the research questions and the right business metrics. Figure 4.2 (and the rest of this section) guides you through how that linking is done and why it's necessary.

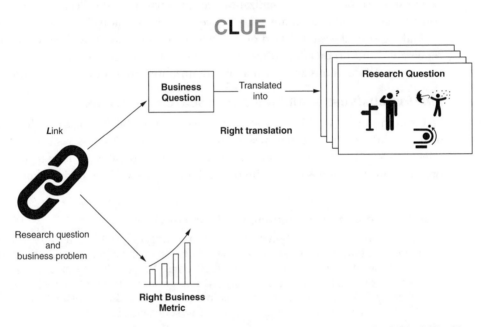

Figure 4.2   Linking business and technology. You must make sure you have the right relationship between business questions and business metrics.

To correctly link a business problem and a research question (or questions), you must ensure that you have the right research question and business metric. Yes, you already thought about the research questions and business metrics in chapter 3 (when doing the *C* part of CLUE), but there you thought about them at the granularity necessary for a triage between the projects. You needed only a level of precision necessary for ranking the projects and choosing the first AI project to run. Now you're running that project and need better estimates.

Additionally, it's possible that the team running the project is a different team than the one that participated in the initial triage. Your new team may have different skillsets and maybe even a different idea about how to approach the problem. Even if the team is the same (as is usually the case in smaller organizations and early efforts), it's now more focused on the specifics of your AI project and able to refine initial estimates.

> **NOTE** This iterative refinement is part of the fail-fast philosophy that I advocated in chapter 3. You'd start an AI project by addressing early the questions that, if you were unable to answer them, would sink a project. Only once you knew that the answers to those early questions justified running the project would you make additional investments—such as detailed refinement of the research questions.

4.2.2 Do you have the right research question?

As already discussed in section 3.3.1, the answer to the right research question needs to support business actions that you would take based on that answer. You determine this through a conversation between the data scientists and business management team, during which you test the research question by describing scenarios of what answers are possible and what business actions are planned based on those answers.

The reason why you're repeating this exercise at the start of the AI project isn't just due diligence, it's also to make sure that the team performing the AI project is familiar with the business problem you're trying to solve.

> **NOTE** If you're a startup or part of a small team piloting AI in your organization, describing possible business actions to the AI team at the start of the project is less important. In a small company, the team members may have already participated in previous conversations about the business objectives. However, in large organizations, it's typical that the team that performed the *C* part of CLUE is different from the AI project team.

When you know that you have the correct research question you're trying to answer, have your AI team discuss how they'd go about solving the problem. You only need to know the high-level outline of the ML algorithms that they're considering so that you can identify which evaluation metrics you would most likely use to evaluate the results of those algorithms. Now we can take a closer look at the metrics you'd typically use (and the ones that you should use) to evaluate an AI project.

4.2.3 What questions should a metric be able to answer?

How do you know that you have the right metrics to run your AI project? You know because good metrics answer the business questions that you would encounter in the project. This section gives examples of some of those business questions.

> **WARNING** It's generally not a productive activity to ask the average AI software team in the industry today, "Do you have a good business case, and are you aware of how well your product is doing in business terms?" What do you expect the team that spent a lot of time and money on a project to say when put on the spot? I expect them to say, "Yes!"

The most important question you should be able to answer when running a project is: "For this project, am I going to be able to get the answers to the business questions that I'm likely to ask?" Here are some typical questions that you might encounter on the project:

- If I release the software today in the state it's currently in, how much money will we make or lose?
- If we can't release a product today, how much better would our results need to be before we could release it?
- Is it worth investing $100 K extra in getting 5% better results than we have today?

A good project metric should be able to answer such questions. But how good is the typical metric used in an AI project today at doing that?

4.2.4   *Can you make business decisions based on a technical metric?*

If this isn't your first AI project, chances are you've sat in on a business meeting in which some technical metric was represented as a measure of progress. If you never were part of an AI project, it's just a matter of time before you sit in on such a meeting. Let's briefly review what this experience typically looks like.

Suppose you're a decision maker on a project, and that project uses as a metric RMSE[1], which is one of the more common technical metrics. The team has presented that the current value of RMSE is 5.143. Quickly, answer the following questions:

- Is it worth investing 5% of the whole project budget into further improving RMSE?
- How much should you improve RMSE?
- Is an improvement of 3.1415927 enough?

If you're in the majority that's not able to answer these questions (or are wondering what in the world is RMSE), then I have several easy questions for you:

- Have you ever made (or have you seen other people make) business decisions impacting an AI project after being at a presentation similar to the one I described?
- How did you establish that the audience at the meeting knew what RMSE was? Note that they need to know it so well that they can immediately apply it to making business decisions.
- What mechanisms were used in such a meeting to ensure that the few people who knew what RMSE is, and knew it well, were the most influential voices in the meeting?

When you're done with the easy questions, let's move on to the more difficult ones:

- Why was RMSE even presented to the audience of that meeting?
- A year from now, how would you find out what the team thought about what an RMSE improvement of 3.1415927 would even mean in business terms?

---

[1] A definition for RMSE is included in appendix A—Glossary of terms.

Making business decisions based on the value of a technical metric isn't trivial. Most businesspeople won't know how to do it. It's not just a problem of having someone at the meeting who's able to translate the value of the business metric into a technical metric. The voice of that person needs to be heard and needs to be influential in making decisions. It's also not clear what business result would be expected from an RMSE improvement of 3.1415927.

> **TIP** A business meeting is not the time to learn new technical metrics. Attempting to do so may even result in a meeting dynamic that looks like an unruly college class headed by a difficult-to-follow professor. Decisions become tentative, people are afraid to speak because they aren't confident they know the class material, and decisions are made based on the personalities of the people present rather than comprehension of the situation.

The preceding example is by no means hypothetical: every single AI project would, at some point, have to decide if further expenditure for improving results would be worthwhile. Similarly, management would have to decide if the project would be worth pursuing further, or if it would be better to reassign the AI team to other projects.

Clearly, the inability to use metrics to answer common and unavoidable business questions means that a metric, while useful for the technology team, is less useful to management. If you find yourself in this situation, you've suffered a case of a technical metric that has escaped into the wild, as figure 4.3 shows.

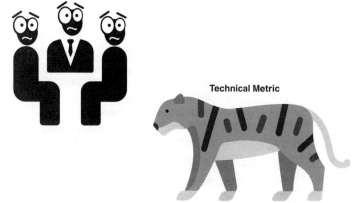

Technical Metric

Figure 4.3 Technical metrics are known to escape into the wild. This is not a reason to invite them to business meetings.

One more problem with presenting technical metrics at a business meeting is the negative impact they have on training new engineering managers of AI projects. Put yourself in the position of a new engineering manager. A new manager can see that most of the other experienced managers are appearing to use the technical metric to make business decisions. No one is questioning, "What does that technical metric have to do with business?" The new manager may be excused if they conclude that the connection between the technical metric and business is evident to all their peers, who instinctively know how to relate RMSE to business decisions—as opposed to being just as puzzled with RMSE as the new manager is.

Many new managers in that position end up trying to learn the technical details of what RMSE is and then try to (somehow) make business decisions based on that. Sometimes, an unfortunate new manager only remembers the conclusion—that some magic happens when RMSE is improved to a value of 3.1415927, which also happens to approximate the value of the constant of π.

> **NOTE** Every data scientist knows that you should never use the value of π when looking to improve RMSE. The right value to use instead should have been e (approximately 2.7182818). All joking aside, in a business context, there's no good value for RMSE; there's only a good value for the business metric—like making a profit.

The previously described situation unfortunately happens a lot today. In some rare circumstances, such as when your company can afford to hire a management team that's so knowledgeable that they know all the technical metrics cold, it might even be reasonable to present the technical metrics directly. Good for you! You're working in a company that's so affluent that you can afford tech-savvy managers.

We are G-MAFIA!

Let's suppose you're a member of G-MAFIA (Google, Microsoft, Amazon, Facebook, IBM, and Apple), or your company is so good that you might as well be a part of G-MAFIA. Maybe your team is so lucky as to be populated by managers who also happen to have PhDs in AI and know well what RMSE (or any other technical metric presented) is.

Run the following experiment: have a meeting, and let the meeting progress and conclude as usual. Note what business decision was made based on the technical metrics presented. Ask people who made the business decision to stay in the room and to write on a piece of paper (*write*, not *say*) what business results they expected from such a technical metric. Then compare the results and check how similar they are to each other. Is there a shared understanding of the data you presented, or was there an expectation of widely different business results?

I recommend you do the exercise anonymously. If you get widely different results from this exercise (by no means an uncommon occurrence), it makes it easier to transition to talking about why the results are different. This is more productive than having a discussion about which people got the right result.

The rest of this chapter shows you how to translate a technical metric to a business metric. When you see how that's done, you'll see why I'm skeptical that even brilliant people are particularly good at doing this right immediately, in real time, in their head, and in the same way.

4.2.5   *A metric you don't understand is a poor business metric*

One of the main problems in a typical AI project is what I call the *technology smoke-screen*, and it works in the following manner:

1   Some technical concept (like RMSE, or some other technical metric) is presented to you.
2   You start by trying to understand what RMSE is.
3   It becomes a game of who'll give up first—the data scientist trying to explain to you what the concept means, or you trying to understand what it means.
4   After a while, everyone is tired, some decision needs to be made, and that decision is made based on the understanding of the concept that has emerged thus far.

> **If you're a data scientist, be empathetic**
>
> If you happen to be a data scientist, how long did you need to learn what various technical metrics mean? How long did it take before you became really comfortable with using them and with understanding what they meant in various problem domains you were working in? How does that time compare with the time you spent on your presentation, explaining what the technical metric means to your business audience?
>
> Is it realistic to expect that the business audience (self-selected for their interest in business) would learn the concept faster than the average student in an ML class in college does? Remember, the college student probably chose that field because of their interest in mathematics!

Most of the time, that situation emerges without anyone intending it. The team is honestly trying to educate management, and if management proceeds down this path, they're contributing to the situation.

Trying to understand a technical metric in such a situation is always a part of the trap. Instead, in this chapter, I'll concentrate on what helps you succeed. It's not a question of what the concepts are that you don't understand. It's a question of *are those concepts something that's relevant to making business decisions?*

The answer to that question for any technical metric is always going to be "No." Any technical metric is either irrelevant to a business decision or is relatable to some other business metric that makes the business decision straightforward. In the former case, the metric shouldn't have been presented in the first place. In the latter case, what should have been presented is a corresponding business metric. The question isn't "What is RMSE?" It's "What is an exchange rate between dollars and RMSE?"

People who know what RMSE is may object, "It's often easy to translate RMSE to dollars!" But if it's easy to translate RMSE to a business metric, then it's also easy to use a business metric instead of RMSE, so you should use the business metric.

WARNING   Sometimes you'll encounter technical metrics you don't understand. Never try to learn that metric during the meeting and translate it to a business metric in real-time. Insist that business metrics be presented instead.

When mental math doesn't work

This sidebar targets the data scientists in the audience. You're familiar with RMSE, and you may counter that RMSE is a simple concept to understand, so why not expect managers to understand it? Certainly it can't be that difficult to learn, right?

Even if we were to agree that RMSE is a simple concept for everyone to grasp, there are still good reasons to always present using business metrics instead of RMSE:

- *If the translation between RMSE and the business metric is easy, why doesn't the data science team just do it before the meeting?* Do you want the full attention of your audience, or do you want them to be performing mental math ("X units of RMSE is Y dollars") while they're listening to you?
- I can't think of a scenario in which presenting results using the business metric would make a strong business case weaker. On the contrary, I could see many business professionals thinking, "If you had a strong business case, you'd try to state it as clearly as possible."
- On the technical side, it's incorrect to assume that it's always trivial to translate RMSE to business metrics.

To translate RMSE to a business metric, it isn't enough for the audience to understand RMSE. The meeting participants also need to understand the *relationship* between RMSE and the business metric. Even someone who understands RMSE may need to concentrate to translate RMSE to the business metric if the relation between the two is not trivial.

If all you need to do is multiply numbers in your head, you may be able to do some mental math on the fly. For example, if your profit curve is, "Every unit of RMSE would cost me \$10," you could argue that such mental math could be done in your head, or even during a meeting. It's much more likely that you'd encounter something like "\$1.21 per unit of RMSE" than friendly, round numbers such is \$10.

Quickly, what is 0.87 times \$1.21?

The manager I just asked responded "Oneish!" Is such a mental calculation what you want applied to your project, after you've spent considerable time trying to optimize a technical metric?

Moving past the linear relation between a business metric and RMSE, what about more complicated relations between RMSE and business metrics? What if the relation is best described by the exponential function? Are you going to ask meeting participants to consult a lookup table, mapping values of RMSE to a business metric?

All of the previous discussion applies even when you're using RMSE, arguably one of the simplest technical metrics to understand. It only gets worse when you're using more complicated technical metrics.

If you have a good business case, and your AI project can demonstrate the ability to achieve a good business result, then present results using a business metric. Any technical metric, if presented at all, should always take a back seat.

Moving past RMSE, you'll encounter many technical metrics in the AI field. Stay focused on business! Running a successful AI project requires knowing some AI concepts but shouldn't require the equivalent of a PhD in AI and ML. The number of managers who'd be able to acquire such a PhD is always going to be limited. Consequently, any argument that a PhD is needed to manage an AI project is actually an argument that a successful AI project is a rarity.

4.2.6 *You need the right business metric*

As explained in chapter 3, it's important to use the right business metrics to measure the progress of your AI project. Surprisingly, often the right business metrics aren't developed early in the project. This section reminds you of the pitfalls of having the wrong business metrics.

One common anti-pattern is to allow business metrics to emerge from the nomination of various team members with no additional analysis. Often, those metrics are transplants that someone has seen used on previous projects.

> **WARNING** It's not uncommon for teams to think that because previous projects used a business metric successfully, they should use the same metric again. A history of past use of the metric is irrelevant—what matters is applicability of the business metric to measure the desired business goal on the *current* project.

Common errors when defining the business metric are as follows:

- Having a business metric that's not related to the business goal at all
- Having a business metric that's too vague to measure the underlying business goal
- Trying to substitute a business metric that's more difficult to measure with a business metric that happens to be easy to measure

The first situation typically emerges when you take or *transplant* a metric from a previous project. An example (exaggerated for effect) is using a metric based on *cost plus* in an early startup. *Cost plus pricing* is common in government and defense contracts, where you might be guaranteed a profit of (for example) 15% above your costs. Clearly, the meaning of high cost in such environments isn't necessarily negative.

Transplant metrics you don't understand are dangerous!

While high cost isn't a problem when you're working in a cost plus environment, making your product and processes costly is usually fatal for an early startup that needs to minimize costs. If such a startup were to adapt metrics from an organization that

(continued)

uses a cost plus model, it would increase its cost of doing business. That applies not only for the obvious metrics (like cost itself) but for the secondary impact of any metric.

As an example of the secondary impact of a metric, imagine that an aerospace manufacturer tracks a "Number of designs approved by an external regulator" metric. That metric may help legal compliance and client communication (intended effect), but it also has a secondary effect of increasing the cost. It may make sense for an aerospace company operating in a cost plus environment to use this metric. But using the metric doesn't make sense for a startup building an iPhone app!

Second, metrics that are too vague to measure business goals are much more common than they should be. They might be vague because they're poorly formulated and aren't correctly measuring a concrete business goal. However, they could also be vague because they're trying to measure ambiguous business goals. An example would be a business goal of our products having a fanatical following, which happens to be better formulated as "We'll have industry-leading retention and referral rates among our customers."

NOTE   A good way to determine if a business goal is too vague is to ask people to state the business goal and then ask "So, how is it (the goal) going?" [3]

The third error of metric substitution happens in practice because you know what an ideal metric would be, but you don't know how to precisely measure it.

Don't use surrogate metrics

The metric you choose should be the exact business metric you want to affect, not some surrogate. If you're doing algorithmic trading on Wall Street, your metric is how much money you made after the actual trades were completed and settled, and all the fees and taxes applied. It's not how much money you'd have made if you were able to instantly complete the trades and didn't have to pay fees and taxes.

4.3   *Measuring progress on AI projects*

You should measure the progress that your analytical teams are making on the research questions by referring to the business metric that measures the success of the business problem you're trying to solve. This section will show you how.

Guiding the construction of a business metric that's capable of measuring business impact should be the overall responsibility of the business leader. Of course, work on it could be delegated, but ownership and responsibility should stay with the executive sponsor of the project. That business metric could be considered a contract among the executive sponsor, the business team, and the data science team.

Defining business metrics is a team sport. Let's look at an example that you can also present to your team and determine if you're lucky enough to have a team that's perfectly capable of choosing the right metrics on their own.

Suppose you're at a university that wants to help students bike between buildings on the campus. A few years ago, as a trial, the university created three bike rental stations at various locations on the campus. The university also collects bike rental data that includes weather information and rental times for each bike. You're probably wondering if there's a way to improve the use of the bikes. How many bikes do you need at each station? To know the answer to that question, you clearly would have to predict what the demand for bikes would be at each station.

For the time being, let's assume that you choose an appropriate ML algorithm to use.[2] Ask your team (and yourself), how would we evaluate how well that algorithm is doing?

If you have a data science team handy, ask them to help you select an evaluation metric they'd use to measure the algorithm's performance. If you want to save time, you might even skip constructing the algorithm and metric and just ask them if they feel that the RMSE could be a reasonable metric to measure the progress of such a project.

Also ask the team if they'd use additional metrics and what they'd report to you when showing progress. And, of course, if you're a data scientist, you might answer those questions yourself.

If you don't have a data science team handy, you can just assume that they advised you to use RMSE. If your team chooses a different evaluation metric, it doesn't matter— regardless of the metric you choose, you can follow the rest of this section with it.

> **NOTE** Be prepared. Your team might not choose the correct business metric. Guide a discussion by asking business questions and how the metric could be modified to better answer those questions. This is a learning exercise, not an exercise in saying "Gotcha!" to the team.

When you've chosen a metric and confirmed that the team will use it to report on the progress of the project, you'll need to make some simple management decisions. Let's try to answer a few questions based on the RMSE. For the sake of argument, assume that the value of the evaluation metric came back as 0.83. Answer these three questions:

1 I'm a student who just finished a class on a Monday, at 5 p.m., in July. What's the chance that there wouldn't be a bike available for me to use?

2 I'm a facilities administrator in charge of the project. How many bikes should I have on the lot to ensure that 95% of the people who'd like to rent a bike can do so?

---

[2] If you're a data scientist, assume that you've chosen multiple regression as your baseline model for this example.

3 I'm the college administrator running the project. What do you think is an important business question to ask for the project? Answer it, under the assumption that your evaluation metric has a value of 0.83.

What happens when you try to answer the three questions? If you know the data science yourself, what answers do you come up with? If not, ask your data science team. How do they do with answering such questions? These are the type of questions that a business is likely to ask on such a project, and if you aren't able to use RMSE to answer them, then RMSE is clearly not the right metric to use for making business decisions on this project.

Now, what would be the right business metric? That depends on the business goal, but I'll provide a business metric for one of the scenarios. The first question to ask is, "What are we trying to achieve with this system?" Are you trying to maximize profit of the bike rental operation? Or are you trying to encourage the maximum number of students who can bike?

> **NOTE** A business metric that's appropriate to use depends on the problem you're trying to solve. You can't define a good metric for a problem you poorly understand, so don't hesitate to ask questions about business goals.

If you're trying to maximize profit, chances are you're charging people to rent bikes, and profit is maximized when you don't have many bikes lying around unused. A good metric will be expected profit (in dollars) after accounting for all costs of bike rentals.

If you're just trying to encourage people to ride bikes, they might be free to rent, and having extra bikes lying around unused is much better than not having enough bikes. The best business metric could be the percentage of the time the rental station is out of bikes.

There's also a hybrid case. Suppose the campus wants to encourage biking, but it also wants to minimize the cost of the program. Then your business metric should be based on making the maximum profit with the constraint that you want to make sure there are always enough bikes per lot during peak usage times.

> **NOTE** Remember this bike example and, in particular, the hybrid business metric. We'll use that metric later in this chapter when constructing a profit curve.

Once you've defined the business metric, it's time to link technical progress to the business metric.

4.4 *Linking technical progress with a business metric*

Linking technical progress and business metrics is done using an artifact known as the *profit curve*. It lets you translate the value of the technology metric into the value of the business metric.

Once you've defined a business metric, if it's the right business metric, you should be able to make a business decision based on it. Suppose your business metric is profit increase. If I told you that an ML algorithm would likely increase profits 10%, you'd have an easy time answering the question: "Is it worth investing $100 K in developing such an ML algorithm?"

But ML algorithms don't operate with business metrics. They operate with the technical evaluation metrics. You'd need to link the business metric you already have with the technical metric that your team has just selected to measure their ML algorithms.

4.4.1 Why do we need technical metrics?

Why do we need technical metrics in the first place? Why don't we just use business metrics directly in the ML algorithms? The reasons for that are both technical and historical and come from the fact that business and technology metrics are intended for different purposes. This section introduces you to *technical metrics*.

Let's quickly revisit chapter 1. ML is a combination of formulation, optimization, and evaluation. An evaluation metric is a technical metric that's optimized by the ML algorithm. Your data science team chooses evaluation metrics based on what's technically appropriate for your project.

> **NOTE** Technical metrics are intended to work well when used with particular ML and AI algorithms. It's not uncommon for the algorithm itself to dictate which technical metrics can be used with it.

Technical metrics have properties that make it easy for the ML algorithms to optimize the value of such metrics. Those properties are mathematical in nature, highly technical, and typically unrelated to business. For example, one of the common properties of technical metrics is that they are differentiable, and many optimization algorithms used in the context of AI and ML would require that the metric be differentiable. Unfortunately, business metrics aren't necessarily differentiable. As a result, you can't use a business metric directly in many of the ML and AI algorithms.

> **NOTE** If you're wondering what *differentiable* means, Google it and read the results until you're satisfied that whoever invented the concept didn't worry much about it having any obvious relationship to a typical business problem you're likely to face.

In addition to the technical reasons, there are also historical reasons why many of the AI and ML algorithms require metrics that don't look like a business metric. When many of the AI and ML algorithms were invented, the use of AI and ML in business wasn't as common as it is today. There were competitions between researchers, such as the KDD cup [80], and originally, technology metrics were perfectly fine for measuring who won such a competition.

4.4.2 What is the profit curve?

A *profit curve* establishes the relationship between the business and technology metrics. It allows you to use a technical metric for your ML algorithms. It also lets you translate the *threshold* of business metrics (the minimum value the business metric project must achieve to be viable) into the corresponding value of a technical metric. This section shows you how to construct a profit curve.

The profit curve, in the context of data science projects, was originally proposed in the book *Data Science for Business: What You Need to Know about Data Mining and Data-Analytic Thinking* [81], although the general concept of establishing mathematical relationships between metrics predates it and was known before [1,3]. Figure 4.4 shows the process of constructing a profit curve.

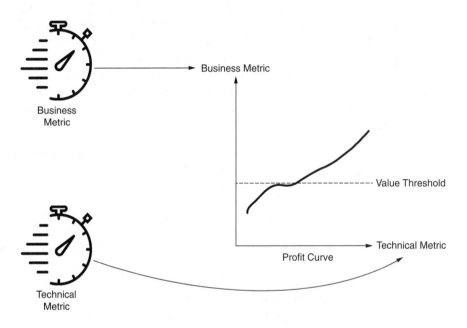

Figure 4.4   A profit curve specifies the relationship between a technical metric and a business metric. It allows you to understand what the technical answer (in the form of a technical metric) means for the business terms.

When defining a profit curve, you'd combine business and technical metrics through a mathematical relationship. That joins technology and business by linking the research question with the business problem you're trying to solve. You can think about it as a form of the exchange rate when answering the question of "How many US dollars is one unit of RMSE worth?" (if your business metric is measured in dollars, and your technology metric is RMSE).

The *value threshold* is the minimum value of the business metric that *must* be achieved for your project to be viable. Suppose the business metric is profit, and the cost of starting the project is $30 K. Clearly, there's no point in starting the business unless it's expected that it would bring in more than $30 K in profit. In this example, $30 K is the value threshold.

4.4.3 Constructing a profit curve for bike rentals

Now that you understand what a profit curve is, we'll construct one for the bike rental example from section 4.3. The construction of the profit curve requires the cooperation of business and engineering. If you don't have an engineering background, here's one area where you'll be learning a little about the engineering side—see the sidebar for more information.

The moment of truth

In chapter 1, I said that an engineering background isn't required for the readers of this book, but that the willingness to learn some engineering concepts is. A profit curve (and some later concepts I present in this book) requires that you understand some simple engineering concepts.

If you're a reader with a business background, I promise to go easy on the complicated math. I have to ask you to have patience, because other readers of this book with a strong technical background (who might even be data scientists themselves) will appreciate it if I go into detail on some technical questions. For occasional content that's specifically targeted toward those readers, I clearly highlight that content as being intended for a technical audience.

This way, the book will provide enough information not only to teach you that some concept like the profit curve exists and how to use it, but will also show you how to build it. Even if that means you'd have to show this book to your chief data scientist.

On the first reading of this book, you're free to skip sections if the content doesn't apply to your level of expertise in AI. You should still be able to learn from the rest of the book all that a manager needs to know about the usage of the concepts I'm describing.

Back to the bike rental example from section 4.3. You need to predict how many rental bikes will be needed on rental lots. As a reminder, you're trying to minimize the number of bikes bought, subject to the constraint that you want to make sure there are bikes available during peak usage times. For simplicity, let's also assume that the rental fleet offers only a single bike model.

The main question for constructing a profit curve is, "How much would an error in prediction cost?" For the technical metric to measure the ML algorithms we chose, let's use RMSE. (In this particular case, take my word for the correct interpretation of what an RMSE measure is in the domain of bike rentals). For our question we'll use: "How many bikes can my prediction be off, on average?"

> **NOTE** If you're a data scientist, you know that RMSE would have a tendency to penalize large errors more, and that, as such, the technical interpretation I'm using might have some caveats and corner cases. In the construction of an initial profit curve, you can disregard the corner cases of technical metrics, as you're just trying to decide how profitable a project is likely to be.

The RMSE given in the bike example was 0.83. This means that we're approximately 0.83 bikes per rental lot off in our demand prediction. To ensure that enough bikes are available, we'd need 0.83 extra bikes per lot. Of course, the number of bikes must be a round number, so 0.83 is rounded to one extra bike per lot, right?

Wrong! If you're looking to ensure that there's always a bike available, you're not interested in the average error in prediction of available bikes. If you're five bikes off in your prediction of demand for bikes at 3 a.m., but the lot is full of unrented bikes, who cares? There are enough bikes for everyone when the lot is full.

What you're interested in is the error of prediction *during peak usage hours*. If there are enough bikes to rent at peak usage hours (let's say 2 p.m.), chances are, there would be enough to rent at 3 a.m. too! Your profit curve in this case isn't

$$Cost\ of\ Error\ Prediction = Price\ of\ Bike * RMSE$$

Instead, it's

$$Cost\ of\ Error\ Prediction = Price\ of\ Bike * Max\ prediction\ error\ during\ peak\ usage\ hours$$

Let's give the quantity "Max prediction error during peak usage hours" a simpler name: *Peak usage hour's RMSE.*

Start simple

For simplicity, this example assumes that all costs associated with bikes are limited to the purchase price of a bike. The profit curve should be matched with the business problem, and if you're purchasing only a few extra bikes, this would be an appropriate level of granularity.

In a more developed example in which many bikes are purchased and maybe even additional lots are opened, the cost of maintenance and the cost of the bike rental spaces are likely to be included as factors in a profit curve construction. Tax treatment of bikes in the form of an accounting concept known as a *depreciation schedule* might also be a factor.

It's also likely that the cost of maintenance per bike would diminish in large bike fleets, so the relationship between extra bikes purchased and the cost of the bike might be more complicated than in this example. If you have a bike fleet measuring in the tens of thousands of bikes, it might be important to model all of those factors.

The point is, *the sophistication of the mathematical analysis during your profit curve construction should match the size of the project.* This isn't a different approach than the one used when you estimated the cost of the project. A project that expects to involve one person for one week of work uses a much simpler cost model than a project expected to require 60 engineers and 200 support personnel for a year.

Figure 4.5 shows you how the profit curve we constructed for the bike rental project looks.

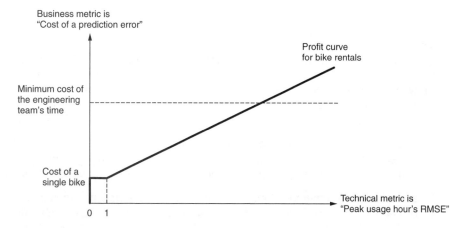

Figure 4.5   Profit curve for bike rentals. Note that in the case of a business metric being a cost, the goal is to *minimize* the business metric.

The construction of that curve is simple but comes with two caveats. The first is that the cost is the same for every peak usage hour's RMSE between 0 and 1. The reason is that you can't purchase half of a bike, so any error smaller than 1 has the same business implication. The second caveat is that any time you're working with business metrics such as cost, *less is better.* When operating with this business metric, the goal of your AI team would be to minimize the business metric. If your business metric was something like profit, you'd want to *maximize* the profit curve.

> **NOTE**   Some organizations prefer this rule: we always build a profit curve in such way that more is better. This is for uniformity and for making understanding and training easier. If that's your preference, use signed numbers; for example, a cost of $10 would be written as –$10.

What about the value threshold you should choose? If you happen to make an RMSE prototype that on the first try has an RMSE of 0, good for you. But if it happens that you have a peak hour RMSE of 1.2, for example, should you try to improve that? It depends on how the cost of your engineering time compares with the cost of a bike. If the cost associated with such a peak hour's RMSE is smaller than the cost of your engineering team's time to look at the problem, then don't worry about improving it. Consequently, the value threshold for this profit curve would be based on the estimate of the minimum cost of the engineering team's time to look at the problem further.

For data scientists in the audience

If you're not a technologist yourself, this sidebar won't make much sense. It's a nod to the data scientists in the audience; skip it, and the rest of the chapter would still make sense without it. If you happen to be a data scientist, please read on.

(continued)

When you look at figure 4.5, the profit curve for bike rentals, you might initially read the graph as depicting a (mostly) linear relationship between RMSE and cost. But a more careful examination of the graph would show that it depicts a linear relationship between *peak hour's RMSE* and cost. Peak hour's RMSE is typically not linearly proportional to RMSE itself. So if the graph depicted the relationship between RMSE and cost (as opposed to *peak hour's RMSE* and cost), it would likely be highly nonlinear.

In practice, you'd extract peak hour's RMSE from an RMSE curve and then would use a mathematical formula to translate peak hour's RMSE to profit. I didn't show that detail in the graph so as not to puzzle readers with a less technical background.

What you need to remember from this discussion is that the relationship between technical and business metrics isn't limited to just a form of the mathematical formula. In this case, the relationship is specified algorithmically as a combination of the formula and RMSE.

(This example is another reason why it's unlikely that even people who know what technical metrics mean will be able to relate technical metrics to business goals in the middle of a meeting.)

Once you're able to express your data science project's progress in terms of a business metric, understanding the value threshold you should select is typically simple. If you're looking to make a profit, the value threshold would be based on that profit actually existing when you take all costs (including costs of capital) into account.

4.4.4   *Why is this not taught in college?*

If you recently had college courses in AI and ML and never heard of a concept such as a profit curve, you might wonder why that's the case. First, some courses (like the ones that use as the textbook *Data Science for Business: What You Need to Know about Data Mining and Data-Analytic Thinking*, by Provost and Fawcett [81]) do teach it. As for the courses that don't teach the profit curve, the reason may be that the profit curve is much more important and applicable to business environments than academic ones. This section explains the differences between these environments.

As shown in figure 4.6, the shape of the typical profit curve in academia is very simple. Once your proposed AI methods get better results than was achieved before, your work becomes publishable. So, a profit curve in academia is typically that your work has no value until you achieve better results than previous researchers.

The shape of the typical profit curve in academia makes it easy to *collapse* the whole profit curve into a single question. That single question is, "Is my technical metric better than what anyone that published before me has achieved?" Replacing the profit curve with that question, and the fact that most of the engineering courses don't talk much about a business environment in the first place, might explain why you didn't encounter this concept in college.

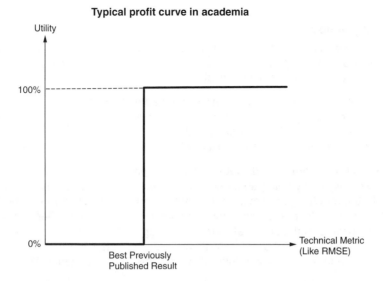

Figure 4.6   A typical profit curve when you're working in an academic environment. Such a profit curve allows you to focus only on the technical metric.

Real world academia is more complex too

The academia profit curve is approximate but probably a good model of the thinking process of an average researcher.

If you have an academic background, you're probably aware that there's an additional advantage to getting research results that are much better than those previously published (as opposed to just slightly better). That would cause a profit curve to not jump immediately to 100% as soon as you got a better result; it would look slightly different after the step from 0% to 100% shown in figure 4.6.

This is true, but it doesn't change the step nature of the profit curve in academia. Researchers try to do the best they can until they're doing better than previous scholars, then they publish shortly after they've achieved the result.

Be that as it may, a profit curve in academia is always going to have a large step around the best previously published result.

4.4.5   Can't businesses define the profit curve themselves?

It's not uncommon for data scientists to assume it's possible for business teams to translate a technical metric into a business metric on their own. This section explains why it's usually better if the data science team helps the business team here, rather than asking the business team to do it on their own.

What would you do?

Let's put ourselves in the position of a business team that's been asked to translate technical metrics to business metrics on their own. I'll give you an example of when I was asked to do something similar myself.

Years ago, I decided to buy a security device that had multiple sensors on it; one of those was an air quality sensor. Pretty soon, the device started sending constant messages about the air quality being abnormal. As I cared about air quality, I decided to investigate the problem, but I didn't exactly have much to go on.

After a few back and forth rounds with technical support, they explained how the device worked. Air quality being abnormal meant that the concentration of harmful chemicals in the air changed compared to what it was the first time I installed the device. What wasn't clear was which harmful chemicals: some really harmful ones were grouped together with some that were fairly benign. I also didn't know what was baseline. Did it just happen that the first time the device was installed, the air was unusually clean, and now it's worse (but still within the bounds of healthy)?

Technical support tried to help by giving advice on how I could calibrate the device to answer those questions. Now, I'm an engineer and not a stranger to analyzing data or calibrating devices. What I needed to do was relatively simple and well within my capabilities. Still, I felt that expecting the customer to perform calibration was an unfortunate demand.

If it was possible for me to perform the calibration, it was also possible for the manufacturer to do so, or at least make the calibration procedure as simple as possible. Instead, the manufacturer has exposed a technical metric (consisting of the "concentration of a group of chemicals") to the user and left it to the user to figure out what to do with that metric. This manufacturer also didn't do well on the question, "Is there a way for me to react to an alert?" I didn't perform the calibration—I bought a different device instead.

The whole purpose of the data science project is to allow management to make the right business decisions based on some quantitative criteria. Don't be like that security device manufacturer that asks their users to manually do the work that they should have automated (see the "What would you do?" sidebar). Even a person who knows how to construct a profit curve might object to the task of manually calibrating a device. It doesn't get better if business users are less current on math and programming than your data science team.

Never present technical metrics to the business audience and ask them to translate the metrics themselves. At best, you're saying, "It's so easy to translate this metric, but I didn't feel like doing it for you." At worst, you're saying, "It's not possible to present in business terms what the project is doing."

The team that's creating a profit curve should consist of data scientists and business analysts. Once you construct the profit curve, use it to present technical results in the form of business metrics to the business audience.

4.4.6   *Understanding technical results in business terms*

Once you have a relationship between the technical and business metric, that relationship is bidirectional. Just as you can use a profit curve to translate the value of the business threshold to the value of a technical metric, you can also translate the value of the technical metric to the business metric. This section shows you how.

One of the outputs of running a typical ML algorithm would be a technical metric. Once you understand the relationship between a technical result and a business result, you can use a profit curve to understand the technical results in business terms. This is the *U* part of CLUE, as shown in figure 4.7.

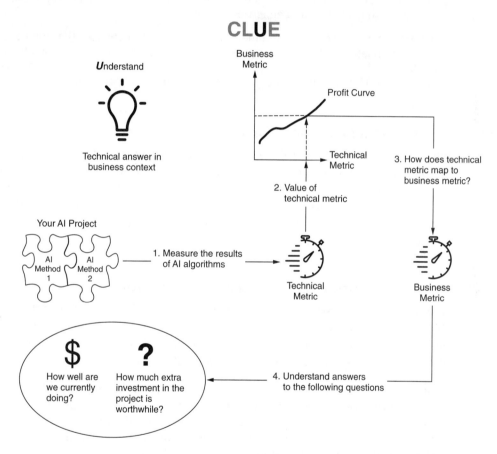

Figure 4.7   A profit curve is a bidirectional relationship. You can use it to answer a business question based on the technical metric.

When you have a profit curve, suddenly it's possible to measure technical progress with business terms. You do that by translating the value of a technical metric to a business result.

Again, suppose your technical metric is RMSE, and your business metric is profit (in US dollars). Let's say you have an RMSE of 0.83. Looking at the profit curve, you see how an RMSE of 0.83 translates into the business metric. And let's say that, in this example, an RMSE of 0.83 is a profit of $1.325 million per year. Now, use the profit of $1.325 million per year to answer your business question.

Is a profit curve limited to supervised learning?

If you're a data scientist, you've probably noticed that many of the examples given of profit curve construction were provided in the context of supervised learning. Although it's easier to construct a profit curve in the context of supervised learning, a profit curve isn't limited to supervised learning.

Any ML algorithm would need some technical metric to optimize. That metric is in some way related to the business result, and that relationship can be found through analysis or experimentation. Typically, supervised learning problems prefer analysis; unsupervised learning problems might be better off with experimentation.

4.5 *Organizational considerations*

While construction of the profit curve is technically simple, you must be cognizant of the organizational aspects of constructing a profit curve. When constructing a profit curve, you must not only consider what's the best mathematical formula to describe the profit curve, but also how best to interact with your organization to get the information you need to construct that formula. This section describes some of the important organizational concerns you must address when constructing a profit curve.

4.5.1 *Profit curve precision depends on the business problem*

A profit curve shows you what your organization currently knows about the relationship between the technical and business metrics you're using on the project. As in any other project management decision, there's going to be a dichotomy between the cost of obtaining precise information and the value of that information.

> **NOTE** You can spend a ton of time trying to construct the perfect profit curve with a precision of up to five decimal places. If you're on a project that's bringing in $1 billion per year to your employer, you definitely should spend that time. If you're on a project that's bringing in $20 K per year in profit, you don't need that much precision.

When constructing a profit curve, the first question should be: "At this stage of the project, what level of precision do we need to make sound project management decisions?" A general rule you should follow is that in the early phases of projects, a profit curve should be approximate. That's the approach that I followed in section 4.4.3.

TIP When you're just starting a project, there are many unknowns. You don't know how much exactly it would cost, yet you're comfortable with estimating cost. You also are comfortable with initially providing a rough cost estimate and revisiting it over time. Use those skills you already have to construct a profit curve.

4.5.2 A profit curve improves over time

A project that's just building proof of concept (POC) and you don't know if it's technically possible is quite different from a project that has been in production for years for a business operation that has $1 billion of revenue per year. If you have the latter type of project, an improvement of 0.1% is typically worthwhile.

> **NOTE** It isn't unheard of for an AI project to be applied to the critical business areas of large companies with revenue of (or exceeding) $1 billion. There are hundreds of companies in this group.

As an AI project progresses through its life cycle, the profit curve is significantly refined. It would be a ridiculous idea for an early startup to hire a full-time economist to construct the best profit curve. But by the time you're making $1 billion per year with some product, putting more effort in getting better profit curves (or hiring full-time economists) is a reasonable thing to do.

As a result, refinements in the profit curve are expected, and they are not a sign that your initial profit curve was in error or that the decisions you made based on that version of the profit curve were wrong. They were the best decisions you could have made based on what you knew then.

Types of data scientists to hire

Leading experts focused on a narrow class of algorithms are worth their weight in gold if they know how to improve the performance of an algorithm by 0.1% that's bringing $1 billion per year to your organization. However, if your question is, "What can AI do to help my business?" you're probably better off with a data scientist who has a command of the wide range of data science methods. A data scientist with that profile has the best chance of finding a use case in which the profit margin would be large and you don't need to get that last 0.1% improvement for the use case to be viable.

A data scientist who was a great fit for an already established AI project inside a G-MAFIA group company isn't necessarily a good fit for an early AI effort, and vice versa.

As your project grows, the economic value of information changes. Large, successful projects need (and can afford) a more refined version of the profit curve.

TIP After refining your profit curve, don't forget to revise old decisions you made based on previous versions. Those decisions were based on a business metric value that changes every time a profit model changes. Perhaps they should be updated based on what you know now.

4.5.3 *It's about learning, not about being right*

The nature of the profit curve is that it should be approximate, and that it codifies the incomplete knowledge that your organization has. The first attempt at the profit curve will likely be the best guess that captures most of the relationship between the technical and business metrics, although it may disregard a few rarely encountered corner cases. It's your job to create an environment in which people feel safe providing their best guess.

Explain to your team (and management) that a profit curve is expected to evolve over time. A good analogy to use is estimating the cost of a project. Such estimates are also expected to change and evolve over the lifetime of the project.

Build an organization that learns over time more about its business domain and codifies that learning with improvements in the profit curve. See *Elastic Leadership* [82] for some of the techniques you can use to build a learning organization.

4.5.4 *Dealing with information hoarding*

Information hoarding is a fact of life for any AI project. Often, some organizational members are going to be afraid that providing access to data and information can result in the loss of their influence and power. This section contains some strategies for dealing with this problem.

If your organization has hoarding problems, it's a safe bet that some of these issues will come up during the construction of the profit curve too. In general, there's no magic wand to resolve information hoarding, as it's a sign of the general organizational culture (and health). Having said that, the rules for getting good information for profit curve construction are the same as the rules for getting any other data in an organization:

- If some parts of the organization are comfortable with working among themselves but less comfortable with working closely with the rest of the organization, you have the problem of *organizational silos*. You'll need the support of higher-level management to break through this problem.
- Identify which organization is in charge of the data you need and which specific people know where that data is.
- People in charge of the necessary data (let's call them data owners) should be part of the team responsible for constructing the profit curve. You don't necessarily need access to all their data; you just need their help in constructing the profit curve.
- If need be, always make the case to the owner of the information that they're better off sharing the data voluntarily. Otherwise, the next best thing is to change incentives—can you affect business metrics on which those owners of information are measured so that sharing the information improves the metric?

In general, resistance to breaking organizational silos always comes down to the fact that you're not important enough to the silo owner, which is almost always a sign that you don't have enough buy-in from higher-level management for the AI project. Consider what you can do to remedy that situation.

4.5.5 But we can't measure that!

One complaint that you often hear when constructing a profit curve is that this AI project is special, and that it's not possible to construct a metric that would measure progress on it. This section presents some of the common arguments you're likely to hear.

The most common objection you might encounter is that the business metric can't be precisely measured. This is typically mentioned in relationship to intangibles such as, for example, customer satisfaction. The solution is given in Hubbard's book [75], which points out that *everything* can be measured. The impression that some things can't be measured is based on the misunderstanding of what measurement is: people believe that the result of measurement is always a number.

> **NOTE** The result of any measurement is actually an *interval.* How tall are you? You say six feet? Is that closer to 5 feet, 9.5 inches, or 6 feet, 0.5 inch? You say 6 feet, 0.5 inch? Is that closer to 6 feet, 0.25 inches, or 6 feet, 0.75 inches? Does it include your hair style? You can't provide a single number even for such a trivial and clearly measurable thing as your height.

Similarly, for intangibles, you measure them using an interval. The interval is just a lot larger. You can attempt to make the case that you can't quantify the value of satisfaction for your early customers to measure the success of your startup. What would you invest in customer satisfaction improvement? Would you invest $0.25 in it? How about $1 billion? You've just quantified that the value of customer satisfaction is between $0.25 and $1 billion. Keep trying; I'm sure you can do better. You can refer to Hubbard's book [75] for many examples of how to measure intangibles.

The next common objection is that the data you need to construct the profit curve simply doesn't exist. For example, it might be that you're trying to measure the profit of some activity, but in your P&L statement, most of the costs your enterprise is incurring are grouped together under the name Overhead. Consequently, you have revenue for some activities but no associated per activity cost, so you can't calculate profit per activity. Or, in the case of a small team, you have a cost for the team but no breakdown of which tasks the team spent its time doing, so you don't know how much the per activity cost was.

When you encounter a situation like that, the right long-term solution is to collect the data you're missing: what were the per activity costs, and which team members spent time on those activities? A short-term solution would have to be based on estimating how overhead cost breaks down among different activities.

Some projects are really different!

There might be a few types of projects in which the value for an AI solution can't be estimated at all. These fall into three categories:

- *Projects that are clearly financially beneficial, so it would obviously be worthwhile to undertake them*—An example is a super intelligent and benevolent AI that's perfectly aligned with the interest of humanity [76,83].
- *Projects for which your profit curve is so simple that the relationship between the technical and business metrics is apparent, and, as such, it's not necessary to construct one*—Such an example is given in section 4.4.4.
- *Projects that are in progress, but it's difficult to see how AI results could be translated to business results*—You'd think that in for-profit businesses such an example would be difficult to find, but let me try my best. Say you're an insurance company that just wrote an AI program that's good at generating haiku poetry.

For the first and second types of projects, you could (and should) skip profit curve generation. Just invest as much as you can afford to invest.

For the third type of project, where you're running an AI project that has no clear relationship to your business whatsoever, such projects are often called *science projects*. Do with them what your organization usually does with the other science projects it encounters.

4.6   Exercises

Question 1: If your organization has run AI projects before, look at some progress reports and the metrics used in those reports. Answer the following:

- If we release software today, in its current state, how much money will we make/lose?
- If we can't release today, how much better do our results need to be before we can release?
- Is it worth investing $100 K extra in getting 5% better results than we have today?

Question 2: Based on the answers to the previous questions, do you feel that your organization is making decisions in its AI projects based on the data, or is it possible that in some cases you had to make important decisions based on intuition?

Question 3: Suppose the cost to start a project is $100 K, and the policy of your organization is that no project that can't create a 10% return on investment is worth doing. If your business metric is profit, what would be your value threshold for the project?

Question 4: Go back to the bike rental example from this chapter. Suppose the estimated cost to assign a data scientist to the project is $10 K, and each extra bike costs

$1 K. How much should you expect to improve the peak hour's RMSE to make it worthwhile to assign a data scientist to the project?

Summary

- Most of the current projects run in businesses today use some form of technical metrics to measure progress and success. But it's difficult for most organizations to use such metrics to make quantitative and repeatable business decisions.
- Link business and technology metrics, which is the L part of CLUE, so that you can measure technical progress in business terms. That's done by constructing a profit curve.
- You should measure and report the progress of your AI project using business metrics. Such an approach helps you understand the AI project's progress in business terms. That's the U part of CLUE.
- Constructing a good profit curve isn't just an exercise in abstract math. If anything, it's more of a detective job in which you're tracking which part of the organization has the information you need and thinking how to get that information.

What is an ML pipeline, and how does it affect an AI project?

This chapter covers

- Understanding an ML pipeline
- Understanding why an ML pipeline ossifies and how to address that
- Understanding the evolution of ML or AI algorithms in larger systems
- Balancing attention between business questions, data, and AI algorithms

In previous chapters, you learned how to select your initial AI project and how to tie technology metrics with business results. Now it's time to understand how to guide the development of the software architecture of the AI project. This chapter teaches you to recognize in which respects the AI system behaves differently from other software systems. To effectively implement an AI project, it's important to understand the technical artifacts and the life cycle of an AI project. I'll start by explaining the most important artifact of the AI project—the ML pipeline.

The ML pipeline describes how data flows through the system, what high-level transformation is done on it, which ML and AI algorithms are applied, and how the results are presented to the user of your AI system. Without a focus on the pipeline's architecture, your project would be saddled with an ML pipeline that emerges from early proof-of-concept (POC) decisions. That's not good, because an ML pipeline quickly ossifies and becomes difficult and costly to radically change.

This chapter shows you how to determine early in your project if the ML pipeline can support your business goals. Finally, this chapter shows the role that AI methods play in the ML pipeline and in which order to make decisions about business, AI methods, data, and technical infrastructure.

5.1 How is an AI project different?

An AI project is a software project that's subject to the same considerations as other software projects. In addition to being an ordinary software project, an AI project always has an artifact called an ML pipeline. Furthermore, an AI project links with the React part of the Sense/Analyze/React loop: it can directly control the system (in the context of a fully automated system) or report the results of the analysis (if a human is responsible for the reaction).

This section explains the concept of the ML pipeline, how the software architecture of an AI project is different from the software architecture of other projects, and how to manage the construction of an AI project's architecture.

5.1.1 The ML pipeline in AI projects

The ML pipeline is a software artifact that addresses several considerations in your AI system. It describes how data flows, performs a high-level transformation on that data, applies ML and AI algorithms, and determines how results are presented to the user. The ML pipeline is essential to your project, and your team must get its design right. To help you do that, this section presents the concept and an example of an ML pipeline.

Your AI software system consists of more than just AI algorithms. It must account for many functions:

- AI algorithms operate on the data. That data needs to be stored somewhere, which may require a technical infrastructure such as a big data framework.
- That data can be *dirty* (meaning there could be various errors and irregularities in it), so it needs to be cleaned.
- Data relevant for your AI system often resides in multiple and different data sources, such as a data lake or various databases, so you need to bring together and combine data from various sources.
- If you're expecting a person to fulfill the React part of the Sense/Analyze/React loop, then the results of an AI analysis need to be presented to the user of your AI system.
- If the React part of an AI system is automated, then you must ensure that the AI system follows some business and safety rules that are specific to your domain.

To demonstrate, let's construct an ML pipeline used in the context of a factory line. That factory line includes many machines that have consumable supplies, such as oil and various parts. The machines are automated and can sense the current level of consumables. You want to order consumables when they're needed. Figure 5.1 shows an associated ML pipeline, simplified for a more straightforward explanation of the concept.

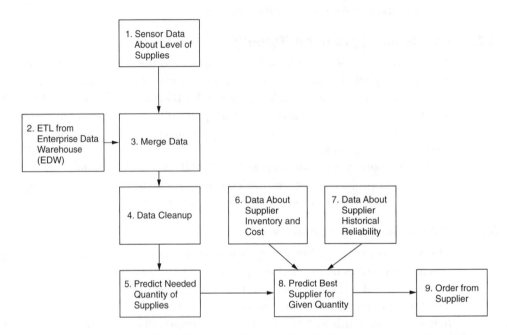

Figure 5.1 Example of an ML pipeline for a factory line. This ML pipeline oversees the automated ordering of consumable supplies from suppliers.

Let's deconstruct what's shown in figure 5.1. Note that the boxes in figure 5.1 could represent interactions both between software systems (for example, communications like invoking other programs and computer systems) and between parts of a single program. The deconstruction would look like this:

- Data about the current level of supplies in the machine are obtained from the sensors in the device itself (box 1).

  The system predicts when a machine will run out of supplies and reorders new supplies. The system needs to know both the current level of the supplies and the historical trend of how fast the machine uses them.

- Data about historical supply usage is stored in the enterprise data warehouse (EDW). From box 1, we get the current level of supplies. An extract/transform/load (ETL) process makes data from the EDW available to the AI system (box 2).

- Sensor data about the current level of consumables needs to be combined with the data from the EDW (box 3).

- Data usually isn't in the exact format that the ML algorithm needs. For example, it might have empty fields, errors, or different formats than the algorithm expects. The ETL process typically won't completely address all of these problems. As a result, you need to do some cleanup of both the EDW and sensor data (box 4).

- Now you need to answer the question, "Based on the current levels of supply and historical usage, when would I need to have new supplies ordered?" To answer that, you'd need to *predict* the usage of the remaining supplies. You apply an AI algorithm to the levels of supply to forecast the expected time when additional supplies would be needed (box 5).

- Based on the forecast, you query various suppliers for their current level and cost of supplies (box 6).

- Because not all of the suppliers are equal when it comes to quality, the system chooses the best supplier (box 8) based on the historical quality metrics (box 7) and the current cost and inventory available from the suppliers (box 6).

- The outcome from the previous step determines the automated order that will be placed with the supplier (box 9).

Real-world ML pipelines are complex

Real-world, enterprise-strength ML pipelines are more complicated and expensive to build. The ML pipeline in figure 5.1 is simplified to highlight only the most critical parts of a typical pipeline used for the automated ordering of supplies.

For production, you'd need to think about additional details in the ML pipeline, so the pipeline could be much more complicated. Even the individual steps in each of the boxes in figure 5.1 are typically more complicated. The process of extracting data might include various data quality checks, ELT/ETL processes,[a] and data cleansing operations. It's also quite possible that some of the source data wouldn't be in the optimal format and would need to be transformed.

In any extensive database of historical data, you'll find data that's simply plain wrong (such as NULL fields that aren't supposed to be NULL and other incorrect data). Remember that you often deal with data that's been accumulated over many years, with many changes in the system and many bugs that made it into the system.

---

[a] ETL stands for extract/transform/load and ELT for extract/load/transform processes. Those processes describe transformation of the data from data sources they're in into system responsible for analytics.

There's no such thing as a universal ML pipeline that would work for every project and every organization. An ML pipeline is customized for each organization and the problem being solved. The structure of the pipeline can be different even when two different businesses are solving the same problem!

Back to our example, the ML pipeline won't be the same even if two organizations in the same business are solving the problem of automated supply ordering. The reason is that both organizations might be using different machines as part of their factory line.

In figure 5.1, the assumption was that data about the historical usage of supplies was stored in the EDW. However, if you have a different factory line, then machines on that factory line may store historical data about supply usage. You might also be able to assume that such historical data is correct and doesn't have any significant errors that need to be cleaned. The ML pipeline for such a factory line would be different; it would bypass EDW and send data directly from the machines to the predictive algorithm (box 5 in figure 5.1). Figure 5.2 shows this situation.

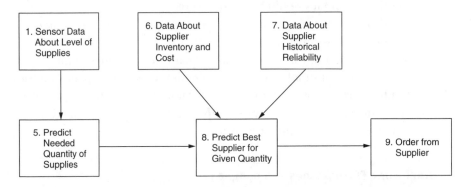

Figure 5.2   Modification of the ML pipeline from figure 5.1 for a situation in which supply levels are stored in the machine itself. You don't need to worry about EDW or merging data and can assume that the historical data is correct, so there's no need to clean the data.

Note that some stages in the pipeline of figure 5.2 play the same function as corresponding stages in figure 5.1. For easier reference, I've numbered such stages identically.

While pipelines are often customized, it frequently happens that ML pipelines used to address similar problems have a commonality in structure. ML pipelines might represent years of accumulated wisdom from your company (or the whole community) and be structured accordingly. For example, natural language processing (NLP) often uses the same general form of ML pipeline [84].

Can we be more formal with an architectural description?

To help readers who are accustomed to the typical architectural presentation done in the industry today, I'm using a simple box and arrow style of architectural diagram, as opposed to the more formal architectural presentation methods (such as the 4+1 architectural view model [85,86]). If you're an experienced software architect and are wondering where the diagrams in figure 5.1 and 5.2 fit into the broader architecture of the system, they're drawn in the context of the development view of the system.

5.1.2 Challenges the AI system shares with a traditional software system

As you've seen, the ML pipeline serves many functions, and it's easy to see why your software engineering team would be interested in structure. This section discusses structural attributes of the ML pipeline that you should care about even if you're a business user.

The ML pipeline isn't just a codification of technical decisions, it's also a codification of the business decisions you make. In figure 5.1, the ML pipeline automatically communicates with suppliers. Someone had to decide which suppliers to use, and contracts with those suppliers needed to be signed. You also needed to work with the suppliers to get access to their systems and APIs so that you could place automated orders. All of those decisions were business decisions that are now reflected in your ML pipeline.

An ML pipeline is costly to develop, not just because of the cost of developing software, but because of the associated costs you incur to obtain data that the pipeline would use. It's also costly in the form of related contracts you need to sign with your business partners.

However, don't forget that an ML pipeline is a part of the larger software system. All the rules that apply to the development of typical software systems still apply. You need competent engineers and architects, and you need proper software development processes. Because an AI project could fail in the same way as any other software system, use the knowledge you already have about managing software projects to help prevent such a failure.

5.1.3 Challenges amplified in AI projects

In some cases, introducing AI can amplify considerations that already exist in traditional software systems. Although those considerations aren't related to AI, they often manifest differently in the context of AI projects. This section provides some examples of those considerations.

Security is important for a software project, but it's even more crucial in the context of an AI project. An AI project can have a lot of data about your users, and a breach of that data can be much more impactful.

AI systems integrated with physical devices warrant additional considerations. AI might need more information than a traditional system would. For example, it's unusual for a website to require access to a video stream of your workspace. A security system using AI, however, might benefit from a video stream. In such a system, you must account not only for the costs and behavior of the ML pipeline but for the costs and behavior of the larger system.

> **NOTE** Imagine that you're selling AI security devices for the home market. Security problems on the device might allow a hacker to get access to the video and audio of your customer's home. Security is a crucial component of AI systems!

When constructing an AI system that controls a physical device, the reactions of that system (in the context of the Sense/Analyze/React pattern) must be safe. If your ML pipeline controls operating parameters of the physical engine, it's typical that one of its steps would be responsible for keeping those parameters within a safe operating range.

5.1.4   Ossification of the ML pipeline

Besides the problems that AI projects share with other software projects, they also have their own problems. One such problem is the cost of maintenance of the ML pipeline. One of the biggest contributors to the cost of an AI project is that the ML pipeline quickly becomes difficult and costly to radically change.

AI software is costly to maintain. There's an inherent tangling between the data and the algorithms used that is more prevalent than in any other type of software project. To address this, if you're a software architect, I highly recommend that you read the article by D. Sculley et al., "Machine Learning: The High Interest Credit Card of Technical Debt" [87], for details about common pitfalls and advice on how to avoid them.

> **TIP**   As a business leader, make sure you have not only the best data scientists you can get, but also the best software architects. They're equally important.

Building the ML pipeline itself also involves costs and challenges. Construction of the pipeline is an early step in an AI project, and data scientists make an early version of the ML pipeline during the initial POC. You may be tempted to adopt that ML pipeline for your production system, but you should be careful when selecting the pipeline you'll use for production. Once the ML pipeline emerges, as mentioned, it rapidly becomes difficult and costly to radically change—it *ossifies*. The more your project progresses, the more difficult and costly it will be to change the structure of your ML pipeline.

> **TIP**   The very nature of the ML pipeline is that it starts ossifying the moment you begin implementing it. *You can't prevent ossification.* The best you can do is engineer an ML pipeline that solves your business problem. What's costly is being caught by surprise with the ossification of the *wrong* ML pipeline.

On a high level, ossification happens for both technical and organizational reasons. On the technical side, the ML pipeline is a complex piece of software that could have many steps. Each of these steps might require specialized skills from the data engineering domain, skills ranging from the area of big data to cloud computing. On the organizational side, ML pipelines, more than most other software artifacts that the organization builds, require agreements across departments and even new contracts with external vendors. For example, let's look at the ML pipeline from figure 5.1.

You can see that in steps 6, 7, and 9, the pipeline interacts with the software systems that your suppliers control. How do you get access to those systems? To gain access to those systems, you need to have agreements with both the EDW team and various suppliers whose automated ordering API you'd use. You need to talk with multiple departments and sign a ton of contracts, and you'll have the legal department on speed dial. The end structure of the ML pipeline reflects the result of many negotiations.

It isn't just interaction with external organizations that gets you. You might have forces inside your organization that would accelerate ossification. For example, you might have to negotiate with other departments within your organization to gain access to data. In the larger organization, even within your department and project, you might see some form of Conway's Law [88,89] acting on you.

> **NOTE** Conway's Law states that any organization that designs systems produces a design whose structure is a copy of the organization's communication structure. If you have five teams, don't be surprised if you finish with a five-stage ML pipeline.

Once an ML pipeline is defined, it's common (and unavoidable) that various parts of it will be entrusted to different people or different departments. It's still rare to find people who have a strong familiarity with both AI and all the pieces of the data engineering needed in the pipeline. Departments will focus on their own area of expertise, not on the ML pipeline as a whole. The overall result increases the rate of ossification, and as time progresses, it's more difficult to make radical changes in the structure of the pipeline.

An ML pipeline once defined would both immediately start accumulating technical debt (in the form of the code that implements it and that's subject to the issues detailed in the article by Sculley et al. [87]) and be subject to human inertia. Agreements people make are the results of significant negotiation. Such agreements are often more resistant to change than the software itself.

> **NOTE** ML pipeline ossification is not limited to large organizations. Even in smaller organizations, if you hire someone specifically because they know Apache Spark [14], it's a safe bet that they'd want to continue using Spark.

An ML pipeline is more visible to the rest of an organization than is the other software the organization builds. As a result, changes in an ML pipeline are more noticeable to the rest of the organization. This naturally makes the management of an AI team more reluctant to change the ML pipeline than it would be for other pieces of software. Once the ML pipeline is defined, your AI team (and broader organization) becomes significantly more resistant to changing the pipeline's structure. Organizational resistance would be even higher toward the idea of completely replacing the ML pipeline with a new and different one, and you'd need good reasons to persuade the rest of the organization that the complete replacement of the ML pipeline was warranted.

> **WARNING** An ML pipeline rapidly ossifies. That's a foreseeable result and the very nature of an ML pipeline. Ossification is unfortunate and can't be prevented. Therefore, it's important that you ensure early in ML pipeline development that it's the right pipeline to solve your business problem.

Because of these characteristics of pipelines, without proper planning, it's easy to end up with a pipeline that's not only inadequate for your needs but also difficult and costly to change.

An ML pipeline could span the whole community

Whole communities and subfields of ML are formed around the pipelines that emerge early, showing that ossification of the ML pipeline can affect not only a single organization, but a whole community. An example is the NLP community, which often uses a relatively standardized form of the pipeline. Historical efforts of the speech recognition community also have led to a standardized pipeline [90]. In some situations, whole AI communities might be facing the possibility that the current standard pipeline needs to be changed. For example, the advance of deep learning caused a need for significant changes in the traditional speech recognition pipeline [90].

The ML pipeline's ossification is compounded if data science and data engineering are in separate groups in the organization. In that situation, data scientists focus on getting the best results and then *throw their AI methods over the wall* to the data engineering group. The data engineering group, in general, doesn't have the knowledge or the mandate to modify the AI methods used, so they implement them as-is. Engineering decisions are made by a cacophony of people working in various teams. None of these decision makers are likely to have the ambition to own the whole ML pipeline. The result is a compromise, a lack of ownership. Figure 5.3 illustrates what may happen when you put such an ML pipeline together.

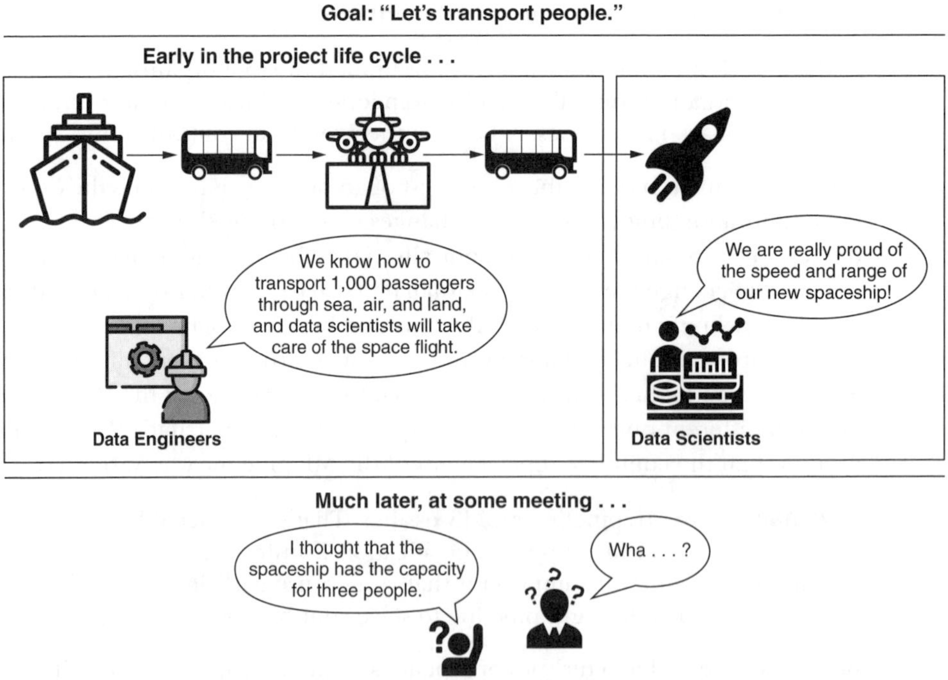

Figure 5.3   An ML pipeline requires data engineering and data science expertise to construct. Specialists in one area might not know another area well, making mismatched elements of an ML pipeline more likely.

5.1.5 *Example of ossification of an ML pipeline*

Let's now discuss the problem of ossification of the ML pipeline in more detail. For that, let's take a hypothetical example of how ossification occurs in real ML pipelines used in business. In this example, you're trying to solve a clear business problem with a simple ML pipeline, and suddenly you must worry about a lot of complicated technologies, each one of them requiring specialists in that technology. The ossification causes I show in this example are something that I've seen (and you may also have seen) in several projects in today's industry.

> **NOTE** The ossification of an ML pipeline manifests as having to deal with complex technologies, AI algorithms, and processes, organizations, and contract details to implement the pipeline.

All the choices I present in this section are reasonable for an ML pipeline like the one in figure 5.4, and every technology chosen is widely used in the industry today. The technologies I discuss will be familiar to many data scientists and data engineers. The point here is *not what those technologies are* but *what ossification is*.[1] Suppose you're running a small team that wants to build an AI-enhanced home security system. The system would look at video from a home and recognize when a person at the home didn't look like any of the family members. You'd also install an application on the mobile phones of the family members and use geolocation to determine if they were at home. To avoid false alarms when a family invited guests, the AI alarms would be enabled only when none of the family members were at home.

Initially, everything looks easy, and the POC proceeds well. There's a video feed coming from the camera, there's geolocation of the mobile phones, and the video stream is enabled when none of the occupants are at home. You ask the owners to take a couple of selfies with their phones so the system can recognize their faces. Finally, you have a good data scientist that's on the team who quickly builds the prototype. If we examine the prototype, we see an early version of the ML pipeline, as shown in figure 5.4.

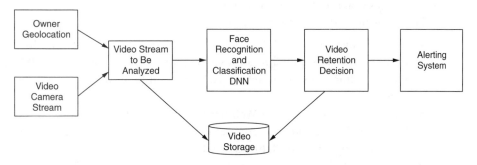

Figure 5.4 Example of an ML pipeline that's used for an AI security system prototype.

---

[1] Don't worry if you're business focused and not familiar with some of the technologies mentioned—I used specific technologies only to make the example concrete for the technologists. What matters for the business user is that even a simple AI project would find itself quickly dependent on a lot of specialized (and expensive) technologies and skillsets.

The initial ML pipeline looks simple when you're brainstorming the project. Then real-world problems hit you. You aren't able to find people with a strong background in the storage of a large amount of video data, but at least you have software architects who are experienced with a big data system and a streaming solution. Your software architects use their previous experience to suggest an Apache Spark [14] based solution on the AWS [11] cloud. The system uses the same ML pipeline that the data scientist used during the POC.

Your data engineering team doesn't know much about video recognition, and your data scientist team doesn't know much about engineering for such a large data volume and video streams from many users, so they make a compromise. The data engineering team will take care of the streaming and will invoke a neural network library provided by the data scientists. The data scientists need to train the neural network on a broad set of images. Initially, you learn that they'll also need a training cluster, and they've used TensorFlow [91].

But what about the training data that you'd use to teach a neural network to recognize images? You initially use a public image dataset called ImageNet [92], but you discover that you need an additional and different dataset with lots of photos of pets so you can better track pet behavior. The good news is that you can mine images of pets from the local humane society's adoption pages, or at least you think so before an attorney from the legal department walks into the project meeting. Two weeks later, you meet with representatives from the local humane society, and they allow you to use their data. You also have a written contract, and it's signed.

Your new best friend from the legal department is also immensely helpful in advising you about the limitations of the privacy policy. You need to secure and anonymize pictures and video streams. You can't have facial images of the minors stored, even with their consent. If you save any photos of the owners accidentally (which happens at the moment they open the door if their phone is off, so the system hasn't noticed yet that they're back home), you must delete them. You're about six weeks into the project. All these decisions might be the right decisions, but you've already made many choices that are difficult to change later.

Let's look at all the decisions that have already ossified in your pipeline:

- You're using the same ML pipeline that your data scientist used for the small POC. Is it the best pipeline for a security system rolled out to 100,000 people?
- Your pipeline is using Apache Spark [14], and you've hired an Apache Spark specialist.
- You've also hired Amazon Web Services (AWS) [11] specialists, but they don't know anything about the competing cloud services, such as Microsoft Azure [13] or Google Cloud Platform (GCP) [12].
- Your neural network is implemented using TensorFlow [91].
- You have a contract with the humane society to use training pictures of the pets.
- Your data scientist spent a month understanding the API interface that the engineering team wants to use because it has some data engineering specifics that the data scientist needs to use.

- You also have an End User License Agreement (EULA) with the user that specifies what your ML pipeline can and can't do.
- You needed a mobile application, so now you have iOS [93] and Android [94] developers on staff.

A couple of weeks pass, and the data engineers come to you. They've found additional dependencies in the system—the data scientist was training AI models on AWS using GPU instances! They didn't notice the dependency on AWS and GPU instances before because the data scientist's deliverable was an already trained AI library. Only when the data engineers looked closely did they find that the part of the system used for training AI models had a dependency on GPU instances. At that moment, you remember that the data scientist did mention it before during a conversation with you and the project manager, but that part didn't seem particularly important at the time, so it fell through the cracks.

Let's summarize the ossifications that have crept into your ML pipeline so far. You're working with the local humane society and using AWS, Spark, TensorFlow, and some specific API library. You're using GPU instances on AWS. You've added specialists in AWS, Spark, iOS, and Android to your team. Your ML pipeline structure is the same one that your data scientist used in the quick prototype for POC. You have three different legal contracts that you must follow in everything your software does, with a nagging suspicion that the next time you see your new best friend, the lawyer, there's going to be another draft of a unique legal contract. That's what you know; probably a few other decisions have escaped your initial attention, and you'll learn about those down the road.

That's how an ML pipeline ossifies in the real world. I placed this example in the context of a small initial effort in a big company. A startup doesn't fare much better, and many startups might not have an attorney to consult about the specifics of the system.

> **TIP** Coincidentally, some of the possible definitions of software architecture that are often heard are that *it's a set of design decisions that must be made early in the project* or *it's a shared understanding of system design* [95]. Because an ML pipeline is difficult to change, you need to think about the ML pipeline as one of the primary artifacts to emerge from your software architecture.

An ML pipeline ossifies because it's not just in software, it's also a determinant of department structures and even business partnerships. The best software engineering practices in the world don't guarantee that ossification won't happen—they postpone it. However, poor software engineering practices are an excellent way to accelerate ML pipeline ossification.

5.1.6 *How to address ossification of the ML pipeline*

As you've seen, it's easy for the ML pipeline to ossify. That ossification is a natural result of how the pipeline is initially constructed and will manifest unless the team takes specific steps to prevent it. How should you manage your ML pipeline development?

Vital for managing the ossification of the ML pipeline is recognizing that *it will happen no matter what.* Ossification of the ML pipeline isn't an error of the engineering team; it's just the nature of the beast. And once ossification has occurred, the cost of changing the pipeline will be high.

TIP   The key isn't to prevent ossification of the ML pipeline. The key is to make sure that you *don't ossify the wrong structure of the pipeline.*

While ossification is unavoidable, with the proper planning and oversight, you can ensure you have the right pipeline so it won't need to be replaced soon. Allowing the pipeline to emerge haphazardly is always an error—pipelines must be designed. Designing the pipeline means you need to make sure that you have the right ML pipeline and that the implementation is technically sound.

You also need the right software architecture

The ML pipeline is one of the most important artifacts of your AI project's software architecture. It's therefore a good practice to perform a dry run of your software architecture. The dry run consists of testing your proposed architecture with use cases before you write any code. The goal is to ensure that the architecture correctly covers the use cases it's supposed to address and that you understand the tradeoffs that you've made in choosing that architecture.

While the larger topic of the software architecture is outside the scope of this book, if you're a software architect yourself and are interested in how you can perform a dry run, I recommend that you check out the Architecture Tradeoff Analysis Model (ATAM) described in *Software Architecture in Practice* [96]. (You may also want to see Wikipedia [97] for a quick summary.)

One part of ATAM consists of using a set of use cases to perform a dry run of the architecture. During that dry run, you can discover various tradeoffs based on a use case and then discuss how the architecture would serve that particular use case. You could think about such a process as a check of the whole software architecture. As a side effect, I've found that a dry run is useful for uncovering software engineering problems you might encounter in the data engineering parts of the ML pipeline.

While a full-blown ATAM analysis is typically more appropriate for organizations that develop a full software architecture in the initial stages of the project, the idea of an informal dry run of the architecture is applicable in the Agile environment and in the context of small companies too.

Pipeline ossification means that you should treat it like a building's foundation. Once you start pouring concrete, there's a limit on the time you have to make any intervention, and you don't get the chance to change your mind a day later. When you're setting up the foundation for a large building, you plan what needs to be done before the concrete arrives.

Consequently, you should plan your ML pipeline early and analyze if it's capable of supporting your business goals. The ML pipeline isn't an artifact you can just let emerge and see what happens after it appears; because of ossification, this is a costly approach. Make a concentrated effort to design the ML pipeline before you begin actual construction. Designing an ML pipeline up front doesn't mean that you can't use Agile methods on your project. It means that if you're using Agile methods, then what Poppendieck and Poppendieck [98] call a "last responsible moment to make a decision" arrives early for your ML pipeline.

Frameworks are emerging around ML pipelines

On the side of the technical soundness of the implementation of an ML pipeline, things are rapidly evolving, and already a set of frameworks are standardizing the way you can code an ML pipeline. I won't take a position on which one is the best one to use, if for no other reason than I expect this area to continue rapidly evolving. For examples of some technical frameworks that are the first step in formalizing the ways we build ML pipelines, see caret [99], Spark's ML Pipelines [100], and TensorFlow Extended [101].

You could argue that the frameworks we have now resolve only some of the technical problems that are associated with the use of the ML pipeline. Also the current frameworks vary in their orientation toward a prototyping focus versus a development or production focus. However, an ML pipeline is already recognized as an essential architectural artifact, and technical frameworks centered around the ML pipeline will continue to evolve.

Allowing a pipeline to emerge from the POC without checking whether it's the right pipeline for your business problem means that you don't know if it can solve your business problem. That's a great way to become the proud owner of the wrong (and ossified) ML pipeline.

It's possible to analyze an ML pipeline early in the project life cycle and estimate its ability to achieve your business goal. Even better, such analysis typically lets you release a first version to the market faster than what you'd be able to do if you didn't think about the pipeline.

> **TIP** As a manager, you need to focus the attention of your engineering groups on the ML pipeline to better understand the results of the analysis of it. That will help you to know how well suited your pipeline is to supporting your business goals.

The design and analysis of an ML pipeline is the most crucial step in properly engineering the entire system. You start by documenting the pipeline you intend to use and then analyze the pipeline's suitability for your business purpose. Chapter 6 shows you how to do that, but before you discover how to analyze a pipeline, let's see why you need to analyze it.

5.2   *Why we need to analyze the ML pipeline*

The ML pipeline defines a user's perception of the AI system as a whole. To improve the results of the ML pipeline, the most important rule to remember is that *a system as a whole is more important than the sum of its parts.* The reason is that the system behaves differently than its parts, and it's possible to have an excellent system using pedestrian (but well-matched to each other) stages in the ML pipeline. Conversely, it's also possible to have a weak system even if the implementation of the individual stages is quite good.

In this section, I'll show you how an ML pipeline behaves when you modify a stage of it. The results of the modification depend on the exact ML pipeline you're using, so, to be concrete, I'll analyze a straightforward ML pipeline, as shown in figure 5.5.

Figure 5.5   A simple pipeline with just three stages, of which only the first two stages affect the end result.

In the figure 5.5 ML pipeline, you collect the data, apply the ML algorithm, and present the output to the user. This is one of the simplest ML pipelines you're likely to encounter in practice, but even modifications of individual stages to this pipeline have educational value.

Suppose you're not happy with the results of your ML pipeline. What do you do if you want to improve the results? You can invest in data (better data or collecting more data) or in a better AI algorithm. How do you know where to invest? As you suspect, the answer would be the dreaded "It depends."

> **NOTE**   There's no universal rule about what works best in all cases to improve the results of the ML pipeline. In some cases, it's better to invest in data. In other cases, it's better to invest in a better algorithm.

The following sections present concrete situations where simple pipelines like the one in figure 5.5 would benefit from improvements in either the data or the algorithm.

5.2.1   *Algorithm improvement: MNIST example*

Suppose the year is 2012, and frameworks that will make deep learning simple to apply have yet to emerge. You have a pipeline like the one in figure 5.5, with an ML algorithm for vision recognition, namely, recognizing handwritten digits on an image. You also have data that's dirty (5% of the data is wrong) because of various errors and bugs in your ingestion pipeline. What should you improve, the data or the algorithm?

To get a feel for how easy it would be to develop an ML algorithm in the pipeline (and how easy it is to improve it), I'll show you an example. Let's see what the ML community as a whole (all academics and quite a few industry practitioners) has achieved on probably the most widely used dataset in computer vision today. That dataset is a Modified National Institute of Standards and Technology (MNIST) dataset [102], which consists of 60,000 handwritten digits from 0 to 9.[2] The MNIST dataset was often used to benchmark computer vision algorithms.

The AI community has tracked the accuracy of the various computer vision algorithms on the MNIST dataset. According to LeCun et al. [102] and Benenson [104], algorithm improvements by the community between 1998 and 2013 resulted in the accuracy of digit recognition improving by only 2.19%—the error rate declined from 2.4% [102] to 0.21% [104].

Although the 2.19% better accuracy for digit recognition the community has achieved on MNIST is a significant improvement for computer vision algorithms, how relevant is 2.19% to us? We have to remember that, in our use case, 5% of our data is wrong. Moreover, the improvement in vision algorithms came at a significant cost. Some of the algorithms used to achieve that 2.19% improvement were the result of the best efforts of the entire ML community! Algorithms that achieved that 2.19% improvement were also difficult to implement in 2012! In the meantime, the initial algorithms in 1998, the ones that achieved about 2.19% worse accuracy, are something that a good intern could develop over a few days.

> **WARNING** If you're already using the best AI algorithm from the well-established academic field, improving it to do better than the rest of the community would be a heroic achievement and not something a team new to AI should attempt.

Achieving a 2.19% improvement in digit recognition can be valuable in a business sense; it might represent the difference between the post office being able to sort most of the mail automatically and having an employee look at numerous envelopes. However, if your data is wrong, how wrong could your total result be? It could be more than 3% wrong (as in, it could be 100% inaccurate).

So, what should you do if you're overseeing a team in 2012 that has 5% dirty data and is working on computer vision? Such a decision is easy. An average industry team would have a much easier time improving the data quality by fixing a few problems in the data processing pipeline than figuring out how to improve vision recognition for 1% of the data. In this case, investing in data cleaning would be better than trying to develop a better algorithm.

Does this mean that you should always start by cleaning your data to get the best data you can? No, not at all. Let's see some counterexamples.

5.2.2 *Further examples of improving the ML pipeline*

Sometimes you're better off cleaning the data; other times, using a better AI algorithm is the answer. Yet other times, you need to improve both the algorithm and the data. *There's no one-size-fits-all rule that you can use for every ML pipeline.*

---

[2] I've used an MNIST dataset as an example of the relationship of data and algorithm improvement in my previous work [103 p56–59]. In this section, I expand that argument in the context of ML pipelines.

Sometimes, your ML pipeline will produce poor results even if the input data is perfect. Suppose you're trying to understand how proficient someone is in constructing a persuasive argument in the text they're writing. The ML algorithm used in the pipeline in figure 5.5 will classify arguments as strong or weak. Currently, understanding the strength of the argument is a difficult problem. Let's assume you built a prototype and found that your first algorithm can correctly distinguish whether the argument is strong or weak in only 66.7% of the cases. The last stage of the ML pipeline would emit an error in one-third of the cases, *even with perfect data!*

There's also a case when you should improve both the algorithm and the data. Such is the case if the algorithm's error rate is 10% (on whatever technical metric is appropriate), and it's also facing 5% of the wrong input data.

No single rule applicable to all ML pipelines tells you whether it's better to clean the data or improve the AI algorithm. Of course, you shouldn't be surprised if engineers advocate for investment in an area they understand. It's often the case that data engineers are biased toward spending more effort on cleaning data, and data scientists prefer to improve algorithms.

5.2.3 *You must analyze the ML pipeline!*

The best strategy for improving an ML pipeline depends on the exact pipeline you're using. You must analyze the pipeline and find what works in your case. You must look at it as a whole system. Here are the questions you need to answer (and the subjects of chapters 6 and 7):

- Chapter 6: Am I using the right pipeline?
- Chapter 7: What area of my existing ML pipeline should I invest in?

If you don't focus your team on thinking about the whole system, they might end up concentrating only on individual parts. Leading a project without a focus on the system can be a costly idea. You should organize the system engineering process to get the ML pipeline right the first time, and you should plan on not changing it often. It would be much more common to change the choice of AI method used in a stage of the ML pipeline. A flexible ML pipeline is one that allows for the natural change of individual methods after getting the data flow right.

The pipeline should be analyzed using the systems engineering methods I describe in chapter 6. The goal of the analysis is to quickly understand if the pipeline can support your business goals and what the right way is to direct work on various elements in the pipeline so you can reach your business goals fast and in a cost-effective manner.

Team dynamic matters!

Leadership requires understanding the incentives you place your team under. If you ask your team in a situation when there's no systematic process to decide where to invest, and they're not comfortable talking about areas they don't know, what would you expect to happen? I'd expect that you'd get an answer in the form of "invest in my area:" data engineers would recommend that you invest in the data, and data scientists would recommend that you invest in better algorithms. Are people on your team comfortable discussing something with which they aren't familiar?

People who understand the whole system are rare on AI project teams today. It's much more common that you'd have smart people that understand parts of the system well. It's your job as a leader to understand the social dynamics this causes.

Unless team members feel that's it safe to ask questions about parts of the system they don't understand, they might opt to talk about only the individual parts they know. Are you running a team in which people are comfortable being wrong in front of their peers?

5.3 *What's the role of AI methods?*

If what matters for the end perception of the result is an entire system, and if the ML pipeline as a whole matters more than an individual AI algorithm, what's the role of advanced AI algorithms? AI algorithms have an active role, but the best way to think about them is that they're pieces of a larger system. In that larger system, every part (including such AI algorithms) is likely to be improved over time.

Today, conversations between AI engineers are dominated by discussions about AI methods. It's common to see data scientists talking for a long time about which methods and algorithms are the best for a given application. It's not uncommon even for larger communities to have this discussion. Different schools of thought in the AI community disagree with each other about which methods are the most promising in the long run.[3]

Currently, deep learning [7,8,106] has a huge mindshare in the AI community. However, a decade ago, methods that became what we know today as deep learning faced much skepticism, even in academic circles. Methods such as Support-Vector Machines (SVMs) [107,108] were much more popular at the time. Even insiders of the AI community are often surprised with what comes next. Methods you're using today can significantly evolve in just a few years.

It's reasonable to assume that this trend will continue—the best method today might not be the best method tomorrow. With all the attention, resources, and investments pulled into the research of new methods, the AI field is growing tremendously. Methods are subject to continuous evolution, and we're finding newer and better methods every day. While AI methods are undeniably mathematical in nature, for managing a data science project, it's better to think about them more as engineering modules than as math.

---

[3] References [105] and [35] provide an overview of the history of AI, including various schools of thought that have emerged in the AI community.

Data science isn't primarily an application of mathematics

If you're a data scientist, I'd like to expand on the point that AI methods are more engineering modules than math. To acquire a deep understanding of AI methods, you need strong mathematical foundations. However, just because methods are formulated in a way that requires an understanding of the math doesn't mean that all you need to do is use mathematical transformations to get an answer to your business problem.

In business and industry, it's highly unlikely you'll encounter a situation in which there's mathematical proof that any method is the correct and definitive way to address your business problem. If for no other reason, it's rare that a real-world industry problem would perfectly match all assumptions of the method. As a result, any practical data science work requires much experimentation. You need to try multiple methods and approaches to determine the best way to address your problem. For that, you also benefit from having a flexible and easy-to-change ML pipeline.

Contrary to the name, data science is *not* a science. It's an engineering discipline. You have to experiment to find what the best method is for your problem. While some methods work better in some domains than others, you already know that there's never a definitive method that's always the best across all possible datasets [67].

The right way to think about AI methods is that they're pluggable modules to be applied at a particular place in the ML pipeline. Each method has characteristics (and for that matter, a limited lifespan) that today makes it a good match for a part of the ML pipeline. You should apply methods in a way that allows for you to replace them with different and better methods as they become available, and you should organize the pipeline in a way that makes plugging in the new methods simple.

Figure 5.6 illustrates the idea of changing the role of methods. A pipeline's structure is a choice that affects the whole organization and, as such, is a focus of the entire team.

The choice of AI methods to use depends on the technical considerations and what the methods can provide. In figure 5.6, which AI method to choose for each of the steps in the pipeline is a technical decision. For example, if a specific step in the pipeline would be to predict a time series value, data scientists might elect to use familiar algorithms such as autoregressive integrated moving average (ARIMA) [109] or long short-term memory (LSTM) [110] for that prediction. Whatever they choose, it's an engineering/technology decision.

The best approach to the engineering of the AI system is to implement methods in a way that acknowledges these characteristics and allows for replacing any method you implement today with better methods tomorrow. The rules of software engineering (including, but not limited to, maintainability and extensibility) apply to AI systems too.

> **TIP** While ML pipelines are subject to ossification, AI methods are subject to rapid evolution. Your systems engineering process should be designed to acknowledge and manage this characteristic. While the pipeline calls for deep up-front analysis, you should implement AI methods in such a way that

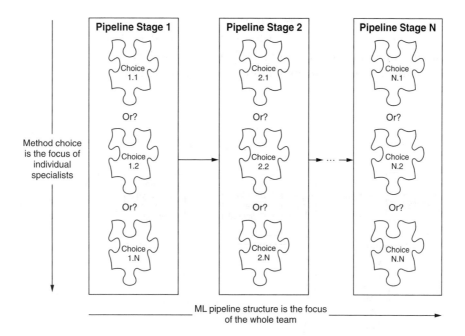

Figure 5.6 The role of methods in the construction of an ML pipeline. The methods that implement a step in the pipeline often change during the lifespan of the pipeline.

it's easy to change the AI method you're using in each step of the ML pipeline. Agile methods typically shine in the implementation of the elements of the pipeline.

In addition to organizing your software to make it easy to change the AI methods, choose frameworks that are also easy to use when developing quick prototypes. The AI community is continuously developing frameworks that are focused on ease of use. Examples of this approach are the mlr package [111] and the caret package in the R programming language [99,112], which focus on easy-to-use implementations of many of the traditional ML algorithms. Another example is the Keras library for deep learning [7,8,113].

What's of interest to the broader team is the question, "Under the assumption that the methods behave in the way that the specialist described them, how would the whole pipeline be affected?" Chapter 6 and 7 show you how to analyze the behavior of the larger pipeline.

5.4   *Balancing data, AI methods, and infrastructure*

I cautioned you in chapter 1 not to overfocus on infrastructure. *Overfocusing* means that you don't have the right balance of attention between data, methods, and infrastructure. Let's see what the right balance looks like.

Balance is based on the order in which you answer questions about your project. This section provides the right order to think about data, AI methods, and the infrastructure you'd use. Figure 5.7 depicts how you should manage an analytics project to balance the business problem definition, AI, and data infrastructure.

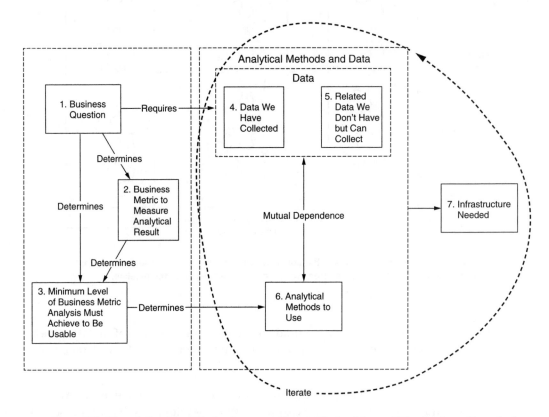

Figure 5.7   The relationship of the business question, methods, data, and infrastructure. The order in which you make decisions is the business AI infrastructure.

In figure 5.7, defining the business question (box 1) and the metrics used to evaluate it (box 2) must be the first step; otherwise, you'll waste time searching for answers to the wrong question. Second, you must define at which value threshold of the business metric you'll have a minimum viable product (MVP) [28] (box 3). Again, the failure to define a threshold is a sure sign that you need to further develop your business case. The threshold value of this metric gives you a milestone in defining the MVP. Note that boxes 1, 2, and 3 are the responsibility of the business team.

Once you've satisfied boxes 1–3, find out what data you have (box 4), what data you need and can acquire (box 5), and the AI methods you'll use to determine the need (box 6). These decisions are in the domain of the data science team.

In all cases where you have a choice among multiple infrastructural components, decide on appropriate infrastructural components to support the data and AI methods that you've chosen. You should define the infrastructure to support the intended analytical approach (box 7).

Figure 5.7 is iterative, with the steps in boxes 4, 5, 6, and 7 repeated. When possible, you should do initial iterations as a POC with a smaller dataset as a starting point.

> **TIP** When starting AI projects, you should first understand which business problems you're solving, which AI methods and data you should use, and how to link business with technology. Choose infrastructure last.

Once you know you have a viable solution, you can scale it to the larger dataset. A combination of the organization's operational practices and data sizes determines the final infrastructure to use.

One exception when you might elect to choose infrastructure first is when there's a tangible link between the business case and the infrastructure solution. Another is when you're working in a company that's so large that it's expecting to run so many AI projects that standardizing on a single infrastructure stack is worthwhile.

Note that you could consider the process shown in Figure 5.7 as an extension to the traditional cross-industry standard process for data mining CRISP-DM process [43] that was defined in the mid-1990s to systematize the approach to data analytics. When you use the CLUE process, it helps you to properly sequence the steps when choosing business considerations, data, AI methods, and infrastructure.

5.5 Exercises

The following exercises will help you to better understand the concepts introduced in this chapter. Here's where teamwork comes into its own. An analysis of the ML pipeline is *both a technical skill and a business skill*, so it's time to find an engineer with whom you'd work in the future and do some of these exercises together. Time spent on that relationship would come in handy on the real project.

Question 1: Construct an ML pipeline for this AI project: the project takes feedback from your customers and analyzes it. If a customer appears unhappy, an alert is issued so that you can contact the customer and try to appease them before they decide to leave. (That part of AI which determines whether a customer is happy or not is technically called *sentiment analysis*.) You already have an AI software library that performs sentiment analysis. The data is in your customer support system, which is a web application.

Question 2: Suppose you implement the ML pipeline from the previous example in your organization. Which departments would be responsible for the implementation of which parts of the pipeline?

Question 3: What business metric would you use to measure the success of the ML pipeline from question 1?

Question 4: What is the history of the coordination between departments from question 2 in past projects that they've participated in? Were projects on which those teams worked successful?

> **NOTE**   The next two questions (5 and 6) are targeted toward data scientists. You can skip them if you don't have data science expertise.

Question 5: As a part of the installation of an AI security product, you're offering a 30-day, money-back guarantee. Your customers have taken a survey about their satisfaction with the product, which they completed as soon as the product was installed. You're interested in predicting if your customers would return the product. During discussions, the team has mentioned that this problem could be solved using either an SVM, a decision tree, logistic regression, or a deep learning-based classification. Should you use deep learning? After all, it's an exceedingly popular technology, has a substantial mindshare, and could solve the problem. Or should you use one of the other suggested options?

Question 6: You answered question 5 using an algorithm of your choice. Suppose the algorithm you chose didn't provide a good enough prediction of a customer returning the product. Should you use a better ML algorithm? Is it now time to use the latest and greatest from the field of deep learning?

Summary

- Every AI project uses some form of the ML pipeline. That pipeline starts by collecting data and finishes by presenting results. The ML pipeline is one of the primary determinants of how the user will perceive the system as a whole.
- The ML pipeline starts to ossify the moment it's constructed. Choosing the wrong ML pipeline, or, worse, letting it directly emerge from the POC, is a costly mistake.
- The success of the AI project is based on the entire system, as opposed to the individual ML algorithms used.
- The user sees the output of the whole system, not the output of the individual AI algorithm. Think about the ML pipeline as a critical architectural artifact and about AI algorithms as important (but evolving) pieces of that pipeline.
- The order in which you make decisions on an AI project should be business first, AI algorithms and data second, and infrastructure last.

Analyzing an ML pipeline

6

This chapter covers

- Determining if you have the right ML pipeline before it ossifies
- Economizing resources in your AI project
- Performing MinMax analysis on the ML pipeline
- Interpreting the results of a MinMax analysis

In chapter 5, you learned that as soon as you construct an ML pipeline, it starts ossifying. Consequently, it's essential for you to ensure you don't have a wrong and inadequate ML pipeline that's incapable of fulfilling the business goals of your ML project. The most critical business question about the ML pipeline is, "How well does this pipeline do in business terms?" This chapter shows you how to analyze an ML pipeline and get an answer to that question.

Once you know how well your ML pipeline does in a business sense, you can analyze it to determine if it can meet your business goals. The name of the analysis you'll want to perform is MinMax.[1] You can do MinMax analysis early in the project, and it consists of two parts, each of which answers a different question:

- *The Min part of MinMax analysis*—If your life depended on releasing your AI project tomorrow, how well would the simplest implementation of your ML pipeline do? Can such an implementation meet your business goals?
- *The Max part of MinMax analysis*—What's the best possible result you can get with the current structure of your pipeline? Before you put effort into the best possible implementation of each stage in that pipeline, would that implementation meet your business goals?

As practical people, we need the answer to these questions in business terms, not in the form of technical metrics (such as 99.9543% accuracy).

In section 6.1, you'll learn why you should care about analyzing your ML pipeline. Section 6.2 shows you how to economize resources devoted to your ML pipeline, and section 6.3 shows you how to use MinMax analysis to determine if you have the right pipeline that's capable of solving your business problem. Section 6.4 shows you how to interpret the results of a MinMax analysis, and section 6.5 shows you how to perform a MinMax analysis. Finally, section 6.6 presents FAQs on MinMax analysis.

6.1 Why you should care about analyzing your ML pipeline

By now, you know that an AI system is more important than the sum of its parts and that an ML pipeline is one of the primary software artifacts that determines the behavior of the system. In chapter 5, you saw that an ML pipeline rapidly ossifies and that allowing the *wrong* ML pipeline to ossify is a costly mistake. That's why managing the ML pipeline must be data driven. The analysis of an ML pipeline gives you that data.

All project management decisions are made under a time constraint (see figure 6.1). When a project is in progress, every day costs both money and opportunity. When accounting for the costs, you must account for all costs—the cost of changing something, and the cost of staying on the current course.

> **WARNING** Inaction is the decision to stay on the current course and can sometimes be as dangerous as taking the wrong action.

The form of ML pipeline you use in your project is one of the most critical project management and software architecture decisions you have to make. If you choose the wrong ML pipeline, you (and your wallet) will know. However, by that time, it'll be too late. Analyzing an ML pipeline early in the project gives you confidence that you're using the right one. To be useful to a team in business and industry, such an analysis must do the following:

- Be easy to learn how to perform
- Be cheap to perform

---

[1] Just in case you're familiar with the Minimax algorithm from game theory [114], you shouldn't confuse MinMax analysis with the Minimax algorithm—they're totally different concepts.

Figure 6.1 **Project management decisions are made under time constraints. Some projects are like the plane in this figure and must correct their course before they crash. Doing nothing can sometimes be as dangerous as taking the wrong action.**

- Provide results that are intuitive to interpret
- Provide a reasonable level of confidence from the information it returns

In this chapter, I'll show you an analysis method that meets these four requirements. The next chapter provides yet another. You, as a leader, need to learn what type of analysis to ask your team to perform and how to interpret the results of such an analysis.

> **TIP** An analysis must be *cheap* to perform. It must balance the cost of analysis (cost of asking the questions) with the value of knowing the answer. This balance is what D. W. Hubbard [75] refers to as the *expected value of perfect information* [79].

Analyzing an ML pipeline is something you should repeatedly do for each AI project and for each ML pipeline you consider for each project. Even if you're a nontechnical reader, spend the time now to understand how analysis works. The understanding you acquire will help you make the best decisions, not only for your current AI project, but for future projects as well. In chapter 8, I'll show you that the methods you'll learn have a far broader application than simply an analysis of the ML pipeline.

Similarities with the stock market

There's another field in which you make decisions under time constraints and with limited and imperfect information. That field is investing.

Let's hear what Ray Dalio, who built the biggest hedge fund in the world, has to say about how to make decisions under uncertainty [29]:

> *"He who lives by the crystal ball is destined to eat ground glass' is a saying I quoted a lot in those days. Between 1979 and 1982, I had eaten enough glass to realize that what was most important wasn't knowing the future—it*

(continued)

> was knowing how to react appropriately to the information available at each point in time."

When building an AI capability for your organization, you'll make many decisions. The goal is to tilt the balance of probability in your favor.

6.2   *Economizing resources: The E part of CLUE*

How do you know that the ML pipeline you're using is the proper pipeline to use long-term? Should you continue using the current ML pipeline, or should you replace it with a different pipeline before it ossifies? Which part of the pipeline should you improve first? You should make such decisions based on the data, and this section gives you an overview of the tools that answer those questions. Those tools are:

- *MinMax analysis*—Answers the question, "Do I have the right ML pipeline to meet my business goals?"
- *Sensitivity analysis*—Answers the question, "How much would my business result change if I modified the implementation of a single stage of the ML pipeline?"

This chapter concentrates on MinMax analysis; chapter 7 presents sensitivity analysis. Together, those two analyses let you allocate your development resources toward the right ML pipeline and the right stage of that pipeline.

Concentrating on your ML pipeline is a logical next step of your project. So far, you've applied the *C*onsider (available business actions), *L*ink (research question and business problem), and *U*nderstand (the technical answer in a business context) parts of the CLUE process. By performing these parts of that process, you've ensured the following:

- Your AI project can viably affect the business. You know that, in your project, there's a way to apply the Sense/Analyze/React loop to your problem and that the React part is possible. Chapter 3 covered this material by describing the *C* part of CLUE.
- Your AI project links the business impact (described with its associated business metric) and the output of the ML pipeline (described by the technical metric). Chapter 4 showed you how to do that by defining the profit curve (the *L* part of CLUE) and how to use the profit curve to understand the business impact (the *U* part of CLUE).
- Your AI project defines the ML pipeline that you're planning to use. Chapter 5 presented the ML pipeline.

What you still need to do is *economize* your scarce resources during the construction of the AI project. To *E*conomize (the *E* part of CLUE), you need to determine that you're using a reasonable ML pipeline for solving your business problem. You also need to decide what the best stages of the ML pipeline are to improve.

MinMax analysis answers the question, "Do I have the right pipeline?" It lets you know what the best possible business result is that you could hope for from your current ML pipeline. It lets you know that the ML pipeline you're making is the one that could support your business goals, and it lets you know that before the ML pipeline starts to ossify.

Unless you already have an ML pipeline that completely solves your business problem, chances are, you need to improve it. You have limited resources, and you need to assign them optimally to get the best overall project results. Sensitivity analysis [115–117] answers the question of which stage of the ML pipeline you should invest in next to get the maximum return on your investment. Figure 6.2 shows you how to integrate your project with MinMax and sensitivity analysis.

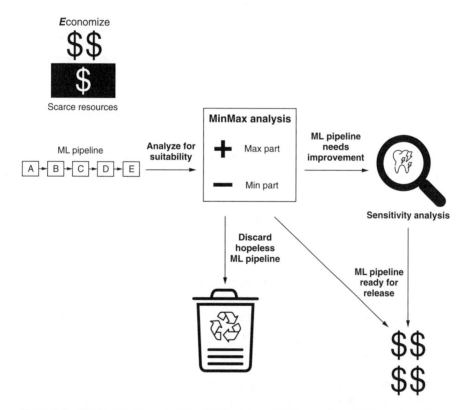

Figure 6.2   The Economize part of the CLUE process. MinMax and sensitivity analyses let you apply your efforts to the right parts of a business-viable ML pipeline.

Figure 6.2 first applies MinMax analysis to determine if your ML pipeline is already producing a viable business result. If not, does the pipeline need further improvement to do so? Or is it, by its nature, incapable of creating such an outcome?

If the pipeline is hopeless, you discard it and try a different pipeline (or a different AI project). Once you know you're working with an adequate ML pipeline for solving the business problem, you use sensitivity analysis to improve the pipeline repeatedly until you're satisfied with the business result.

All the earlier steps in figure 6.2 require the close cooperation of data science, data engineering, and the business team. The team that works on the analysis of the pipeline should initially consist of representatives from all three areas. The goal is to reach a point where a shared understanding about the link between business and technical metrics emerges. The team that manages the ML pipeline should consist of management and engineering leaders (to include data scientists and data engineers). The goal of forming this team is to have an ongoing shared understanding of the technical characteristics of the data science pipeline and to guide deployment of resources based on those characteristics.

> **TIP**   This approach of analyzing and improving the ML pipeline is by necessity iterative. You might perform early iterations of analysis while the proof of concept (POC) is still in progress. If you're using Agile [118,119] or iterative software development methodologies, you could consider analytical work to be part of the first iterations of the project.

6.3   *MinMax analysis: Do you have the right ML pipeline?*

A fundamental analysis you should always perform on any ML pipeline, MinMax analysis answers the question, "What's the best and what's the worst result that an ML pipeline of the given structure can achieve?" This section provides an overview of MinMax analysis.

> **NOTE**   I use the term *MinMax analysis*, but know that this type of analysis is sometimes also known as *Best Case/Worst Case analysis*. Section 6.6.4 elaborates on this terminology.

MinMax analysis shows in an early stage of the pipeline's life the expected range of results it can achieve. For the question, "Should I continue with this ML pipeline," the analysis answers with either "yes," "no," or "maybe." Knowing that you have the right ML pipeline so you don't spend a lot of time and money on building the wrong ML pipeline is a beautiful thing.

> **DEFINITION**   MinMax analysis is a type of analysis that determines if your ML pipeline is already meeting your business goal, if it needs improvement to be able to meet the goal, or if it's incapable of meeting the goal.

MinMax looks at the structure of your ML pipeline and assesses its business viability. For the ML pipeline that's analyzed, the Min part answers the question: "If I release the simplest implementation I can make, what would be the business result?" The Max part answers the question: "What's the business result I'd get with the best possible implementation?"

TIP Before you try anything, it's always an excellent idea to ask, "What's the best that can happen if I succeed, and, knowing this, is it worth it to even try?" The Max part of MinMax analysis answers that question.

To perform a MinMax analysis, you need an ML pipeline structure and a profit curve. With the profit curve, you have a business metric, which is a way to relate a technical metric to business. You also have the threshold (the minimum level of a business metric that you need to reach). Figure 6.3 shows an overview of MinMax analysis.

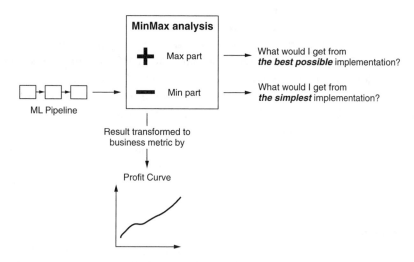

Figure 6.3 A MinMax analysis consists of the Min part (–) and the Max part (+). It uses a profit curve to transform the technical metric into an expected business result. The result of this analysis determines the viability of your ML pipeline.

At a high level, MinMax analysis consists of the following:

1 It measures how well your ML pipeline does on the problem you're trying to solve. You measure the ML pipeline using a technical metric.

2 It expresses the output of the ML pipeline in business terms. You use the profit curve to form an *U*nderstanding (*U* of the CLUE, as explained in chapter 4) of what the measured result is in business terms.

3 It repeats the earlier two steps twice more: once for the Max part and once for the Min part. The Max part uses the best possible implementation at every stage of the ML pipeline. The Min part uses the most straightforward implementation at every stage.

Once you've performed the analysis, you'll know what the most straightforward ML pipeline can achieve in terms of the business. You'll also understand what the best implementation of your current ML pipeline can achieve. If the best isn't enough to make the business viable, you know it's time to discard the ML pipeline.

The following sections show you how to perform a MinMax analysis. But first, I'll present an example ML pipeline that we can use for this analysis and then show you how to interpret the results.

6.4   *How to interpret MinMax analysis results*

MinMax analysis answers the question, "Is it worth continuing with the development of the current ML pipeline?" Therefore, every team leader must know how to interpret the results of a MinMax analysis. Performing this analysis is of interest only to a subset of readers who want to perform the analysis themselves or to better understand the details. Consequently, I'll first show you how to interpret the MinMax analysis' results, and then, in a later section, you'll learn how to perform the analysis.

This section first gives you a concrete scenario of an ML pipeline that solves a real business problem. Then it asks you to make concrete decisions from this scenario: should you continue development of the ML pipeline or not? These examples highlight that the result of the analysis can point not only to the ML pipeline being adequate or inadequate for addressing your business problem, but also to the need to improve it before it can solve the business problem. Finally, once you've seen an example of interpreting the MinMax analysis, it provides a summary of rules for performing MinMax.

Understanding the details

Deciding if your technology is able to solve a business problem is inherently a multidisciplinary problem. You must understand the details of the business problem because decisions in the business can't be made without considering the financial impact and the business and domain rules. First you need a basic understanding of the technical solution. Then you need to decide if that solution is profitable.

As a result, a realistic scenario for a MinMax analysis would be a little bit more complicated than other scenarios in this book. Taking the effort to comprehend the details of the analysis is worth it, though, as the easiest way to save a ton of money on an AI project is to abandon the wrong ML pipeline before it costs you dearly.

6.4.1   *Scenario: The ML pipeline for a smart parking meter*

Let's talk about a concrete business scenario with all of the details of a business problem that needs to be solved, and the financial implications of various decisions your system makes. I'll start by describing the business side of the problem and then show you the outline of the ML pipeline that solves the problem.

Your company makes smart parking meters. The parking meters have a camera, which can be used to take photos of license plates. Your client is a city. It has many plans and possibilities for these parking meters, but for the time being, it issues automatic citations if someone overstays their visit.

The city is primarily interested in compliance with the parking regulations, not citation revenue. For our scenario, the city has agreed to pay for the initial installation of the meters and give you a yearly bonus for any meter with fewer than 50 overstays per year. The bonus in itself is large enough that your company is perfectly content with that bounty being the sole source of revenue related to smart parking meters for the city.

The economics of the smart parking meter is that you make a profit of $3 per citation, and you have to pay the city $20 for every incorrect citation that it issues. For the smart parking meter business to be practical for your company, the value threshold is $100/year (per meter) or getting the bonus from the city, which is the preferred choice. The best current estimate is that there are at least 300 overstays per year for each parking spot, with the maximum profit per meter at $900 if all citations are correctly issued.

> **NOTE** As you learned in chapter 1, you should be careful not to extrapolate past data into future data when the deployment of AI technology might change the reality of that speculation. Would the same number of overstays continue once you started issuing citations? Alternatively, would parking overstays disappear instantly?

To be on the safe side, you decide to assume that the number of overstays would collapse. Instead of using 300/year, you assume there would be at least 51 overstays/year. You're hedged by the city if there are 50 or fewer overstays, so 51 overstays/year is the worst-case scenario for you. Figure 6.4 shows the simple ML pipeline you'll use.

Figure 6.4 A simple ML pipeline for the automated parking meter that takes a picture of the license plate, checks if parking is legal, and issues a citation if not. The examples in this chapter use this pipeline for the analysis.

The ML pipeline shown in figure 6.4 uses a camera and image recognition. However, because we're working with a physical device in the real world, there are a few complications:

- The quality of the camera image depends on the time of day and weather. (Reflections from the sun, light, and rain are all factors.)
- Citations are issued using a cellular network, so the parking meter has a cellular modem. For this example, we'll assume that the ticketing stage of the pipeline always works perfectly.[2]

---

[2] In practice, it's possible that some citations would fail because of communication errors or problems with the citation system. To simplify this example, I'm disregarding those issues.

Parking rules are a bit more complicated than what I initially described. In fact, they're complicated enough that the ML pipeline shown in figure 6.4 needs a rule engine to support those parking rules.

> **NOTE** In this chapter, we're initially covering a basic case of MinMax analysis. In the basic case, it's safe to assume that your profit curve is such that a higher value of the technical metric would always result in a higher value of the business metric. Section 6.5.5 will show you what to do if this assumption isn't met.[3]

In some cases, you can make decisions based only on the Min or the Max part of analysis. In others, you'll need to examine both the Min and the Max part of the analysis before making a decision.

> **NOTE** Before you see the set of hypothetical results of the MinMax analysis, remember that for the parking meter to be profitable, the threshold that you need is at least $100 per year from each meter to make it practical. That threshold was based on assuming there would be 51 overstays per year, which is your worst case of overstays, and that would *not* be few enough for the bonus from the city to kick in. (The city pays for no more than 50 violations.)

In the first scenario for this example, you know that with the most straightforward meter you can construct, and the simplest implementation of video recognition of the license plate, 97% of citations will be correct. Unfortunately, 3% will be wrong. Based on your profit curve, your data scientists tell you that they've completed the Min part of the MinMax analysis and found that the expected profit per meter is $117.81 per year (for 51 illegal parking citations per year). Because your threshold was just $100 per year, you know that your ML pipeline is viable, and that the AI system would make a profit in an "as-is" form of the pipeline. You don't need to worry about the Max part of MinMax, because the ML pipeline you have today is already good enough to support your business goals.

To release or not to release?

If the Min part of your MinMax analysis shows that your current ML pipeline is already producing a value that exceeds your threshold, you might choose to release your product. Alternatively, for various business reasons, you can decide not to release it. This is now a business decision that might require more analysis.

As another consideration, parking meters have parts that can complicate business decisions; for example, once the meters are deployed, you can't easily replace the cameras. However, if you know that you already have the best camera you can get, and you can update the software in the meter remotely, you can treat the meter as a conventional software system. In this case, you should release at once and, if needed, build a better vision recognition system down the road.

---

[3] For data scientists in the audience—your profit curve is monotonic, but there's no requirement for the relation between the technical metric and the business metric to be linear.

Let's now look at an alternative scenario: someone has decided that instead of putting a camera in the parking meter itself (so that it's just a few inches from the license plate), they'd reuse a security camera on the roof of the building near the parking lot to look at all the parked cars. With such a system, you don't even need to install new physical parking meter devices with cameras!

The city mandates that they like the idea and would use it, as it would save them from having to pay for installing new parking meters with cameras. All other parameters, such as the cost of citations and the $100 value threshold, stay the same. Your company decides that it would still want to do business with the city under those conditions.

Then you get the images from the existing security camera on the roof. It turns out that the camera takes fuzzy and distorted images only once every few seconds. It's a fisheye lens camera intended for security systems. There are also obstructions that affect the view of the parking lot, and you now need to map the image from the camera to determine which car is in which parking space.

You ask engineering what they think. Your team performs a MinMax analysis again. This time, they know they're facing a difficult technical challenge and wonder if even the best implementation of the current ML pipeline would be able to solve it.

The team first performs the Max part of the MinMax analysis. The analysis shows that with the images you have, your system will issue 89% correct citations and 11% incorrect ones. With 51 overstays per year, the profit per meter would be $23.97 per year. Your ML pipeline isn't going to work.

Panic time! Can engineering construct a different ML pipeline? They try, but none are business practical if you use images from the existing security camera. If you can't get better pictures, you don't have a viable AI project.

> **TIP** Canceling a project in cases like this isn't a bad thing at all. This example shows you exactly why you should perform the MinMax analysis early in the project. When would you rather talk with your boss about canceling the project: when you've spent 3% of the budget (time and cost) and can prove it can't work, or when you've spent 105% of the budget and realize it's going nowhere? If you're destined to fail, fail fast, and start something more productive.

Your boss is reasonable and understands that the idea of using images from the security camera installed on the roof is a nonstarter. The boss makes some phone calls and comes back to you with good news! You'll be able to use much better cameras placed around the parking lot instead. Multiple cameras will be positioned in such a way that you don't have to worry about obstructions. You ask the team to repeat the MinMax analysis with the same ML pipeline, but under the assumption that you'd be using better cameras.

This time, the Max part of MinMax shows that the best that's possible with such a system is 98% correct citations, with 2% incorrect. And at 51 overstays per year, the profit per meter would be $129.54 per year. (Remember, the Max part provides a result corresponding to the best implementation of the ML pipeline.) The Min part, however, analyzing the simplest pipeline you can construct, shows that you'd have only 91% correct citations, with a profit of $47.43 per year. The simplest implementation of the ML pipeline isn't going to work, but maybe you can improve it.

The project should continue, but there's a question of how difficult it will be to improve the ML pipeline. We'll discuss that next.

6.4.2 *What if your ML pipeline needs improvement?*

The results of the MinMax analysis are often conclusive about the business value of your ML pipeline. In the previous section, you saw an example where the Min analysis showed that the pipeline was already providing viable business results. You also saw an example in which the ML pipeline was inadequate to meet the business goal. However, sometimes results are inconclusive: your ML pipeline needs improvement to meet your business goal.

This section describes the last of these situations. Figure 6.5 shows an overview of applying MinMax analysis for the case in which an ML pipeline needs improvement.

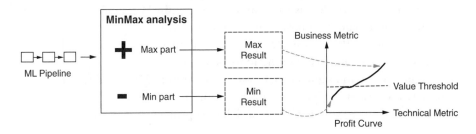

Figure 6.5   Here, the Min analysis doesn't reach the value threshold, but the Max analysis exceeds it. It might be possible to improve this pipeline enough to make it business-viable.

In figure 6.5, the result of the analysis shows that with the ML pipeline you're using, the Min implementation isn't good enough, but the Max analysis shows that the current structure of the ML pipeline can be improved to provide an acceptable business result. In this situation, you can say that the ML pipeline passes the Max analysis and fails the Min analysis.

An ML pipeline that makes you money with a minimum effort on your part is a good thing to have. An ML pipeline that doesn't make you money even when you use the best techniques possible in each of its stages is a good thing to abandon early. However, what happens when you're in between and you know that the Max is good enough, but your Min isn't? You need to improve your ML pipeline before you can release your AI product, so you'll need to perform a sensitivity analysis on it (as detailed in chapter 7).

6.4.3 Rules for interpreting the results of MinMax analysis

In the previous section, you learned how to interpret the results of the MinMax analysis. If we were to summarize how we made those decisions, we could form a set of rules for interpreting the results of the MinMax analysis. This section summarizes those rules. Let's first agree on some terminology:

- We'd say that the Min part of the MinMax analysis *passed* if the most minimal implementation of the ML pipeline you can make already has a business value that exceeds the value threshold on the profit curve. The minimal ML pipeline is business-viable.
- We'd say that the Max part of the MinMax analysis *passed* if the best possible implementation of the ML pipeline will have enough business value to exceed the value threshold on the profit curve. The best possible implementation of your current ML pipeline will be business-viable.

Different combinations of the results of the Min and Max analysis have different business meaning. Table 6.1 summarizes the possible results of a MinMax analysis and their business impact.

Table 6.1 Summary of the possible results of a MinMax analysis. Each of the results has direct implications for your business.

Min result/Max result	Max passed	Max failed
Min passed	The ML pipeline is business-viable.	This combination can't happen.
Min failed	The ML pipeline needs improvement to be business-viable.	The current ML pipeline isn't suitable for solving the business problem.

6.5 How to perform an analysis of the ML pipeline

Now that you know how to *interpret* the results of the MinMax analysis, let's talk about how to perform the analysis. How did we get the numbers from the previous section that are the result of the MinMax analysis? By analyzing an ML pipeline. This section shows you how to perform such an analysis.

> **NOTE** If you're a manager without an engineering background, you might want to skim through the rest of the description of MinMax analysis to get a basic understanding of what your team will do during it. If you're a manager with an engineering background, you should be able to understand (or even perform) this analysis.

The first step in analyzing an ML pipeline is to make sure you have all the prerequisites. You need a logical diagram of your proposed ML pipeline. You also need the technical and business metrics you're using on the project and the profit curve.

You analyze an ML pipeline by running data through it and then using a profit curve to measure the result in business terms. The general process for the analysis (figure 6.6) is the same for both the Min and Max part of the MinMax analysis, and even applies to the sensitivity analysis of the ML pipeline.

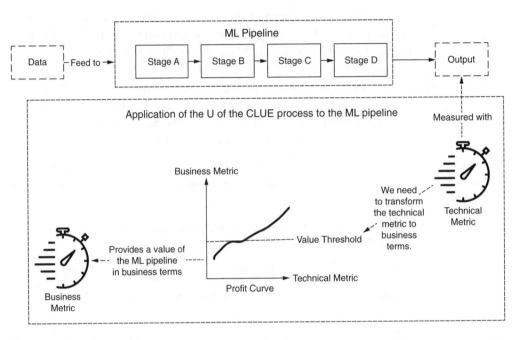

Figure 6.6   Analysis of an ML pipeline. This analysis tells you what the current ML pipeline can achieve for the business. Both the Min and Max part of the MinMax analysis use the same process.

The analysis shown in figure 6.6 measures the results of the ML pipeline in business terms. That's done by processing real data with your current ML pipeline, measuring the output using technical metrics, and then transforming that value into the business metric. Another way to think about this analysis is that you're feeding the ML pipeline with real data and are then applying the *U*nderstand part of the CLUE process to measure the result.

The same process from figure 6.6 would apply to both the Min and Max parts of the MinMax analysis. What changes is not how you analyze the ML pipeline but the implementation of the stages of the ML pipeline.

Now that you understand the overall process for analyzing an ML pipeline, let's see how to perform the actual analysis. Section 6.5.1 shows you how to perform the Min part of MinMax analysis, and section 6.5.2 shows you how to perform the Max part. Section 6.5.3 discusses how to account for trend estimates and safety factors during the performance of the MinMax analysis. Section 6.5.4 introduces different types of profit curves you may encounter in practice. Finally, section 6.5.5 shows you how to apply MinMax analysis to profit curves that have a complex shape.

6.5.1 Performing the Min part of MinMax analysis

To perform the Min part of the analysis, you should first construct the simplest implementation of your ML pipeline. The goal is to build an ML pipeline implementation that you can test with real data.

How much effort should you put into preparing the ML pipeline for the Min part of the MinMax analysis? The effort should be insignificant compared to the size of the whole project. The general rule is that it should take no more than a few people a couple of weeks of effort, regardless of the project size, costing not more than 5% of the total project budget. If you're a small company, it can mean the best that one person can do in a few days.

The liberal use of duct tape is the key. Use a pipeline implementation that you can construct fast. If commercial off–the-shelf (COTS) products can help you, use them. Ask yourself, can you use someone else's product at any stage of the pipeline to implement needed functionality? You're looking to get the system working with the minimum effort needed so you can see what business result is possible with such a system.

Once the analysis is complete, it's time to apply techniques that you learned in section 6.4 and interpret the results of the analysis. If you already have an ML pipeline that's giving you results that exceed the threshold value of the business metric, your pipeline is business-viable as-is.

> **NOTE** What happens if the amount of effort you need to spend to construct even the simplest ML pipeline is large? Without that simple implementation, you can't perform the Min part of the analysis. Therefore, the result of your Min analysis is zero—*the current* implementation of your ML pipeline has zero business value. Without making improvements, you have nothing.

6.5.2 Performing the Max part of MinMax analysis

If what you have today isn't good enough to release, you clearly need to improve your AI system before it's business-viable. It's time to perform the Max part of the MinMax analysis and determine if your ML pipeline is something you can improve enough to achieve your business goal. This section shows you how to perform this part of the analysis.

For the Max part of MinMax analysis, the idea is that for an ML pipeline with the given structure, the best possible result for the pipeline as a whole is the one in which every single one of its stages has the best possible implementation. Look at stage B of the ML pipeline shown in figure 6.6. Suppose that stage is given an image and handles visual recognition of digits on the image. For the Max analysis, you'd look at what the best result is that anyone else has achieved recognizing digits and use that as a proxy for what the best possible result is that your stage B could accomplish if you were to put considerable effort into it.

Best-so-far is an upper limit of reasonable expectation

For the sake of argument, let's assume that the best result anyone has gotten so far for some stage of the ML pipeline (let's call it stage B) is 99.22% accuracy. Suppose you construct an ML pipeline using that stage, and when you perform the Max part of the MinMax analysis, you find that your ML pipeline isn't business-viable. However, if you could improve the accuracy of stage B by just 0.5% (to an accuracy of 99.72%), you'd have a business-viable ML pipeline. Should you assume that your team would be able to achieve that 99.72% accuracy?

For most teams in the industry, it's risky to bet that a team can improve on the best published result achieved in the field of AI so far. That means that any ML pipeline that can't produce acceptable business results when every single stage is using the best possible implementation known is, by its structure, unsuitable for solving your business problem. Such an ML pipeline has failed the Max part of the MinMax analysis. If you need to exceed the best historical result to get even a minimally viable product, it's well past time to abandon such an ML pipeline.

The Max part of the analysis is especially crucial in the early stage of building a new business or product. At this stage, you're estimating the total costs of your project and your pipeline, and, chances are, you're overlooking some costs. If your ML pipeline fails the Max part of the MinMax analysis even when your total costs may be underestimated, that ML pipeline surely can't support a viable AI product.

The most important question during the Max analysis of the ML pipeline is, "What is a reasonable proxy for the best possible result in such a stage?" Let's look at some of the ways to find a good proxy.

The Max part of MinMax analysis has its root in competitive benchmarking [1,120]. Competitive benchmarking means that you're looking for a proxy, someone who has a similar problem, and you measure how well they solved it. Here are some sources we'll investigate in more detail that you can use as a proxy:

- The best results achieved so far in business, industry, or academia on a problem similar to one you're trying to solve
- A person performing the task you need your AI to perform

WHAT'S THE BEST RESULT FOR PROBLEMS LIKE YOURS IN ACADEMIA OR INDUSTRY?

What's the best published result in academia or business for a task like yours? What you're looking for is an organization that had the same problem as the one you have and how well they solved it.

When looking at the industry, you're looking for not only the COTS products you can buy, but also what's best that other companies (even if they aren't your direct competitors) were able to achieve when tackling the problem you're facing. When you're looking at academic papers, you're looking at the best published result. In both cases, the key is that you're trying to find what's the best someone else has achieved when solving the problem *that looks as much as possible like yours.*

TIP If you're considering a COTS product for some stage in the pipeline, ask the vendor what the best result is that they've seen achieved with their product for a problem such as yours. A vendor that's confident that they're supplying a tangible business value for a business case like yours should recognize that question as an opportunity to distinguish themselves.

The idea of using academia or industry as a proxy is that if the world's best experts were unable to achieve more than 80% accuracy on some task, it's reasonable to assume that you won't do better than 80%.

  As for which proxy to choose, you're typically better off using a proxy that's more like your problem—proven industry use is always a stronger proxy than an academic paper. On the other hand, an academic paper describing a situation that's precisely like yours might be a better proxy than industry use on a less-related problem.

How similar is your situation?

You must work carefully to ensure that the problem you choose to use as a proxy is similar to your situation. The proxy must be closely related, and you must understand under which conditions the advertised result was achieved. Pay special attention to any simplifications that the authors of an academic paper might have introduced.

B. Hu et al. present an example in their paper on time series classification [121]. Accelerometer data can be used to recognize the motions and gestures of an actor. The question here is, how do you know when one motion starts and another one ends? The answer to that particular academic community, at one point in time, was that they'd use what's technically known as *pre-segmentation*.

That community was interested in classifying gestures under the condition that it was already known when the gesture started and stopped. That was known because the actor was asked to perform the gestures on cue. *To get more precise pre-segmentation, some actors were even using a metronome!*

The only problem is that recognizing gestures if accelerometer data is pre-segmented with the help of the metronome is much easier than understanding accelerometer data coming from a smart watch (such as an Apple Watch). If you were using a former community's results as a proxy for what's possible with a smart watch accelerometer, you'd stop wondering why you were unable to get gesture recognition accuracy anywhere close to what that academic community was able to achieve.

What if during the Max analysis your team misses the absolute best result published? For example, it was in some obscure scientific paper. That doesn't matter; the finding of Max that your team made is still considered the Max for your organization, and that Max isn't affected by the existence of some obscure paper. What you're looking for during Max analysis isn't the absolute Max known to humankind. You're looking for a practical or industrial Max—the one your actual team might be able to get when they try to implement the given stage of the pipeline. Your team can't implement algorithms from papers they don't know about.

HOW WELL WOULD A HUMAN DO SOLVING YOUR PROBLEM?

What if you have no example whatsoever that's like your problem? If no one has solved a problem like yours before, it's dangerous to assume that you can make an AI product that would do better than a human. Instead, see what a person can do when given a small subset of the data. Use that person as your proxy.

Take a human and show them the same data that the stage of the pipeline sees. Ask them to play the role of the pipeline stage, then measure what the human-powered stage achieves. That's your estimate of the maximum that an AI algorithm would be able to do.

> **NOTE**   Although it might be possible to get a *better-than-human* effect on some tasks, at the time of this writing, such situations are infrequent, often newsworthy, and, even when achieved, usually produced by teams that already consist of people who are among the best AI researchers in the world. It's much more common that the results from your AI algorithm would be worse than that which a person could achieve.

6.5.3   *Estimates and safety factors in MinMax analysis*

The nature of the Max part of the MinMax analysis is that you're estimating what can be achieved if every stage of your ML pipeline has the best possible implementation. This section addresses those questions that often present themselves when you're estimating what you can achieve. For example:

- When you're performing a MinMax analysis and your project is to be released in 18 months, should you account for trends in the improvement of hardware or AI algorithms?
- How should you use expert opinions during a MinMax analysis?
- Should you add any safety factors to your results?

USING TREND ESTIMATES IN A MINMAX ANALYSIS

Sometimes you might look at a trend in improvement and estimate what the continuation of such a trend would mean at the time you deploy your project. For example, the cost of data storage is declining, and if your project is shipping in two years, you can account for a decline in data storage costs and conclude that you'd be able to afford to store more data than you can today.

You can also apply trends to the improvement in AI algorithms. In some cases, there might be a clear trend that AI algorithms are getting better. For example, right now, AI is getting better in the recognition of images and video streams, and it's doing that rapidly. Estimating trends is especially tempting to do if the results of your Max analysis are failing with a small margin from the business viability threshold you're trying to reach. For example, you need accuracy of 96%, and currently the best you have is 95.5%, but you think it will be 96% in two years.

I'm not a fan of estimating trends in your early AI efforts; I tell most of my clients not to attempt to do so. To predict trends in some field successfully, you need more expertise than you're likely to possess at the time you're starting early efforts in that field. I'm talking about not only technical knowledge, but also knowledge of how good your organization is at assimilating new AI technology. Finally, for trends to be significant, the project typically needs to be long enough that it would be longer than your first AI project should take.

ESTIMATES BASED ON EXPERT OPINION

It's always a good idea to ask an expert for their estimate of the Max result that you can get in some stage of the pipeline. Such experts could be consultants or academics. They might also point out not only what the best possible result is in some stage of the pipeline, but how to achieve it.

Another advantage of an expert opinion is that they might know an area well enough to tell you not only what the current best result is, but what the trends are in the particular research area. Is this an area that's rapidly improving its capabilities (such as the image recognition community)? How much training is necessary for your team to achieve those results?

Be careful to contextualize expert advice. Did the expert answer the single question in isolation, and does the expert understand your particular situation well?

Experts are expensive and busy, and it's tempting to try to save money by asking them a straightforward question that your team constructed. The problem is that now your team has to handle contextualizing both the question and the answer in an area where they have less expertise than the expert.

Answers you get in such situations may also give you a false sense of security: you're likely to believe that the answer is correct because it's coming from a recognized expert. However, the contextualization part (done by lesser experts) could be an essential part of the problem. Asking the right questions is difficult, and a lot of what makes an expert an expert is that they know which questions to ask.

You encountered the problem of contextualizing the question before in chapter 3, when we were formulating research questions for solving business problems. Just like the executive and the data scientist needed to talk in chapter 3, you'll need to speak with an expert to make sure that the question (asked correctly) reflects your needs.

I believe that saving money on expert advice is a "penny wise, pound foolish" approach. Budget what it takes to get enough time with the expert to explain the problem you're facing so that expert can contextualize the answer. If you have the right expert, you can explain to them the specifics of your business situation in a few hours.

Finally, be careful to understand what the form of the answer is that you get from an expert. Is it fact, expert opinion on the situation, or just an estimate? You already know that I'm not a fan of trend estimates on initial AI projects, and my opinion doesn't change much just because the estimator is a technical expert in the field.

> **WARNING** If you get an estimate, be aware that most people (and most experts) aren't particularly accurate estimators. It's worth reading D. W. Hubbard's book [75] for data showing that most people are poor estimators, a discussion on why humans are poor estimators, and ways for people to become more accurate.

SHOULD YOU ADD SAFETY FACTORS DURING YOUR ANALYSIS?

Sometimes academic results can't be replicated fully in the industry setting. You might also be skeptical that your team can create an AI solution that will produce results on some task that are close to what a human working on the same task can do.

In such a situation, you might want to introduce a safety factor, such as, "We assume that we can reach only 50% of the best published result." Of course, it's not clear what this safety factor should be—why have we chosen 50% as a safety factor and not 80%? A safety factor is a good idea when you understand the problem well enough that you can describe where the uncertainty is coming from and how much uncertainty there is. However, when you don't know how much uncertainty there is, a safety factor is just a guess.

> **WARNING**   Be careful when you encounter safety factors that are round numbers (like 2, 3, 10, or 50%). They look too suspiciously round to be the result of a technical analysis of the problem, and those numbers might be just a guess.

6.5.4   *Categories of profit curves*

In the examples of profit curve analysis presented thus far, we've assumed that the profit curve is monotonic—that when technical metrics increase, the business metric (such as profit) also increases. This is the most common real-life situation, but this section will demonstrate what to do when the profit curve and technical metrics have more *complicated* relationships.

> **NOTE**   This section is of interest to both the general reader and the mathematically inclined reader. To facilitate the broadest audience, I'll use everyday terminology to describe some of the concepts more simply. I ask for patience from my mathematically inclined readers—you already know the basic concepts I'm describing, as well as the corner cases, and can add the underlying mathematical rigor yourself.

Profit curves can have different shapes. We're particularly interested in the four categories in figure 6.7. Let's discuss the categories of profit curves shown in figure 6.7:

- In a linear profit curve, the relationship between the business metric and the technical metric is a straight line.
- In the monotonic profit curve, when the technical metric increases, so does the business metric. However, the function describing the relationship between the technical metric and the business metric is not a straight line—the profit curve can take many shapes. Every linear profit curve is a monotonic curve, but not vice versa.
- The next more complicated profit curve is the non-monotonic profit curve. This curve has segments in which the business metric increases when the technical metric does and other segments in which the business metric decreases when the technical metric increases. Graph (c) shows one type of non-monotonic curve you may encounter in practice.

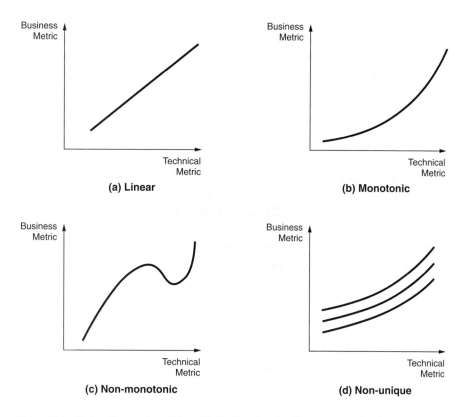

Figure 6.7 **Various types of profit curves. The linear and monotonic profit curves are simpler to optimize than the non-monotonic profit curve. Avoid non-unique profit curves.**

- The final example is a profit curve that's non-unique (ambiguous)—there's no unique relationship between a given technical metric and revenue. You'll encounter this type of profit curve when a technical metric fails to measure business considerations vital to you.

You know the shape of the profit curve for your project; your team constructed it.[4] Let's give some concrete examples of when you'll encounter the kinds of profit curves shown in figure 6.7:

- You'll often encounter a linear profit curve (graph (a)) when a simple and direct relationship exists between your technical metric and your business metric. For example, a linear profit curve would happen when you have a rule of the form, "Our yearly cost is given using the formula *$100K * RMSE*."

---

[4] While a profit curve may in some cases be experimentally derived, that's an advanced technical topic that isn't practical to cover in this book because of the intended target audience and space. Some of the technical topics relevant to experimental derivation of profit curves include design of experiments, response surface analysis, and Bayesian optimization.

- You may encounter a monotonic (but nonlinear) profit curve when you're predicting some value—the better your prediction, the more valuable it is. Graph (b) shows an exponential relationship between a technical metric and a business metric—where a small increase in prediction accuracy will result in a massive increase in profits. You'll face that situation often in the financial markets.[5]

- Another example of a non-monotonic curve is in robotics, where the profit curve will look like the curve shown in graph (c). In robotics, there's a concept of *the uncanny valley* [122]. Consider two robots, the first with a doll-like face, and the second robot with facial features (and facial movement) similar to a human's, but not a perfect facsimile. We tend to think that the second robot with more sophisticated facial modeling would be more popular, but the opposite may be the case [122]. Some people have an instinctive, negative reaction to the second robot.

- Another example of a non-monotonic curve is of automated systems that require close human supervision. Think of a security system that uses AI to highlight suspicious activity. Still another is when workers are supervising automated machines and robots. Transportation systems (such as planes) can also be subject to the same phenomena [123].

  When (for legal or practical reasons) you have to have a human fully dedicated to supervising your system (and being bored for a significant amount of time), you may see shapes similar to graph (c). The combined system of AI and a human will perform *worse* when an imperfect AI makes occasional errors (but still makes them) than when the AI makes more frequent errors. The reason lies not in the performance of the AI system but in the performance of the human supervising the operation—humans tend to get bored and inattentive and therefore may be slow to correct problems when they finally do occur. Or they may simply be out of practice in how to react to the errors of the AI system.

- Yet another example of a non-monotonic profit curve is in some situations where the business metric is profit. Sometimes, reaching a higher value in the technical metric may be expensive and require additional capital expenditure. Suppose that further improvement of your technical metric would require you to buy access to costly additional data sources. This creates a "dip" in your profit curve where the further improvement of your technical metric is possible only after you buy costly additional data (and, therefore, reduce profit at that point).

As a general rule, monotonic profit curves are simpler to deal with, and if you have a choice, you should prefer them. If you have two *equally good* technical metric/business metric combinations to choose from, of which one is monotonic and the other is not, choose the monotonic combination.

---

[5] Note that the reason for an exponential relationship may be that large improvement may be difficult, or even be believed to be impossible. It's likely that because of competition, once you show that the improvement is possible, your competition will try to catch on, and the shape of the curve may quickly change. Chapter 7 shows you how to operate with a profit curve that changes over time.

WARNING *Never make business decisions based only on a technical metric that you can't relate to a business consideration you care about!* Otherwise, you're deciding to maximize the number (technical metric), not to optimize business outcomes.

In your early AI projects, or while your AI team is still gaining experience, you should prefer use cases that have simple profit curves. That's for both technical reasons (monotonic profit curves are simpler to analyze) and business reasons.

NOTE A complex profit curve may be an indication of a weak business case for AI, in which monetization isn't straightforward. But it can also be an indication of a business case that's so strong that it's worth your while to perform a detailed analysis of the profit curve. Or it can be merely a technical coincidence—as in "That's just what the relationship between these particular business and technical metrics is." I don't start with any preconceived notion, but when I see a non-monotonic profit curve, I always ask myself, "Why does the profit curve have this shape?"

Sometimes you don't have a choice—the only technical metric/business metric combination that works for you is non-monotonic. The techniques shown in the next section will help your data science team address that situation.

6.5.5 *Dealing with complex profit curves*

Now let's talk about the details needed to construct the more complex profit curves. This section describes the technical aspects of dealing with non-monotonic and non-unique profit curves.

NOTE I assume in this section that the reader is already familiar with confusion matrices and F-scores in the context of natural language processing (NLP). You can find more information in Leon Derczynski's paper [124].

Let's first deal with how to recognize a non-unique profit curve. A non-unique profit curve happens when no unique mathematical relation exists between the business metric and the technical metric that you're using. An example from the legal field is *e-discovery*, in which AI is used to help to save on the cost of lawyers reviewing documents. We can use AI to check a large number of documents. If an AI system can *reliably* flag the text that's unrelated to the litigation, it can produce dramatic time savings for lawyers, and cost savings for the litigant.

Suppose now that you're working for a law firm. Your business question is, "Can you estimate the maximum amount of money that AI can save me during the discovery phase of litigation?"[6] Your savings in e-discovery are proportional to the percentage of the documents that AI correctly classifies as "unrelated to the lawsuit"—the true negatives.

AI systems analyzing documents are part of the broader field of NLP. One metric that the NLP community typically uses is the F-score [124]. Unfortunately for our

---

[6] To keep this example simple and on-point, let's assume that this is the only question you care about and disregard the costs of AI making a legal mistake. Of course, if enough cost savings are coming from this first question, and the legal firm decides to explore this AI system, further business questions will be asked.

business case, the F-score doesn't account for true negatives! It's quite possible for two different AI systems, with a widely varied number of true negatives, to have the same F-score! In our business case, that means that there's no unique relationship between the F-score and the amount of savings AI can provide. The same F-score may save 10% of attorney time or 80%! You can't use this F-score to construct a "cost-saving/F-score" profit curve. Although you can use the F-score to measure other characteristics of this system, it's certainly not a good technical metric for a profit curve in which the business metric is cost savings.

> **NOTE**   If this is the case, why do people use F-score at all? Because the F-score makes sense in many areas of information retrieval, *but not in our particular business case.* F-score is often used in the context of NLP [124], so if you're debating which *technical metrics* to use, it's a reasonable starting point. The broader teaching point is that just because a certain technical metric is widely used, doesn't automatically make it a useful metric for your profit curve.

Now, let's explore some non-monotonic profit curves. You must perform MinMax analysis of the non-monotonic profit curve differently than the analysis of the monotonic curve. If your curve is non-monotonic, then the MinMax analysis approach you should undertake is shown in figure 6.8.

Remember that the term *Min* in the MinMax analysis refers to the minimum configuration of your ML pipeline (every stage has a simple, minimal implementation), not to the minimum value of the business metric. You always want to get the best value of the business metric you can get with your ML pipeline! Therefore, when performing

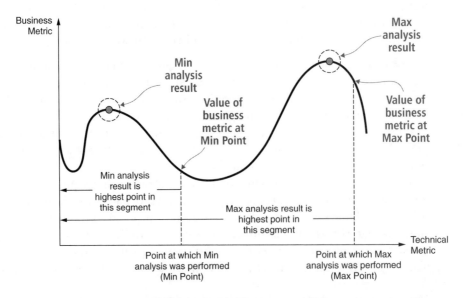

Figure 6.8   MinMax analysis of a non-monotonic profit curve. The Min analysis result is the best value of the business metric on the segment [0, Min Point]. The Max analysis result is the highest value of the business metric on the segment [0, Max Point].

MinMax analysis in figure 6.8, the result of your Min analysis is *the best value you've seen on the whole interval* [0, Min Point] *between the start of the curve and the point at which you've performed the Min analysis.* Similar logic applies when performing the Max part of the MinMax analysis on the whole interval [0, Max Point].

Once you get a handle on MinMax analysis overall, MinMax analysis on the non-monotonic profit curve isn't difficult to perform. However, it's more labor intensive than working with a monotonic profit curve! And the work doesn't stop with MinMax analysis—a project with a non-monotonic profit curve typically has special considerations. For example, if the profit curve has the shape in figure 6.7 part (c), because a human supervisor may become bored and inattentive, how are you going to address that boredom?

When mental math doesn't work

The more you climb the ladder of complexity in the profit curves, the more difficult it is to comprehend relationships. Simple nonlinearity in a profit curve already makes mental math impractical. It's much worse when the curve is non-monotonic!

When you fail to present a well-defined profit curve, you're forcing meeting participants on your team to perform mental math to figure out what the technical metric means in business terms! I know I can't concentrate on the central topic of most meetings while simultaneously performing the mental math required for nonlinear, non-monotonic profit curves as a "side activity." I suspect that many people stuck in such a position will skip the mental math altogether and settle for "Let's just improve the technical metric." Any nonlinearity in the relationship between the technical metric and the business metric then gets ignored, or at best *approximated*.

That means that any AI project that fails to construct a profit curve, but happens to have a non-monotonic profit curve, is optimizing for the wrong thing! That's especially unfortunate when the precise optimization of the technical metric was a costly activity, which was then followed by an approximation!

I heard a joke about the series of successive approximation, back when I was in my first year of college. The joke was: "Engineering is about using a micrometer screw gauge to take a measurement, then marking where to cut with a piece of chalk, and finally using an axe to cut at the marked spot!"

6.6 FAQs about MinMax analysis

When you understand the basics of performing MinMax analysis, we need to address some practical questions about performing that analysis. This section presents answers to the following common questions:

- Should MinMax be the first analysis of the ML pipeline when a more complex analysis might provide more precise results?
- Should I perform the Min or the Max part of the MinMax analysis first?
- Is a MinMax analysis something that only big companies can afford to do?
- Why do you use the term MinMax analysis? Why don't you call it Best Case/ Worst Case analysis?

6.6.1   *Should MinMax be the first analysis of the ML pipeline?*

Let's start with the question of whether MinMax should be the first analysis of the ML pipeline. If you're familiar with the fields of systems engineering and industrial process control, you might be familiar with the several types of analysis that could be suitable when analyzing the ML pipeline. So why use MinMax analysis instead, when a more complex analysis might provide more precise results?

I'll discuss some alternative types of ML pipeline analysis in chapter 7. Those types of analysis might be more potent than MinMax is, as described here. However, MinMax is simple to learn, is cheap to perform, and provides a reasonable estimate of the suitability of your pipeline. It's a good tradeoff between complexity of analysis and precision of results.

> **WARNING**   There's no point in performing an analysis of an ML pipeline if that analysis is overly complex to learn and expensive to implement, regardless of how precise the results of such an analysis might be. Analysis that perfectly predicts the future is worth something only if its results will be available before the future has already arrived.

6.6.2   *Which analysis should you perform first? Min or Max?*

Let's talk about the order in which you should perform a MinMax analysis. Do you schedule the Min or Max part of MinMax analysis first? These parts are independent, so for the validity of the analysis, the order of the Min and Max parts of the analysis doesn't matter much. When I implement MinMax, I use the process shown in figure 6.9 to account for factors such as the difficulty of Min and Max parts and prior opinions about expected outcomes.

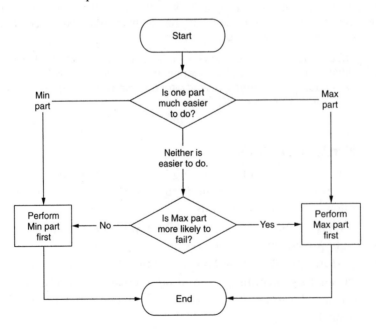

Figure 6.9   The order in which you should perform a MinMax analysis on the ML pipeline. Perform the part of the analysis that can provide conclusive answers first.

Each one of the Min and Max parts can be conclusive in itself regarding whether you're using the right pipeline. The conclusiveness of either part of MinMax analysis helps you to avoid the need to perform the other part. If the Max analysis is easy to do and it fails, you don't need to perform the Min analysis. Figure 6.9 shows scheduling the parts of a MinMax analysis so that you start with the more straightforward component of the analysis, which also provides conclusive results.

6.6.3 Should a small company or small team skip the MinMax analysis?

Another question is, "Shouldn't small companies minimize process overhead by working on AI algorithms and the ML pipeline itself and then see what happens when they deliver it?" Yes, it's better to skip analysis of the ML pipeline . . . if you can be certain you're working on the right ML pipeline! The problem is that in the absence of the MinMax (or equivalent) analysis, you *can't* be certain that you're working on the right ML pipeline. Because smaller companies and teams have less money and resources to recover from mistakes, *MinMax analysis is even more critical for small teams.*

When you're constructing an ML pipeline for an AI project, you're working in a new area that inherently has significant risks and for which best practices are still emerging. Very few people have done enough AI projects to be able to intuitively construct the right ML pipeline on the first try, and for many problems, the number of ML pipelines that wouldn't work overwhelms the number of ML pipelines that would work.

So how do you know that you're working on the right ML pipeline? You can take a risk, but if you're wrong, then you'll finish with a flawed ML pipeline into which you've put much effort and that is now ossifying.

> **TIP** Knowing if you have an adequate ML pipeline is even more critical in the context of the small company! A proper MinMax analysis is the most important technical step of an AI project, and choosing to skip it is taking a risk, not streamlining the process.

A similar argument applies to sensitivity analysis: How do you know which pipeline stage you should improve? It's vital to use sensitivity analysis in companies of all sizes. The next chapter elaborates on this.

6.6.4 Why do you use the term MinMax analysis?

Multiple terms are used in business and industry to refer to MinMax analysis. It's also known as Best Case/Worst Case analysis. These terms are often heard in ML circles.[7] However, while working in the industry, I've found that the Best Case/Worst Case terminology is problematic because it's often unclear from which point of view (business or engineering) the best case is to be measured.

---

[7] As an example of use of Best Case/Worst Case in the context of ML algorithms, the best case result for an ML algorithm is discussed in [112].

Look at the ML pipeline we've analyzed in this chapter. What is the best case, from the business point of view? That the most straightforward technical implementation of ML pipeline would solve the business problem. That's the ML pipeline we used for the Min part of the MinMax pipeline. However, from the engineering point of view, you could argue that the Min result is the worst case. I've known many engineers and statisticians who argue precisely that. The ML pipeline you have today establishes the lowest limit (worst case) of how well the AI of your product would behave if you released your product today.

All of this discussion is of keen interest to some engineers, and they have good reasons for that: imprecise terminology is a root cause of a lot of the problems in their profession. While I empathize with the argument, from a pragmatic point of view, I prefer to use the term MinMax analysis.

6.7   *Exercises*

The following exercises help you get a better understanding of the concepts introduced in this chapter. By its nature, interpretation of the results of a MinMax analysis is straightforward. Analyzing the ML pipeline is *a technical and business skill*, so it's time to form a team consisting of a business specialist and an engineer and do some of these exercises together. All of the exercises in this chapter use the ML pipeline given in figure 6.10.

Figure 6.10   An example of an ML pipeline. We'll use this pipeline for the exercises in this chapter.

You'll also need to refer to the information provided earlier in table 6.1 (which is repeated here for your convenience as table 6.2).

Table 6.2   Summary of the possible results of MinMax analysis

Min result/Max result	Max passed	Max failed
Min passed	The ML pipeline is business-viable.	This combination can't happen.
Min failed	The ML pipeline needs improvement to be business-viable.	The current ML pipeline isn't suitable for solving the business problem.

Answer the following questions.

Question 1: Note that in table 6.2, you don't have any guidance for the situation in which the Min part of the MinMax has passed, but the Max part of the MinMax failed. Explain why this is the case.

Question 2: For the ML pipeline in figure 6.10, assume that the value threshold at which the project becomes business-viable is $1 million. Determine whether the pipeline is worth pursuing if the results of the MinMax analysis are as follows:

- **Scenario 1:** The Min part is $2.3 million, and the Max part is $23 million.
- **Scenario 2:** The Min part is $500 K, and the Max part is $1 million.
- **Scenario 3:** The Min part is $500 K, and the Max part is $2 million.
- **Scenario 4:** The Min part is $1.1 million, and the Max part is $900 K.
- **Scenario 5:** The Min part is $500 K, and the Max part is $900 K.

Question 3: If you're a data scientist or technical manager, take a technical problem of your choice and construct an ML pipeline for it. Perform the Max part of the MinMax analysis for it.

Question 4: If you're a data scientist or technical manager, look at the examples given in section 6.4.1 and perform a MinMax analysis as described in that section. Determine where the dollar amount given in that section comes from. Hint: a profit curve was constructed from the confusion matrix of the classifier.

Question 5: How would you classify the use of AI in the context of saving litigation costs during the e-discovery process described in section 6.5.5? Use the taxonomy of AI uses introduced in section 2.5. It's shown in figure 2.5, duplicated here as figure 6.11, which summarizes the taxonomies discussed in that section.

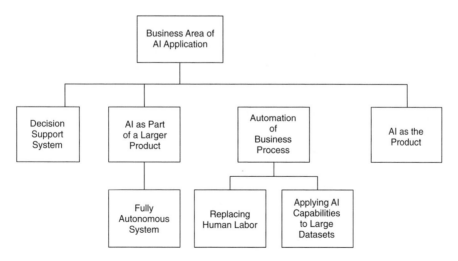

Figure 6.11 AI taxonomy based on the high-level role it plays in business. You could use this taxonomy to guide you in eliciting available business actions you can help with AI. (This figure is a repeat of figure 2.5.)

Summary

- Project management is about making the best decisions based on the information you have now, and usually with a time constraint. To get an early indication of the business value of your ML pipeline, you should analyze it using MinMax analysis.
- To economically allocate resources in your AI project, you need to determine if you're using the right ML pipeline and then improve the right stages of that ML pipeline as needed. The former is done using a MinMax analysis, and the latter using sensitivity analysis. This is the *E*conomize part of the CLUE process.
- MinMax analysis allows you to determine if your ML pipeline already meets business goals, needs improvement to be able to meet those goals, or is incapable of meeting those goals.
- MinMax analysis helps you implement the "If you're going to fail, fail fast!" policy on AI projects.

Guiding an AI project to success

This chapter covers

- Performing sensitivity analysis on the ML pipeline
- Assessing advanced sensitivity analysis methods
- Accounting for the effects of time in your pipeline
- Organizing a project so that "If you fail, you fail fast"

This chapter answers the questions: "What should I do when my ML pipeline needs improvement, and how do I know that I'm improving the right stage of the ML pipeline?" Such issues almost always arise for an AI product that's already on the market, and your goal is to continue to improve an AI product's user experience.

The same questions arise during the initial development of the AI project when your current ML pipeline needs to improve to meet business goals. Technically, this situation happens when the Min part of MinMax analysis is failing, and the Max part is passing. (Section 6.4.3 describes details of such a scenario.)

In this chapter, I'll show you how to improve your ML pipeline. The key is to correctly decide the stage of an ML pipeline on which you should concentrate your improvement efforts, which allows you to economize your resources. The *Economize* part of the CLUE process addresses how to best direct your resources.

- In section 7.1, we look at how sensitivity analysis shows you which stage of your ML pipeline needs improvement.
- Section 7.2 completes our journey through the CLUE process.
- Section 7.3 discusses advanced methods for performing sensitivity analysis and when you should use them.
- Section 7.4 shows you how to manage the growth and maintenance of the ML pipeline past the release of your AI project.
- Section 7.5 addresses how you should balance a set of AI projects and your current project by reinforcing your winner projects and cutting off your losers.

7.1 *Improving your ML pipeline with sensitivity analysis*

When you know that you need to enhance the results of an ML pipeline, the question arises as to which part of the pipeline you should upgrade. Do you need cleaner data with fewer errors or a better AI algorithm? You have limited resources and can't just say, "Let's improve everything in the ML pipeline at the same time and see what happens." You need to choose a stage of the ML pipeline to improve. This section introduces the tool that would guide you through the quest for what is the best stage of the ML pipeline to improve next. That tool is called *sensitivity analysis*.

> **DEFINITION** *Sensitivity analysis* shows how refining a single stage of the ML pipeline improves the result of the pipeline as a whole. Sensitivity analysis guides you to the stage of the ML pipeline you should upgrade first.

At its core, sensitivity analysis answers the business question: "In which stage of my ML pipeline should I invest for the maximum payoff?" Knowing the answer to that question allows you to economize resources put into pipeline improvement.

Let's look at an example. Suppose you have the pipeline in figure 7.1, and you want to improve the result (the output from stage E) of the pipeline.

Figure 7.1 An example of an ML pipeline. We use this pipeline as a base example for sensitivity analysis. (This repeats figure 6.10 for the reader's convenience.)

In effect, you're asking, "What's the payoff if I improve each stage of the pipeline?" For example, if stage A is 1% better, what's the improvement in the overall pipeline? You'd then ask the same question for stages B, C, D, and E. Sensitivity analysis is the tool you use to answer these questions, and it allows you to replace intuition and gut feeling with the data-driven approach.

TIP Sensitivity analysis gives you the business value of developing a stage in the ML pipeline. Sensitivity analysis of every stage allows you to rank the pipeline's stages by how much overall improvement in your business each stage will cause when it's improved.

Based on the results of sensitivity analysis, you can prioritize the stages of the ML pipeline and create a backlog of tasks needed to improve it. Once you have that backlog, you'll use the project management methodology you ordinarily use to manage the rest of the project. With sensitivity analysis, you transform the problem of improving the ML pipeline into management decisions similar to the ones that you make daily. This approach applies regardless of whether your environment is Agile or not. You're balancing the cost and time of upgrading a stage in the ML pipeline with the business benefits.

NOTE I've written the next sections, 7.1.1 and 7.1.2, for readers with an engineering background, so some simple introductory calculus-level concepts are ahead. You can skip over the details of those sections if you're only looking to get an idea of how your team should perform sensitivity analysis.

In the following sections, I present two advanced methods for how to do sensitivity analysis:

- Section 7.1.1 covers local sensitivity analysis. Your team should use local sensitivity analysis when you expect that only incremental improvement in a stage of the ML pipeline is possible.
- Section 7.1.2 covers global sensitivity analysis. Your team should use global sensitivity analysis when you expect that a wide range of improvement in a stage of the ML pipeline is possible.
- Section 7.1.3 presents an example of interpreting the results of sensitivity analysis.

A manager making the decision about which stage of the pipeline to improve next is primarily interested in interpreting the results of sensitivity analysis (which is described in section 7.1.3); the type of analysis performed is of secondary interest. A technical expert performing a sensitivity analysis, however, must know how to choose the correct form of analysis—local or global.

7.1.1 Performing local sensitivity analysis

Local sensitivity analysis answers the question: "What would be the business result if I were to improve one stage of my current ML pipeline just a little?" This type of sensitivity analysis is appropriate when you expect that only small, incremental improvements in a specific stage are possible. An example is when you (or the broader community) already put so much effort into improving a specific stage of the pipeline that you believe that the days of substantial improvement in the results of that stage are behind you.

As an example, let's assume we want to improve the ML pipeline in figure 7.1 and want to find which stage of the pipeline, when improved, would result in the best overall performance of that pipeline. To do this, we would apply sensitivity analysis to every stage of the ML pipeline.

> **NOTE**   Sensitivity analysis of a single stage is much faster to perform than it would be to actually improve (for all possible results) a particular stage of the ML pipeline. Therefore, we can use sensitivity analysis as a guide for which stage of the pipeline to improve next.

Let's look at analyzing stage B from figure 7.1. Suppose that stage B classifies its input into a couple of categories. Let's assume that the technical metric for measuring stage B's ability to classify the input into the correct categories should be classification accuracy. Furthermore, suppose that you're currently achieving an $x\%$ classification accuracy in stage B. Figure 7.2 illustrates this method of sensitivity analysis.

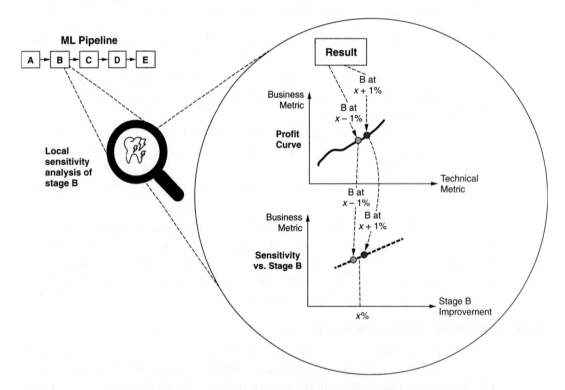

Figure 7.2   Local sensitivity analysis. For small improvements in the response of stage B, this analysis assumes a linear response in the ML pipeline. If a gain of 0.5% in stage B results in a 1% improvement in the pipeline's result, then a 1% gain in stage B would result in a 2% improvement in the entire ML pipeline.

What happens to the output of the last stage (stage E) of the pipeline as you change the classification accuracy of stage B in the vicinity of $x\%$? What happens at $x - 1\%$ and $x + 1\%$? You perform the local sensitivity analysis by simulating improvement in the results of stage B.

You perform this type of sensitivity analysis locally, near the point at which the accuracy of your classifier is $x\%$. You get the result of the whole pipeline when you change the output of stage B to have an accuracy of $x - 1\%$ and $x + 1\%$ and then measure the effect of the change in stage B to the output of the ML pipeline. You use the profit curve to transform technical metrics into business metrics, and, finally, you plot the relationship between changes in stage B and the business results of the whole pipeline.

> **WARNING** The profit curve and the *sensitivity versus stage* curve are two totally different curves. The former shows you how the business metric changes when the technical metric measuring the whole ML pipeline changes. The latter shows you how the business metric changes as a function of the improvement in the individual stage.

How to get 1% worse (or better)

To get a 1% worse output, you take the classifier as-is and run the output of the classifier through a random number generator. The random number generator should be tuned to decrease the total accuracy of the classifier by 1%. To get a 1% increase in accuracy, you can use humans to review the results and correct them.

You can also use a commercial off-the-shelf (COTS) product or service that achieves better results than you're currently able to produce.[a] Such a COTS product or service doesn't have to be capable of playing a permanent role in the production version of your ML pipeline. For the purpose of the analysis, it doesn't matter if, for the reasons of cost, performance, or the complexity of integrating the COTS product with the pipeline, you can't incorporate the COTS product in the production version of the ML pipeline. The COTS product just needs to be useful for experiments that can yield a one-time increase in accuracy of 1%.

---

[a] You should always survey the commercial landscape before investing significant resources in building in-house solutions. Therefore, you should already know what these COTS solutions are.

When performing local sensitivity analysis, you're assuming that in the vicinity of $x\%$, the response of the whole ML pipeline is linear. If a 1% change in stage B causes a 1% change in the output of the ML pipeline, then a 2% change in stage B would cause a 2% change in the output. With this approach to sensitivity analysis, you understand the behavior of the whole ML pipeline's output *in the vicinity of stage B's classification output being $x\%$.*

This approach to sensitivity analysis is most appropriate when you're expecting that any improvement in the results of the sensitivity analysis would be incremental and that increasing performance by 1% might be nontrivial.

> **NOTE**   A typical example of this situation is when the pipeline stage you're improving is an implementation of some AI algorithm. Your team may also have worked on improving that stage for a while. Here, the assumption is that even a small improvement in the metric might be a struggle.

In the example I've just used to illustrate local sensitivity analysis, there's nothing magical about a 1% metric improvement. You don't have to use a 1% improvement; you could also use 0.1%, 1.5%, 2%, or some other percentage. What's essential is that you use a percentage increment that's a fraction of the total possible improvement in the stage. For example, if the potential gain is limited to 0.1%, you can use the increment of 0.05%.

7.1.2   *Global sensitivity analysis*

Often, there's no reason to believe that you'd be limited to small improvements to a particular stage of the ML pipeline. Maybe it's possible to improve a stage by 30% or 60%? Global sensitivity analysis helps you understand how your ML pipeline reacts to drastic improvements in a single stage.

One example of the source of a potential dramatic improvement in a stage of the pipeline is when you don't have any implementation of that stage yet, but you know that there are multiple possible implementations of the stage that would provide drastically different results. Another example is when you're improving the pipeline stage that's performing data cleansing. At least, theoretically, if you put enough effort into such a stage, you can completely clean the data.

> **NOTE**   In practice, there are limits to how high a data quality you can afford and achieve. Still, you have significant control over how much you could improve the quality of your input data.

When significant improvements in the results of one stage are possible, local sensitivity analysis isn't appropriate, because you're looking at the ML pipeline's response over a wide range. Instead, you should test the whole range of values you have available with an interval between test points. Figure 7.3 shows this approach to sensitivity analysis.

Global sensitivity analysis is performed similarly to local sensitivity analysis, but instead of carrying out analysis at two points ($x - 1\%$ and $x + 1\%$), you analyze over a range of values that the stage can produce. With this approach, you can better accommodate nonlinear relationships between changes in a single stage of the ML pipeline and the output of the ML pipeline as a whole. The disadvantage is that you need to put more work into the sensitivity analysis because you're analyzing more points. So how many points (and in what interval) should you use?

As far as the interval is concerned, it comes from comparing the current level of performance to the maximum level of performance you think is possible (or 100%, if you have no reason to suspect you can't reach 100%). Regarding how many points you need

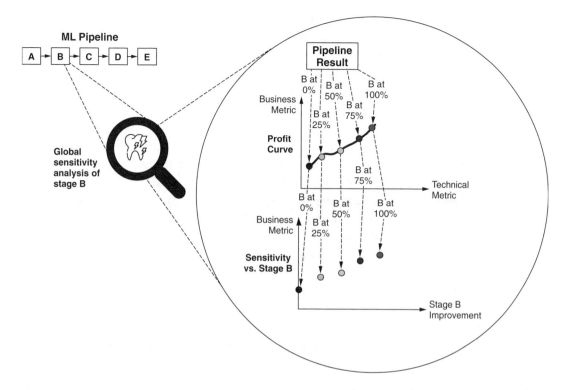

Figure 7.3 Global sensitivity analysis uses a wide range of values. You perform global sensitivity analysis when there's no reason to believe that only small improvements are possible in some stages of the pipeline (in other words, you believe drastic improvements are possible).

to perform the analysis, that's determined by how much effort you need to carry out the analysis per test point. The recommendation is to start with at least three points and use as many points as you can accommodate within the available time frame.

Once you've completed sensitivity analysis for every stage of your pipeline, you have data on how changes in individual stages of the pipeline can affect your business value. This data gives you a massive advantage over people who improve the output of their ML pipelines based on "experience and intuition."

7.1.3 Example of using sensitivity analysis results

Suppose you have the ML pipeline from figure 7.1, and a MinMax analysis has shown that you need to improve it further to reach your business goal. You have an estimate from the development team about how long it would take to improve each stage of the pipeline (and how much each stage could be improved). Those improvements would take significant time: something on the order of occupying a majority of the team for weeks to improve each stage. You want your product released soon, so you want to implement only the improvements for which the payoff is reasonable.

Let's suppose that the business metric is profit in dollars per unit, and you need an improvement of $3/unit to reach the value threshold. Also, assume you have the following results from the sensitivity analysis:

1   Stages A and B could be substantially improved. It was simple to simulate various improvements in them. However, after performing global sensitivity analysis, neither one of these stages significantly affects the results of the pipeline.

2   Stage C can be improved by only about 1–2%. It takes the engineer an hour of work to perform sensitivity analysis at a single point. The result of that analysis is that for every 1% improvement in stage C, based on local sensitivity analysis, the whole ML pipeline would improve by $10/unit/%.

3   Stage D also can be improved only slightly (1–2%), and it takes the whole team two days to perform analysis at a single point. Local sensitivity analysis at two points has shown that sensitivity for a 1% improvement in this stage is $.05/unit/%. The difficulty of improving stage D is comparable to that of improving stage C.

4   Stage E can't be improved at all beyond its current level. (It's just providing notifications.)

In this example, I would choose to improve stage C: it has high sensitivity and appears to be equally easy to upgrade as stage D. Most importantly, I believe that a reasonable and achievable amount of improvement in stage C would bring me to my business goal.

7.2   *We've completed CLUE*

As you learned in section 6.2, the combination of MinMax analysis and sensitivity analysis is how you *Economize* your scarce resources, which is the final *E* of CLUE. MinMax analysis tells you that you're working on the right ML pipeline. Sensitivity analysis helps you work on the right stage of that pipeline.

> **TIP** If you're a data scientist, you may have noticed recursion here. You can think about MinMax and sensitivity analysis as if you're using data science to predict how your ML pipeline would behave.

CLUE is an integrated process, and each one of its stages depends on the previous stage. Figure 7.4 shows the dependencies in CLUE.

The *Economize* part of CLUE uses the *Understand* part (in the form of a profit curve as shown in figure 4.4). The *Understand* part requires business and technical metrics to be *Linked*. Finally, you worked on the right business problem, which is where the *Consider* part of CLUE comes in.

> **NOTE** The end goal of the CLUE process is a reduction in regret down the road. CLUE organizes your AI project in a way that ties business and technology. CLUE prevents foreseeable waste, such as working on the wrong business problem or chasing technical solutions that can't deliver the anticipated business results.

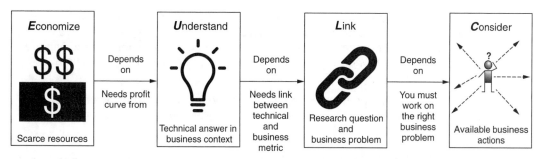

Figure 7.4 Dependencies between the parts of CLUE—subsequent stages depend on the correct implementation of the previous stages. Following CLUE enables you to work on the right business problem, choose the proper ML pipeline to solve that problem, and always work on improving the right stage of the pipeline.

At every point during the project, CLUE helps you to focus on making informed decisions based on the information that's cheap to collect but has a predictive power for the technical outcomes that are possible for your ML pipeline. It allows you to answer questions such as, "How likely is this ML pipeline to deliver acceptable business results?"

NOTE CLUE helps you to make decisions based on the best information that's either available at present or easy to collect quickly.

Even if you elect to use a different process other than CLUE, such a process must address the same problems that CLUE does: you must work on the right business problem, understand the results in business terms, and economize your resources based on the information you have (as opposed to gut feeling). If you fail to address any of these considerations, you're taking a chance with your project results.

In the absence of data, personalities take over!

Not using data to manage the development of your ML pipeline means that you're handling its development based on gut feeling or on how much you trust personalities in your team who are advocating for particular actions.

Remember that it's typical for few team members to understand the whole ML pipeline, but most team members only have an extensive understanding of the part of the pipeline they're personally working on. It's human nature for team members to be more comfortable advising on how to improve the part of the system they understand instead of the part they don't understand.

Adjudicating technical proposals in the area where you're missing technical expertise is the worst kind of situation for the manager to sort out. While advocating for their

(continued)

opinions, team members will present qualities of leadership, integrity, maturity, persuasion power, and expertise. Those qualities are genuine. *They're also entirely unrelated to what part of the ML pipeline might be the most productive stage to improve.* Deciding based on understanding people can put you on the wrong track here.

The gods of ML pipelines have a sense of humor. They will often assign the stage of the ML pipeline that's the most productive stage to improve to the least persuasive member of your team. Then those gods will happily let you live with the consequences.

The whole point of using a process like CLUE is to substitute the need for an intimate knowledge of AI algorithms and details of AI systems with a set of metrics that allows you to understand technical decisions in business terms. Remember the example of the factory manager from chapter 2? The manager who wasn't as good a factory worker as the shift foreman but still knew how to run the factory? That manager used data and management know-how to run the factory.

With the data CLUE provides, you can also use data and management skills to run your AI project. Applying CLUE offers a more scalable approach than asking managers to learn intricate details of AI and data engineering at the level that would be necessary if technical knowledge were the only tool you'd be using to adjudicate technical arguments.

Managers are human too

Naysayers may tell you that no matter what, you need an intimate understanding of AI to lead an AI project. I beg to differ, especially if those AI skills come at the expense of leadership skills.

Besides, if such naysayers are right, we'd never have a widespread AI revolution in many areas of business and industry. Do you believe that there are enough people who have the ability, time, persistence, and focus (and some of the other, less flattering qualities needed) to quickly get to a PhD level of understanding AI? Ah yes, those people are supposed to have also learned how to be good leaders. But AI is also improving rapidly, necessitating extensive and continuous technical education to stay current with it. After finding time to learn all of that, where would such people get the time to do the needed work?

We're asking for a combination of qualities that few people possess, and "let's teach the details of AI to managers" doesn't scale. On top of that, we need such managers not only in top technology companies, but in every field that's supposed to be applying AI in the next few years.

I don't think it's realistic to expect that we'd be able to teach the details of AI to as many leaders as we'd need to deliver that AI revolution. We need to find a way to lead AI projects that doesn't require significant AI expertise, or we won't have many successful AI projects.

Maybe there are managers who have a fantastic intuitive feel and work on projects in new areas for which there has been little opportunity for experience (such as is the current case with most AI projects). I'd let you take a guess as to how numerous such managers are. However, I'd say that for people who don't have such an intuitive feel, managing projects based on processes such as CLUE makes them better stewards of management and software architectural responsibilities than managing on gut feeling alone.

7.3 Advanced methods for sensitivity analysis

The previously introduced methods for pipeline analysis are quick to do and could help you learn early on if your pipeline is the right one to use long-term. I recommend that when you're starting with CLUE and AI, you use the sensitivity analysis methods described in section 7.1. However, as you get more proficient with sensitivity analysis, you might be interested in more precise (but also much more complicated) ways to perform sensitivity analysis. This section discusses those methods.

Complex topic ahead

This section describes advanced methods that require substantial process engineering experience to apply successfully. It's intended for advanced readers who already have a process engineering background or for teams that have already implemented CLUE and want to get better at it.

My goal is to teach you to recognize when you have a situation where these advanced methods might be needed, and give you just enough understanding of these methods so that you know what kind of help to ask for from the experts.

Sections 7.3.2 and 7.3.3 are the only parts of this book that I feel are relevant only for the large company with a significant investment in AI tools, technology, and infrastructure. You would need an expert in the area of process engineering to apply many of the topics described in these sections, and there's no way to learn that expertise from a single chapter or, for that matter, from a single book.

If you don't have the budget to afford such experts, I also include some references that will give you a head start on how to learn to do these things by yourself. To get the most from those references, you'll still need an engineering background (and much patience).

Once you've developed the initial ML pipeline and invested a lot of time and money into it, you may be willing to spend more time analyzing ways in which you can improve that pipeline. This is where the more advanced analysis methods are useful. In specific scenarios, those methods could provide better analytical results, albeit at the price of an increase in the complexity of the performed analysis. A roadmap through the rest of this section follows:

- Section 7.3.1 shows you how to detect the presence of nonlinearity.
- Section 7.3.2 talks about interactions in the ML pipeline.

- Section 7.3.3 introduces the concept of design of experiments, a technique that can discover and address interaction but requires significant process engineering knowledge to apply successfully.
- Section 7.3.4 addresses common critiques that you might encounter when performing sensitivity analysis.
- Section 7.3.5 advises on the best practices for improving your ML pipeline by enhancing the quality of your data.
- Section 7.3.6 presents the applicability of some recent advancements in the field of sensitivity analysis for ML pipelines.

There are two significant sources of errors in sensitivity analysis: nonlinearity [125, 126] and the interaction between pipeline stages. When you encounter nonlinearity, the results of your local sensitivity analysis are subject to error. When you meet interactions, changing two stages of the pipeline can result in significantly different behavior if you change them together rather than if you change one at a time. Let's look at each source briefly.

7.3.1   *Is local sensitivity analysis appropriate for your ML pipeline?*

Local sensitivity analysis, described in section 7.1.1, assumes that the response of the whole ML pipeline to the change in a single stage is linear: if a change of 0.5% in stage B produces a 1% improvement in the entire pipeline, then a 1% improvement in stage B would result in a 2% improvement in the ML pipeline. If the assumption of the linearity of the pipeline's response were violated, then your sensitivity analysis results would have an error in them. This section shows you how to detect when the assumption of linearity is broken. When that is the case, local sensitivity analysis isn't appropriate, and you should replace it with global sensitivity analysis.

Informally, a nonlinear response means that the output on the profit curve could change faster (or slower) than would happen if the response were linear. Figure 7.5 shows a situation in which the system's profit curve increases in nonlinear (superlinear or convex) fashion and, for a given percent increase in the performance of a single stage of the pipeline, you get more than that percent increase in the response on the profit curve.

Why does convexity of the response matter? Because, as you can see in figure 7.5 when you have a convex response, the farther away you move from the point at which you perform the analysis, the larger the error. In an extreme case, the error could be so significant as to invalidate the results of the analysis. You might even miss that the improvement in that stage of your ML pipeline would provide a considerable return. Such low-probability, high-impact events are commonly referred to in business circles as *black swans* [127].[1] So nonlinearity matters when the significant payoff is missed. Figure 7.6 shows a situation in which local sensitivity analysis misses the convexity.

---

[1] In Europe, it was believed for a long time that all swans were white, until someone traveled far enough to see a black swan. A single black swan, while rare, had a large impact on dispelling this theory.

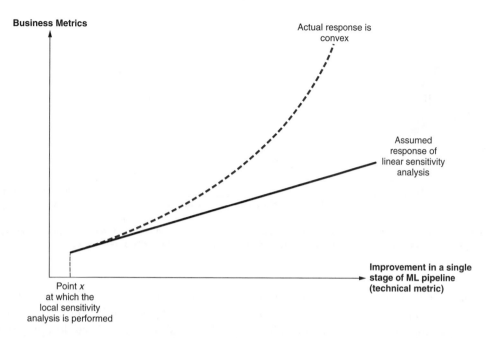

Figure 7.5 Convexity in the ML pipeline's response. The further you move away from the point at which analysis was performed, the more significant the error in your analysis. Never extrapolate far from the point from where your local sensitivity analysis was performed.

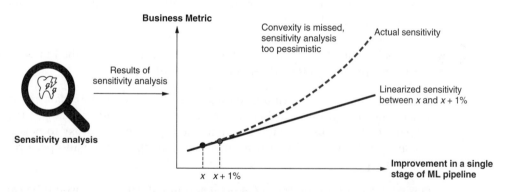

Figure 7.6 Sensitivity analysis with convexity present. Localized sensitivity analysis performed at only two points, *x* and *x* + 1%, has missed the convexity because you can always draw a line between two points.

There are heuristic techniques that you could use to show that you might be having a nonlinear response and that are particularly appropriate for situations in which nonlinearity is likely to highly skew the result. One heuristic consists of replacing local sensitivity analysis with performing global sensitivity analysis at three points and seeing

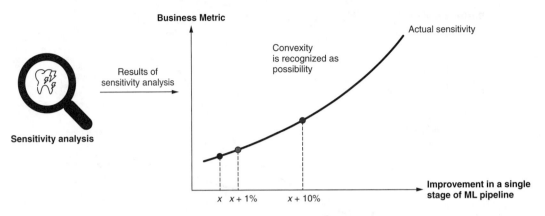

Figure 7.7   Global sensitivity analysis in the presence of convexity. At a price of the increased complexity of the analysis, global sensitivity analysis could detect the presence of nonlinearity of response.

whether the response is linear or if there are indications of convexity/concavity. Details of this technique are explained by Taleb et al. [126]. Figure 7.7 shows the application of that heuristic. Coincidentally, any global sensitivity analysis could apply the same technique (described in the Taleb et al. paper [126]) to detect the nonlinear response.

How much do the possible errors in the linear sensitivity analysis matter for your ML pipeline, and does the fact that linear sensitivity analysis could miss convexity mean that you should always perform global sensitivity analysis? I take a pragmatic view and remember that all project management decisions need to be made under time constraints. The key difference between local sensitivity analysis and global sensitivity analysis is that the former requires two points (such as x and $x + 1\%$) to perform, while global sensitivity analysis (and the heuristic approach described in Taleb et al.'s paper [126]) requires at least three points to complete.

> **TIP**   If I know that performing sensitivity analysis at one more data point is cheap and straightforward, I always perform global sensitivity analysis. If it's expensive (for example, when I have to use a human as a proxy to perform the analysis), I use local sensitivity analysis where appropriate and perform it at just two points.

If sensitivity analysis of the ML pipeline at additional data points would be expensive, the only situation in which I worry about convexity is when I don't have a clear winner after analyzing the rest of the pipeline. However, in such a case, I schedule improvement of the stage that has convexity in front of the stages that have a similar sensitivity analysis result but don't exhibit a convex response. That gives the (possibly) black swan a chance to work in my favor.

> **NOTE**   You shouldn't think about nonlinearity as a danger to your project. Convexity means that it would be easier to achieve a business goal than if the

sensitivity of the stage was linear. The impact of missing concavity during the sensitivity analysis is limited. Your project should be organized so that, "If you fail, fail fast." Therefore, if a stage improves slower than you expect it to, you find that out early and stop working on that stage.

7.3.2 *How to address the interactions between ML pipeline stages*

Sometimes, the result of changing two things at the same time is very different from changing them one at the time. That happens when there's an interaction between two variables. This section provides an example of interactions and advice on how to address them in the context of analysis of the ML pipeline.

One example of interaction is that when you buy a laptop, you care about both the weight of the laptop and the speed of the processor. The lighter laptop is always better, all other things being equal. The faster processor is always better, all other things being equal. However, if you put a speedy processor in a tiny (and light) laptop, the processor might start overheating, as there's not enough volume in the laptop for the processor to cool appropriately. Making a small but powerful laptop is also expensive. As a result, a tiny laptop with a mighty processor might not be worth building (or buying).

> ### What's the effect of the interactions?
>
> In the presence of interactions, an analysis that changes only a single variable at a time (such as the output of a single stage of the ML pipeline) can be invalid. Furthermore, you'll encounter statisticians and data scientists who would point out that the presence of interactions affects the results of MinMax and sensitivity analyses.
>
> That's true, but how is it relevant to the analysis your team could perform? You can perform interaction analysis only if your team knows how to perform interaction analysis. Even if interactions are present, if you don't know how to find them, you would have to accept the risk of interactions (and its effect on MinMax and sensitivity analysis).

My advice is that determining how much to care about interactions depends on the team you have. If your organization has significant knowledge of process engineering and the ability to quickly analyze the behavior of your ML pipeline at multiple points, then I would advise that you perform interaction analysis. In practice, that usually means a well-funded team in a large corporation working on a project in which a small change in the ML pipeline could provide a huge financial payoff.

For teams just starting with AI and sensitivity analysis, my advice is to not worry about interactions initially and concentrate on what happens with the ML pipeline when you change only one factor at a time. Two Six Sigma resources from ASQ [21,22] give some starting points on the process and a profile of people who have good experience in designing experiments for detecting interactions, which brings us to the broader topic of the design of experiments ([24]).

7.3.3   *Should I use design of experiments?*

Design of experiments (DOE) [24] is a methodology that has been successfully used in the area of process engineering for decades to improve quality, cost, and the efficiency of processes such as manufacturing physical objects. When you have a factory line costing millions of dollars to run, you want to know that it's running optimally. DOE is about conducting experiments, the results of which show you how to improve your factory line. This section introduces you to DOE and advises when DOE is applicable to an AI project.

Historically, software development didn't use DOE much. Some reasons for that are that DOE is a complex topic that's unfamiliar to software engineers. More importantly, instead of DOE, the cost of implementing a pseudo-experiment ("let's just try it and see what happens") was small in terms of software; for example, it was easy to change a configuration parameter to see how your database reacted.

> **NOTE**   Pseudo-experiments have many weaknesses. For example, they could miss interactions. Also, they're sensitive to background processes; if a background process runs at an inconvenient time, it can impact the results of your pseudo-experiment. Unlike pseudo-experiments, a proper experiment conducted under the DOE methodology would provide correct answers even in the presence of interactions and background processes.

With recent AI projects, the cost of "just trying something" has drastically increased. It's not unheard of that a large project in a large corporation might use hundreds of machines to train some complicated AI algorithms [128]. Running such a system costs a lot of money, and, as the price of hardware infrastructure starts rivaling the cost of running a factory, the methods used for running the factory may become relevant for software engineers too.

DOE allows for many advantages compared to pseudo-experiments. Using DOE enables you to better manage an expensive ML pipeline development.

So should you use DOE on your project? For most AI projects, I don't recommend DOE because it's complicated to perform right and requires experts with specialized training to implement it correctly. The cost of the experiments (and those experts) is too high to justify this approach on an average AI project today. Furthermore, if you've never thought about the management of your ML pipeline systematically, the methods already presented in this book would be a huge step forward.

> **NOTE**   If you look at the history of how the field of process engineering developed, it also started with simple experiments and built DOE theory and knowledge later.

However, if you're running a massive AI operation, and your capital investment in the team, hardware, and infrastructure rivals the cost of running a factory, and if the results of every decision you make regarding the management of your ML pipeline are of correspondingly high stakes, I'd reverse that recommendation. Instead, my advice would be to work with an expert who knows both AI and process engineering. Such an expert can advise you on a case-by-case basis about what's right for your system. You're already spending so much money on running your system that you should design experiments in it properly.

7.3.4 *One common objection you might encounter*

This section is about a criticism that you're likely to face and why that criticism is both correct and mostly irrelevant for the practical use case of ML pipeline analysis. The criticism is that it's possible to construct an example in which sensitivity analysis would indicate results that, while useful, aren't the best possible result.

Let's look at an example. Suppose you have a situation in which you performed global sensitivity analysis at five points, and there's an unusual situation in which interactions have caused the sensitivity curve in figure 7.8.

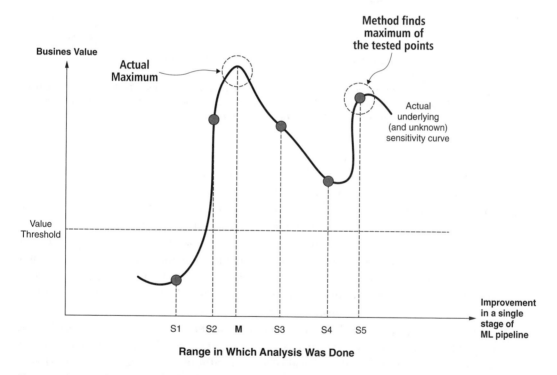

Figure 7.8 Sensitivity analysis performed in locations S1–S5 but missing the actual maximum at point M. It doesn't matter; you're above the value threshold, so you're still making money. No cheap analysis performed on only a few points can avoid this problem.

In figure 7.8, you've performed the analysis at five points, S1–S5. The best result that you got is the maximum of the five points you looked at (S5). However, it's not the absolute maximum of the underlying function, which is the location *M*.

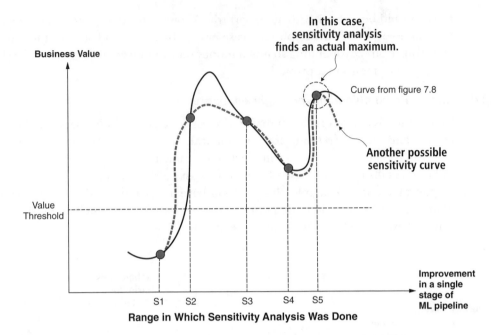

In this case, sensitivity analysis finds an actual maximum.

Business Value

Curve from figure 7.8

Another possible sensitivity curve

Value Threshold

Improvement in a single stage of ML pipeline

S1   S2   S3   S4   S5

Range in Which Sensitivity Analysis Was Done

Figure 7.9 If the underlying curve has a shape given in this figure (as opposed to figure 7.8), sensitivity analysis will find the actual maximum. You never know the shape of the underlying curve, so it doesn't matter what the maximum of that curve is. What matters is that you're above the value threshold.

While the previous example looks convincing, think again. In practice, do you have access to the "truth," represented as the actual underlying sensitivity curve in figure 7.8? No, you don't! That real sensitivity is unknown and unavailable to your project; all you have is the result of sensitivity analysis in points S1–S5. The underlying sensitivity curve stays hidden and might as well have been the curve in figure 7.9.

I could construct many counterexamples, but these have one thing in common: the criticism I mentioned assumes that you already know the whole shape of the curve in figure 7.8! In practice, you never have access to the underlying sensitivity curve. If you did, you wouldn't wonder about the stage in which to invest in the first place, you'd just read it from the sensitivity curve.

Which brings us to the difference between mathematical theory, which is what the original objection in this section was based on, and practical project management. The objection raised is a theoretical objection without any actual advice on what to do. While critics can point to some methods that could find a max value of the underlying curve, when you ask for details, you'd learn that such methods would require performing sensitivity analysis at many points. The number of points at which you analyze is a determinant of the cost of analysis, so such methods are often too expensive to be practical for guiding improvement decisions in an ML pipeline.

Practical people need solutions, and in this case, the answer is recognizing that you're already familiar with the problem. It's the same problem as if I ask you, "So, what's the maximum amount of money you could have made in life?" Well, maybe if you were introduced to the right people, you might have founded a company more prosperous than Google is today, but you'd never know. You don't know the "income sensitivity" curve of your life that answers that question.

> **NOTE** In life, you never know if you've made as much money as it was possible to make. The only thing you know is if you made enough money to live comfortably or not.

Like with life, with a project the question isn't "What's the maximum value of the curve?" Remember, you're on a rich hunting ground (section 3.1.1), and you want to make sure that the AI project you invested in is profitable. You also need to decide based on the best information available *at the time when you must make an investment decision.* If sensitivity analysis doesn't find the maximum value but still allows for constructing a profitable pipeline, that's called success in the business.

> **NOTE** It's *rare* that you encounter an ML pipeline in which sensitivity analysis would miss so many profitable areas that you'd be stuck and unable to improve it.[2] It's even rarer that an ML pipeline in which that happens is easy to bring to profitability. Such a rare pipeline isn't a rabbit that's easy to hunt, and you're on the rich hunting ground. Try something else.

Sensitivity analysis involves maximizing the information available to you at present and allows you to determine if the next action you take is profitable or not. That's all you need to run a successful AI project.

What about unsupervised learning?

You may be asked if sensitivity analysis (as well as MinMax analysis) is only applicable to supervised learning. The answer is that it's relevant to any type of AI because you can always construct a profit curve for unsupervised learning too.

Suppose that your product is analyzing data and creating clusters from this data. Afterward, the clusters are presented to humans, who use them as one of the inputs to a decision that needs to be made under a considerable time constraint. An example of that would be a system that uses AI to cluster types of fault in a complex transportation system.

In such a situation, the more clusters you present (and the more difficult it is to see what's common in each cluster), the less value the system has for the user. Clearly, there's a relationship between the output of a system and the value to the user. It may happen that you'd have to perform an experiment with the help of actual users to determine the value to the user. The results of that experiment can be described in the form of a profit curve.

---

[2] You'd have to encounter such a situation not only in a single stage of the ML pipeline you're analyzing, but in multiple stages at the same time.

7.3.5   *How to analyze the stage that produces data*

Some of the stages in your pipeline are likely to be operations with the data, and every AI algorithm you use would take data as an input. You can typically improve the quality of such input data. This section provides advice on how to analyze how data improvement affects your ML pipeline.

Your goal when conducting global sensitivity analysis or the Max portion of a MinMax analysis should be to get the best data you can. Here, the best is across all dimensions—larger dataset, better-targeted data, cleaner dataset.

> **NOTE**   If you're building an AI-powered physical device, such as a camera, better might mean having a superior sensor in it. If you have a problem with a fuzzy picture, can you get a better camera? If you have a problem with obstructions, can you get more cameras?

It's often the case that better data could beat the better AI algorithm [129], so checking what happens when you have cleaner data is essential.

How to clean all that data?

An issue sometimes arises in the big data space: how do you measure what the impact of getting cleaner data would be if your data volume is substantial? It's not like you can ask humans to clean 1 PB manually! Moreover, while you may launch a project to clean 1 PB of data, by the time you get the answer, you've also spent a ton of time and money to do so, so the economic value of that information is low.

Fortunately, there's a simple solution: collapse two stages of the pipeline into one. Suppose that one stage of the pipeline ingests image data and another applies object recognition based on deep learning to those images. It's exceedingly difficult to answer the question, "What would be the result of applying this deep learning network architecture if I had perfectly clean image data?" So trying to improve the ingestion phase is difficult.

However, it's much simpler to answer the question, "What's the best result that we can achieve with image recognition if we look at the data and algorithm together?" You simply look at the best vision recognition results achieved so far on any dataset. By collapsing two stages of the ML pipeline into one (data ingestion and recognition), you've transformed a complex question into a simple one.

7.3.6   *What types of sensitivity analysis apply to my project?*

Sensitivity analysis is a complex topic and an area of active research in the computer science community (for example, see *Global Sensitivity Analysis: The Primer* [117]). You're likely to be interested in how some of the latest research can help you perform better sensitivity analysis. This section presents the criteria you should use to determine its applicability for your project.

The most important question that you should ask when presented with any research in sensitivity analysis is, "How much work would it be to apply this method?" Only the methods that are easy to implement (compared to the total size of your project) have a practical value for project management of the ML pipeline.

TIP If your analysis is so complex that performing it costs you as much as building the ML pipeline, you might as well just build the pipeline and see what happens.

The largest source of cost in ML pipeline analysis is the number of points at which the analysis needs to be performed. Consequently, global sensitivity analysis techniques that require analyzing thousands of points are far less applicable (especially for an AI team with limited experience in process engineering) than the methods described in section 7.1.

A handy trick

While it can be difficult to make data or results *better*, it's often straightforward to make them *worse* by introducing errors into them. The trick is that instead of making the result of the ML pipeline's stage 1% better and analyzing at the points x and $x + 1\%$, you make the result 1% worse and analyze at the points $x - 1\%$ and $x\%$. If you use this trick, you're assuming that the behavior of your pipeline is as similar when the output of a stage slightly improves as it would be if the output slightly declined.

Suppose that you're conducting global sensitivity analysis at points 33%, 66%, and 100%. Once you complete analysis at 100%, you could purposely corrupt the output data of that stage to perform analysis at points 33% and 66%.

The same trick applies to local sensitivity analysis. If your pipeline is already producing results in a stage that are, for example, 95% accurate, don't conduct sensitivity analysis at points 95% and 96%. Instead, perform it at 94% and 95%. It's far easier to introduce an error in the outputs of your current stage than it is to improve it.

You could use this same trick to adapt sensitivity analysis methods that require evaluation at thousands of points to an analysis of an ML pipeline as you construct the results for a single point (the very best point), and then degrade those results to simulate other points.

However, be advised that the technique presented in this sidebar has subtleties and traps that are easy to fall into. Errors you introduce in the output aren't just random errors. They must have similar statistical properties as the errors that the actual implementation of a stage in the ML pipeline would have. You need experts to avoid this trap.

My advice is that you shouldn't attempt this technique until you have people on staff who have significant experience with sensitivity analysis, process engineering, and analysis of statistical distributions.

7.4   *How your AI project evolves through time*

The techniques of MinMax and sensitivity analysis presented so far were focused on AI projects that would be delivered fast. All other things equal, you should prefer projects that can be delivered to your real customers quickly [28], and that's especially the case with your initial AI projects. However, once delivered, that AI project could be in the market for a long time. Furthermore, sometimes your AI project is breaking new ground, and it simply takes a long time to deliver it to the market. This section shows how you should modify methods presented so far when you're leading long-running AI projects.

Section 7.4.1 discusses how time affects your project. Section 7.4.2 shows you how to modify the Understand part of CLUE to account for the influence of time in long projects. Section 7.4.3 shows you how to diagram a change in the business value of the project through time.

7.4.1   *Time affects your business results*

In managing a project, we often focus on the sequence of steps we need to execute to succeed. We think about time in the form of the project deadline, and we think about deadlines as a responsibility of engineering. This section shows you a different way of thinking about time so that you can consider together the engineering and management decisions that affect your project.

In many projects, time becomes an afterthought that's present only as a deadline. The management and engineering teams negotiate the deadlines. Once settled, deadlines become the problem of project managers and engineering. That results in a divorce between the impact of time on the value of what's delivered and the technical management of the AI project. Engineering focuses on not missing deadlines. Management concentrates on making contingency plans if deadlines are missed, and it might occasionally surprise engineering with the request for a new feature. Instead of integrating technical decision-making with the business results, the relationship between teams becomes detached, if not outright politely adversarial.

A better way to address the time dimension is by including a time to complete the project directly in the metrics that you're managing and optimizing. If the time needed to complete the project matters, you should be able to quantify at least a range of how much it matters. Once you quantify the influence of time on your project, you can incorporate time in the profit curve.

> **TIP** If you can't quantify precisely, use estimates. See D. W. Hubbard's book [75] for ways to quantify "intangibles" in the business.

The value of the project (and the value threshold it should meet) changes over time. For example, AI capable of indexing and searching the internet had immense business value in 1998 (before Google). Today, the value of such AI is much smaller. Both the profit curve and the value threshold of your project, therefore, evolve over time.

Those variations become significant when you're talking about more extended periods, such as successful AI projects that could be on the market for many years.

If a project faces a range of delivery dates, you shouldn't use a single profit curve for the whole duration of the project. You should have multiple profit curves that reflect the changes in the business value at various times. Figure 7.10 shows a set of profit curves for a project running for two years.

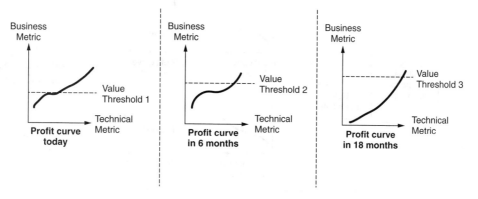

Figure 7.10   A set of profit curves for a long-running AI project. Both the shape of the profit curve and especially the value threshold change with time.

You should manage the ML pipeline with time in mind. Even an approach as simple as "if done before June 1, accuracy x is worth $\$y$; if done later, it's worth $\$z$," when applied to the profit curve, would give you a quick way to address the time dimension.

> **WARNING**   A deadline is at best an imperfect way to account for time. An Agile process by itself doesn't address such a dynamic of deadlines; it only enforces more common checkpoints between engineering and business teams. Even on Agile projects, you must purposely focus on the longer term implications of the ML pipelines you're choosing.

7.4.2   Improving the ML pipeline over time

At some point, you'll deal with much longer AI projects. Those projects could last for an extended period, and, as seen in section 7.4.1, the profit curve can change as time passes.

> **WARNING**   On a longer project, the profit curve typically shifts over time to account for the opportunity cost of a delay. You must account for that shift when evaluating the business value of the project.

To account for that change, you estimate how long it would take to deliver an improvement in a stage of the delivery pipeline, and then you use the appropriate

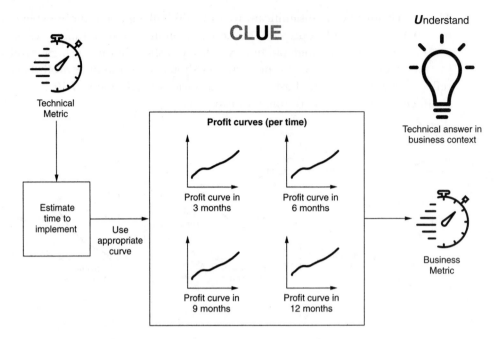

Figure 7.11   Modification of the U̲nderstand part of CLUE to account for long delivery times. The project value changes with the time it takes to deliver it. You must use the profit curve corresponding to the time when you would release software to calculate the value of the improvement.

profit curve that reflects the value the improvement would have *at the time the AI project is released* (as opposed to today). Figure 7.11 describes this process.

Once you account for the influence time has on your profit curve, the scheduling of the improvement in your pipeline is simple. You schedule the stages in the ML pipeline to be improved in the order that allows you to reach the value threshold as soon as possible and to stay above the value threshold as the project is progressing.

> **NOTE**   Just like the value of the improvement of a stage in the ML pipeline changes with time, so does the value threshold. For example, your value threshold could be $5/unit in the first six months, and then decline to $4/unit. Don't forget to account for the changes in the value threshold when building your schedule.

7.4.3   *Timing diagrams: How business value changes over time*

On longer projects, the business value of the project changes over time as well. You can represent the change of business value over time with the help of a *timing diagram.* This section gives an example of constructing such a diagram.

This example assumes that the value threshold is based on the value of your AI product to your end user and is expressed in the profit your end user makes per unit.

I would also assume that you're trying to capture a rapidly expanding market that's expected to have a high lifetime value for the company that establishes the standard solution. Therefore, the goal of your corporation is market presence. Your goal is to release a viable product as soon as possible, and to keep it continuously viable, not worrying about profit in the next 24 months. Corporate leadership expects that profit will come later, when your product is established as a standard.

Let's look at a scenario in which a change in the value thresholds over time is given in table 7.1. You can extract that information by applying the process shown in figure 7.11.

Table 7.1   Values of stage improvements for your end user

Stage name	Improvement value today	Improvement value in 6 months	Improvement value in 12 months	The time needed to complete stage improvement
A	$7	$4	$3	2 months
B	$30	$27	$21	11 months
C	$14	$10	$7	3 months
D	$10	$8	$6	6 months

The value and time needed to improve a pipeline stage are given in table 7.2. You can construct the value threshold change by reading the value thresholds from the corresponding profit curves in figure 7.12.

Table 7.2   The value threshold the unit has for your customer. You must exceed the value threshold for a customer to buy your product.

Value threshold now	Value threshold in 6 months	Value threshold in 12 months
$5/unit	$14/unit	$15/unit

Figure 7.12 shows the timing diagram of the value that your ML pipeline is expected to have for the end user. Note that there are two reasons why the business value of the ML pipeline changes: improvement in the stage of the ML pipeline and the passage of time. Increases in the pipeline utility at 2, 5, 11, and 23 months are caused by completing improvements in stages A, C, D, and B. Dips at 6 and 12 months are caused by the passage of time as the business value of the improvements in your pipeline stages decline.

A timing diagram allows you to determine what's expected for the value of your ML pipeline at every point in the future. That information helps you answer the question of in which order you should improve your pipeline stages if you have a long-running project.

This technique is useful both in the early stages of the project, when you're choosing the best ML pipeline for your research question, and when you need to manage the development of a new ML pipeline that would replace the current ML pipeline in

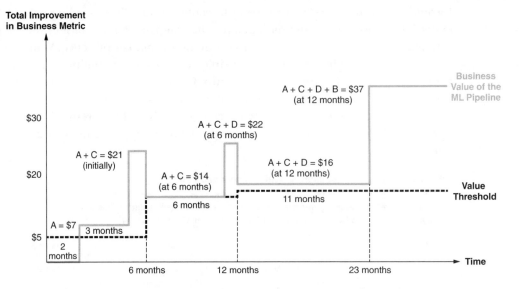

Figure 7.12   Improving the ML pipeline accounting for the time parameters given in tables 7.1 and 7.2. The order of improvement of the ML pipeline stages should be first stage A, then stage C, then stage D, and finally stage B. That order allows you to release a viable product after only two months.

your project. In the latter case, you could use a diagram like the one in figure 7.12 to tell you how to manage incremental improvements that you want to make in the old ML pipeline and estimate the point when you could expect that a new pipeline would be able to take over the job of the old pipeline.

7.5   Concluding your AI project

Managing projects requires many estimates, such as how long some functionality would take to implement, how complicated some AI algorithms would be to apply, and how much business value implementation would provide. Sometimes, everything happens as estimated and planned. Other times, reality refuses to comply with our wishes, and we find that estimates don't work out. This section shows you what to do when the problem is much more complicated to solve than you initially thought it would be.

Today, if you're running your initial AI projects, your team is likely to be the first team in your company to use powerful AI techniques to address your business problems. This also means that if the project proves to be challenging to complete, your initial estimate of its complexity, although correct in the light of what you knew then, will need to be modified based on what you've learned now. Instead of continuing a project that's difficult to implement, you should pause it and try something simpler.

On early AI projects, you're on the rich hunting grounds, and you should think like a hunter (section 3.1.1)—don't spend time chasing mammoths, catch rabbits instead. If you're hunting for a while and figure out that an animal you're following is a mammoth that's quite good at camouflaging itself as a rabbit, you should abandon the chase and find a rabbit.

If you're going to fail, fail fast

Your project management approach should be biased toward failing fast. You should make the tradeoff of accepting the possibility of giving up too early and missing a potential solution if that means you'll avoid situations in which you're stuck for a long time on something that doesn't work in the end.

Remember that the primary way AI initiatives die is that they persist in problematic projects for far too long and have nothing to show for it at the end (section 3.1.1).

You should always *timebox* how long to allow your AI project to proceed before you pull the plug if you encounter difficulties. If research questions turn out to be much more difficult to implement than initially estimated, you shouldn't persevere in pursuing the answers. Instead, pause the current project and start working on more straightforward research questions instead.

With this approach, you're trading the possibility of putting on hold a project that potentially could result in a functional solution (but could also finish as a considerable time waster with nothing to show for it) to try more straightforward projects first. However, when using this technique, it's vital to understand what you found when you put the research question on hold. *You've decided to put that research question on hold; you haven't found that there's no business value in pursuing that research question further.*

Unfortunately, organizations often have a habit of classifying results of research projects as binary categories—"yes/no," "works/doesn't work." To correctly use the timebox approach, you need to understand that the initial analysis of research questions has three possible results:

1 *Yes*—This approach is worth pursuing further. We should put many resources into it.

2 *No*—We've tried enough things to be confident that this is the wrong approach, and it's not expected to work. Don't put any additional resources into it.

3 *Maybe*—With the time we put into the *initial* investigation, we were unable to show that this approach works. However, we didn't investigate this long enough to know that it won't work even if we try harder. If we have more money and time later, we should revisit this problem.

NOTE It's crucial that your results be reported and tracked in the three-state logical form of yes/no/maybe. That's because you'd never reopen questions answered with "no" but might resume questions answered with "maybe" at a later date. Correctly making this distinction is the only way the "be willing to abandon difficult projects early" approach works.

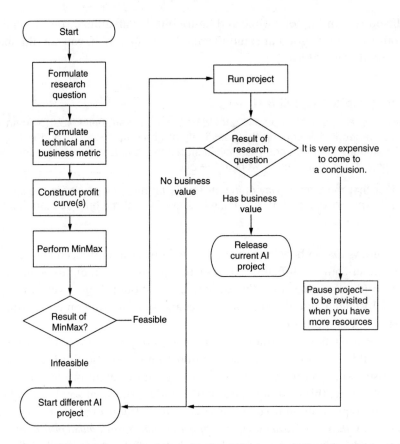

Figure 7.13   Running an AI project with the ability to put challenging projects on hold. This approach allows you to quickly cut your losses on projects that prove to be more difficult than anticipated and, instead, allows you to try a more straightforward project.

Down the road, when you have a successful solution that you're looking to improve later with more resources, you might decide that some of the maybes are worth a second look. Figure 7.13 summarizes the process of running a project using this three-state, yes/no/maybe classification of results.

7.6   *Exercises*

The questions in these exercises refer to the ML pipeline in figure 7.14, which is a reproduction of figure 6.10 (and figure 7.1).

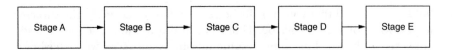

Figure 7.14   An example of an ML pipeline. We will perform sensitivity analysis of this pipeline. (This is a repeat of figure 6.10 for the reader's convenience.)

Question 1: This question gives you the results of the sensitivity analysis for the pipeline in figure 7.14. Assume that the business metric is profit and the value threshold is $2 million/year. The results of your MinMax analysis are the Min part being $1.9 million/year and the Max part being $3 million/year. You decide to perform a sensitivity analysis. Why is it necessary to perform the sensitivity analysis? You've worked on all the stages for a while, and you've reached a point where it's more and more challenging to improve any of the stages. Determine in which stage of the pipeline you should invest if the results of the sensitivity analysis are as follows:

- Stage A would require 6 months to improve by 1%. When you improve stage A, the overall improvement in the ML pipeline will be $10 K/%.
- Stage B would require 2 months to improve by 1%. When you improve stage B, the overall improvement in the ML pipeline will be $200 K/%.
- Stage C would require 1 year to improve by 1%. When you improve stage C, the overall improvement in the ML pipeline will be $800 K/%.
- The ML pipeline doesn't show any appreciable improvement in results when stages D and E are improved. When does such a situation occur in practice?

Question 2: This question gives you the results of the sensitivity analysis for the pipeline in figure 7.14. Assume that the business metric is profit and the value threshold is $2 million/year. The results of your MinMax analysis are the Min part being $1.9 million/year and the Max part being $3 million/year. You decide to perform a sensitivity analysis. You haven't constructed any prototype or tried to clean the data. Determine in which stage of the pipeline you should invest if the results of the sensitivity analysis are as follows:

- Stage A would require 3 months to improve by 2%. When you improve stage A, the overall improvement in the ML pipeline will be $200 K/%.
- Stage B would require 2 months to improve by 1%. When you improve stage B, the overall improvement in the ML pipeline will be $100 K/%.
- Stage C would require 1 year to improve by 1%. When you improve stage C, the overall improvement in the ML pipeline will be $800 K/%.
- The ML pipeline doesn't show any appreciable improvement in results when stages D and E are improved.

Question 3: Your AI project is investigating if, by installing an IoT sensor to monitor a vehicle's sound, you'd be able to determine what kinds of changes in tone would indicate a mechanical problem in the vehicle. You've deployed a sensor in 150 vehicles and waited for a month. Only a single vehicle had a mechanical problem. After the month-long investigation, your data scientists tell you that from the data collected, they can't predict breakage of the vehicles, and that a single broken vehicle is an insufficient dataset. Does this mean you can't make an AI that can predict vehicle breakage?

Question 4: Suppose you have two ML pipelines. Your business metric is revenue. The value threshold is constant at \$10 million/year. You have two parallel teams that could work on both ML pipelines. Pipeline 1 would deliver \$20 million/year, and pipeline 2 would provide \$30 million/year. The cost of the team to develop the pipeline is small compared to the lifetime profit expected from the AI project. Your organization can implement pipeline 1 in 4 months and pipeline 2 in 1 year. Determine which of the two pipelines you should release, and when. Also, draw a timing diagram showing these two pipelines.

Summary

- Sensitivity analysis answers the question, "In which stage of my ML pipeline should I invest?" There are two forms of sensitivity analysis: local sensitivity analysis and global sensitivity analysis.
- Local sensitivity analysis is applicable when you believe you can improve a stage of the ML pipeline only a little.
- You should perform global sensitivity analysis when you think that a stage in the pipeline could be significantly improved.
- CLUE is an integrated process that addresses important considerations of managing an AI project. Each part of the CLUE process depends on the previous sections of CLUE, so you must perform the *C*, *L*, *U*, and *E* in order. To make informed decisions based on data, you need a process such as CLUE.
- On a long-running project, the business value of your solution changes with time, so you'd need to construct multiple profit curves to account for value at different times. You can use timing diagrams to visualize how the business value of your ML pipelines evolves over time.
- The answer to your research question isn't limited to yes/no. It could also be, "Unknown at this time with the resources we can devote to answering the question." Don't be afraid to put such a project on hold and revisit it at a later date.

AI trends that may affect you

We're close to completing our journey through this book. You've learned how to select a business problem that can be solved with AI and how to run a successful AI project. A series of successful projects allows you to build an AI organization that's instrumental for the success of your business.

As your organization matures, you'll have to incorporate new developments that inevitably arise over time. This chapter highlights upcoming trends in the field of

AI that are likely to affect your future projects. Here's the organization of the rest of this chapter:

- Section 8.1 shows the evolution of the term *AI*.
- Section 8.2 provides some considerations when AI is used to run physical systems.
- Section 8.3 explains why most AI systems today don't make decisions based on causal relationships but only on whether events occur in close proximity.
- Section 8.4 highlights why most AI algorithms in use today weren't designed to combine data sources with differing levels of veracity.
- Section 8.5 keeps you out of trouble by showing you how an AI system's mistakes are fundamentally different from human errors.
- Section 8.6 discusses AutoML—the point where automation meets AI system construction.
- Section 8.7 generalizes what you've learned about AI and its relationship to other fields of business.
- Section 8.8 summarizes humans' role in guiding AI systems to business success.

8.1   *What is AI?*

The concept of AI and what AI is continues to evolve. In this section, I discuss "What is AI?" and present some of the current answers. Now, why did I leave this question until the very end of the book? Why not just insert a figure (like figure 8.1) that you've likely seen?

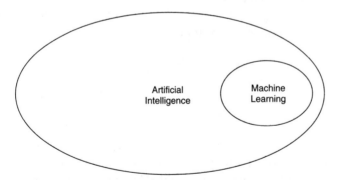

Figure 8.1   AI versus machine learning (ML). As you can see, AI is a superset of ML.

The answer to that question is that figure 8.1, while technically correct, doesn't tell the whole story about AI. Currently, AI is often used as a marketing term. And from the perspective of marketing and funding, it has been beneficial over the last couple of years for your product to align with AI.

NOTE Sometimes a connection between AI and a company's product is drawn even when that connection is tenuous at best. One survey [130] found that approximately 40% of the companies in Europe that are classified as AI startups don't use AI in any way that's material to that company's value proposition!

How can a company boast a connection with AI even if it's not creating much with AI? One reason is that a multiplicity of definitions for AI are floating around. No single definition has won universal acceptance. I'll present some statements often heard about AI and then let you make up your own mind on how compatible these definitions are.

- One definition given by the Wikimedia Foundation [131] (and having its origin in the book *Computational Intelligence: A Logical Approach* [132]) is

  "Computer science defines AI research as the study of 'intelligent agents': any device that perceives its environment and takes actions that maximize its chance of successfully achieving its goals."

- Another definition is from Kaplan and Haenlein [133]:

  "Artificial intelligence (AI)—defined as a system's ability to correctly interpret external data, to learn from such data, and to use those learnings to achieve specific goals and tasks through flexible adaptation . . . ."

- In this book, I've used the definition that "AI solves problems that historically could only be solved by a human."

Sometimes, once a problem that was previously considered AI is solved, that issue is no longer perceived to be part of AI—a phenomenon called the *AI Effect* [134]. An example would be chess. In 1997, a computer won a chess match against a world champion [135]. Today few people consider the ability of computers to defeat chess champions to be a part of advanced AI.

There are also many viewpoints on the relationship between AI and ML. Here are some of those views, none of which is universally accepted as *correct*:

- AI is a broader field than ML. While ML involves working with algorithms, just as AI does, AI is also heavily used with robotics [136].
- AI deals with more modern algorithms and techniques than classical ML. Based on that idea, newer technologies (such as deep learning), when applied to visual recognition or natural language processing tasks, are considered part of AI.

The relationship between AI and ML continues to change over time, and, as you can see, there's no universally accepted definition of AI. Depending on what year we're in, when we declare that some technique is part of AI or is no longer part of AI, AI's meaning changes. I expect that what's considered a part of AI will continuously be in flux.

NOTE The question "Is this part of AI?" is academic. For business purposes, the relevant question is: "What business benefits can I attain by using these methods?"

8.2   *AI in physical systems*

When AI is used as a part of a larger physical structure, considerations arise that are absent in a pure software system. Those considerations are that AI could cause physical harm and that collecting data for training and improving AI needs to be done differently than when you have a nonphysical system. This section elaborates on those considerations.

For example, AI is applied in physical systems to autonomous vehicles [38] and the Internet of Things (IoT) [46]. Companies ranging from Google to Tesla and Uber have autonomous driving projects. Autonomous cars aren't possible without AI, and a fully autonomous vehicle requires capabilities superior to what AI can provide today. AI is also used to analyze data harvested from IoT devices (an example being smart thermostats such as Nest [36]). Let's take a look at some of the related concerns.

8.2.1   *First, do no harm*

When you're controlling heavy metal objects moving with substantial speed, it's imperative to keep people safe—humans are vulnerable in collisions with metal objects. As AI becomes more widely used, the diversity of those heavy metal objects will increase. Today we mostly talk about robots and cars [38], but it's possible that in the future those objects could include ships, planes, buildings, and drones.[1] When using AI in any of these examples, you must address safety.

Unfortunately, most of the current AI algorithms don't inherently guarantee safety. Quite the contrary! During training, most of the widely used AI algorithms will attempt any action that the system under their control can take. Only after "seeing" the result of that action (which can be harmful), will the AI algorithm try to adjust its behavior. Even then, there are significant limitations on how much the algorithm can change.

While the previous approach might be acceptable if you're building an AI for research purposes (such as an AI that learns to play old computer games better than a human [137]), such cavalier treatment of human safety doesn't work when applied to autonomous vehicles. You can't let an autonomous car learn to drive by letting it drive in the physical world and drive itself right off a cliff—or worse!

Local vs. global models

One taxonomy of AI methods divides models between those that are global versus those that are local. In the global models, there's a limited capacity to instruct the algorithm to change the results for only a single input without affecting the results for other inputs (more on global models in section 8.5). You can't say to the algorithm, "Only for this particular picture, that's a child (who happens to be in a funny costume), but don't change the result for any other picture!" But in the case of local

---

[1]   There's nothing magical about metal objects. The need to keep people separate from objects remains even when those items are made of carbon fiber.

models, it's possible to change the response of a single input without affecting the results for the other inputs.

Many methods used in AI today are global methods. If you're classifying pictures on the web, this rarely matters. However, if safety is critical in your problem domain, this is a massive problem. You don't have an effective way to prevent a global model that *mostly* works from performing a few harmful actions.

Building safe AI systems is an area of active research, and there's no simple, universally applicable approach that makes the use of AI safe in *all* physical systems. That's why it costs a fortune to create AI for safe self-driving vehicles. Although there's no simple set of rules that you can use to ensure the safety of AI-controlled physical systems, this set of heuristics can help:

- Always start an AI project analysis with the Sense/Analyze/React loop (chapter 3), because it forces you to start with enumerating the possible actions that the physical system controlled by AI can take.

- You need a simulator of the physical environment that AI is in. You can't train AI algorithms by unleashing a few AI-powered vehicles on the unsuspecting public! The simulator allows you to train the algorithms in an environment in which the training errors that the AI system makes aren't catastrophic.

  Simulators are typically challenging to build and have a substantial cost. The design of such a simulator (and its cost) should be addressed early in the project. It's not unheard of that a simulator is more complicated and costly to develop than the rest of the AI algorithm.

- Whenever possible, limit the AI system to a small set of actions that are easy to manually review for safety. A typical example of an AI system with a small set of actions is a control system for an AI-powered oven: it can turn heaters on and off, change the heating element temperature, and turn the convection fan on and off.

- A global AI model is almost never self-sufficient. To ensure safety, you *must* be able to guarantee that whichever action is determined to be harmful will never be taken.

  By their nature, global methods don't allow you to change the outcome for only one scenario. In a global model, the moment you modify the result of an individual situation, the whole model changes, possibly introducing different harmful conditions.

  Unfortunately, many of the most influential models we use in AI today (such as deep learning models) are global models. Therefore, you may need to combine a global model with a method that can restrict undesirable actions. One way to do that is by using a rule engine to compare the output of the system to a list of prohibited actions [138].

While all the methods advised in the previous chapters of this book are fully applicable to physical systems using AI, they can't, themselves, guarantee that the system is *safe*. Safety must be ensured using human judgment, knowledge, and experience.

> **NOTE** An AI-powered physical system operates best in a simple environment with simple actions. If the system looks "boring" because all of the actions it takes are easy, that's perfect. Do you want the car you're a passenger in to be *creative?*

A physical system using AI is a physical system first and an AI system second. Such physical systems must be designed with safety and reliability guidelines appropriate for their field of use. (For example, an autonomous car falls under the rules and regulations of automotive engineering.) When it comes to designing safe systems, domain experts with safety and systems engineering backgrounds have the last word for the foreseeable future.

AI isn't magical pixie dust that you can spread on physical systems to resolve safety concerns. If anything, for many AI algorithms used today, physical safety is an area of weakness rather than strength. I recommend that you follow the progress of AI algorithms addressing physical safety to see if this situation changes in the future.

In the meantime, only human involvement can ensure the safety of physical systems. Projects that use AI to control physical systems must have significant research and development (R&D) components to ensure safety. Part of that R&D effort must address the question, "How do we combine AI algorithms with existing best safety practices in our field?"

AI is always a component of a larger software system

Starting in 2019, and ongoing at the time of this writing, Boeing has been struggling with the grounding of one of its plane models worldwide [139]. The reasons for grounding the planes were related to problems in the Maneuvering Characteristics Augmentation System (MCAS), a computerized component of the flight control system [140]. The MCAS was implicated as one of the links in a chain of events that resulted in two plane crashes with mass fatalities [141]. Although the MCAS system isn't an AI system, it highlights the high stakes inherent in developing safety-critical flight control software. Building safety-critical software systems isn't trivial, even if there's no AI involved.[a] And it only gets more difficult when you add AI to the mix.

Before you implement good AI-based control of a physical system, you must first master the development of good software for controlling physical systems. All the rules of good software engineering must be respected first.

---

[a] The 737 MAX grounding is still an ongoing story as I'm writing this sentence—for example, the Wikipedia page covering it currently has 749 references [142], with more likely to be added by the time you're reading this book. The events that occurred are tragic, and I'm not taking any position on MCAS development, or regulatory and certification processes. I'm only pointing out that developing safety-critical software is a high-stakes and nontrivial activity.

8.2.2 *IoT devices and AI systems must play well together*

In chapter 1, I showed you why looking with AI for something in the data is a fantastic way to spend money, only to finish with non-actionable insights. In chapter 5, you also saw that AI methods and data are inherently dependent on each other. This chapter shows you why the typical IoT project [46] is in danger of falling into those traps unless the architecture of the AI solution is designed in close cooperation with the device's composition.

IoT is about building physical devices that are connected to the internet. Those devices can also have an AI component controlling their behavior. AI is typically trained using data collected across the whole population that uses the device. In addition, multiple individual IoT devices, such as smart lights and smart locks, can participate in workflows like "Turn on my smart lights automatically when my smart lock unlocks the door."

IoT and AI naturally fit together because AI can provide additional functionality to the device. One example of such a system in which IoT devices benefit from AI is a smart alarm system (for example, the one discussed in section 5.1.5). On a larger scale, smart cities [143] use IoT sensors to collect data, then they use AI to manage assets and resources more effectively.

Creating IoT devices requires a broad range of expertise. Depending on the type of device, a development team might need expertise in software, electrical, and mechanical engineering. You also need to arrange for the manufacture of such devices and manage suppliers and distribution chains. With so many things to handle for the typical IoT device, AI could easily become an afterthought. Often, the high-level design of the device is finalized before AI experts are consulted.

Unfortunately, IoT devices designed in isolation from AI can easily create the dreaded "collect data, then run some analytics" model often used in unsuccessful AI projects. Most of the data your AI will use comes from sensors on the device itself. If the device's design is finalized before considering AI, you've already locked yourself into which data you'll have access to *before* you've even considered the dataset you'll need to produce actionable analytical results! This significantly reduces your options once you do start thinking about AI, because you'll then commonly fail to collect the data the AI really needs. For example, if you don't incorporate a temperature sensor, you won't know the local temperature at the location of your IoT device.

Even if you have the right sensors on the IoT device, often substantial differences exist between collecting data in an IoT setting and in the enterprise setting. In the case of an enterprise project, you'll often just aggregate the data that your enterprise is already collecting, usually in some type of data lake. This makes the collection and retention of the data reasonably cheap.

Collecting data in the IoT environment is almost always more expensive than in an enterprise project. In the case of IoT projects, to collect data, you'll first need to include a sensor in the device. Such sensors increase the cost of your device, but it doesn't stop there. If your device is a small, battery-powered sensor communicating over a cellular network, then transferring data could also be costly in terms of bandwidth and latency.

> **WARNING**   Collecting data from IoT devices is costly, and you should plan which data your AI needs within the design of the IoT device. Deploying AI as an afterthought to the existing IoT device is a fast track to regret.[2]

When applying AI to the IoT domain, you need to understand that the physical device can be difficult or impossible to alter after it's deployed in the field, whereas the AI portion of the system consists of software that's much easier to improve. To account for that discrepancy, during the design of the system, you should not only consider what the first version of your AI system will do, but also look at the features you'll ideally want to develop in your AI system down the road. Consider embedding all the hardware sensors you'll need in later versions of the AI side of the system into the initial IoT devices that you deploy in the field. That allows your customers, through a software update, to get additional functionality from the devices they've already purchased.

Examples of the "ship hardware now on which later software can capitalize" policy range from manufacturers who continually improve the software on smartphones to the automobile industry. Some of the Tesla models already include all the hardware that's expected to be necessary for self-driving [144], but the autopilot functionality itself continues to improve over time.

8.2.3   *The security of AI is an emerging topic*

The security of AI systems is rapidly improving. In addition to the security practices that your organization integrates with any other software system, AI brings many specificities of its own.

In recent years, we've learned a lot of surprising things about the security of AI algorithms. Deep learning systems can be tricked into misclassifying images by adding small changes to the image that are imperceptible to the human eye but can cause an AI to misclassify the image entirely [106,145]. To learn more about this area (also known as *Generative Adversarial Networks* or GANs), some good starting points are the Goodfellow et al. book and paper [106,146] in appendix C.

Recently, it was demonstrated that a similar attack is possible, not only by subtly changing images but also by putting a physical sticker on an object [147]. What if this sticker is applied to a traffic sign, tricking an autonomous vehicle into thinking that a stop sign is a 50 mph sign?

Attacks against deep learning classifiers aren't limited to images; similar attacks are possible with text classifiers in natural language processing (NLP) [148]. Another interesting development is the ability of the user of an AI system to recover some of

---

[2]   The keyword here is that data collection should be *planned*. Don't just throw in sensors to collect data you have no plans of ever using. Sensors have an embedded cost. That cost is not only the monetary cost of the sensor itself but the cost added by the need to secure the device and its sensors from unauthorized access. Furthermore, you must account for how the presence of the sensor impacts users' privacy.

the data that was used to train the ML models [149]. While we're at it, why stop at the data? Why not steal the whole AI model that your organization has developed? Security problems aren't limited to deep learning algorithms; for example, model stealing could be done with many other kinds of frequently used AI and ML algorithms [150].

It's not clear what future developments await us in the field of AI security, and it's a good bet that new developments will emerge by the time this book is in print. What's also clear is that the security of AI systems is a young field that still may hold many surprises in the future. Indeed, some of the aforementioned security problems of AI came as a surprise to everyone, including AI researchers and experts.

Instead of asking your team if a particular AI algorithm is secure (for quite a few of the modern ones, the correct answer is "unknown"), you should understand that this is a rapidly evolving field, and the answers you get today can change tomorrow. Ideally, in your first projects, you should use AI on the types of tasks in which security is ensured through the larger system of which the AI algorithm is but a part. Right now, AI algorithms themselves are difficult to secure against attack.

8.3　*AI doesn't learn causality, only correlations*

The Achilles heel of AI as it's currently practiced is that the conclusion of an analysis is typically not driven by learning the connection between cause and consequence. Instead, AI learns that there's a correlation between events—that the consequence occurs together with the cause.[3] This section explains when this difference matters and when it's safe to ignore it.

The majority of AI methods used currently aren't capable of establishing and explaining the exact causes of particular events [25,151]. You could think about these AI methods on a high level as pattern-matching mechanisms that are good at recognizing patterns. AI algorithms recognize that the cause and consequence occur together; they might even recognize that the cause occurs before the consequence. But AI algorithms don't understand the difference between cause and consequence, or how the underlying system that's undergoing analysis actually works. Furthermore, popular AI methods (like many deep learning methods) can't even account for *known* causal relationships [25,151]—there's no way to force a deep learning system to respect a causal relation that the domain expert already knows is there!

You could say that a focus on correlation was historically encouraged in at least some parts of the AI community. In 2008, a widely quoted article [152] advanced the argument that if you have all the data so that you can predict what's going to happen, does it matter why? As a corollary of that approach, theory (and theories about causality) was declared to matter much less.

---

[3] Here, I use the word *correlation* to mean that there's some form of relationship (or co-occurrence) between events. I'm not implying that AI would necessarily calculate a correlation coefficient, only that AI would learn that these events occur together.

You never have all the data

Unless you possess special skills such as clairvoyance, you'll never have all the data about all possible outcomes! To start with, you're missing data about results that have yet to occur. These results have yet to happen in the period that's usually termed *the future*. Most of us also have a tough time even collecting data about all the outcomes that occurred in the past.

The reasons for this incompleteness range from the data not existing in the first place to data being too expensive to retain or being private. Lacking such data, we train our AI models preferentially with data that describes outcomes to which we have the best access (those that are often limited to the most common outcomes or well-publicized rare outcomes).

Even if you take the position of "a correlation between events is all that I need," it's questionable whether your dataset will include enough data to guide you through all the scenarios you'll encounter.

Sometimes, the relationship between cause and effect doesn't matter much. Is your goal to profit from the world as it is, without any ambition to change it? Do you have sufficient data describing the situations you're likely to encounter in practice? Then you can argue that your AI system doesn't need to worry about causation. If you're in the business of selling shoes and want to sell your shoes to someone who'd soon need a new pair of shoes, you don't need to know the causes of people needing new shoes. You might be perfectly content with knowing that, "Person *x* buys new shoes every 18 months."

AI, as practiced today, could even guide you through a change, if such a change was something that the AI system had seen before. For example, if your goal is to improve your half-marathon times, a hypothetical AI system on your smart watch might be able to predict your running time improvements. AI can even guide you through developing habits that will improve your running times, such as stride lengthening or reducing heel strike. AI can coach you because the system has access to the time results of many runners. The AI system can therefore match habits that will lead to your improvement with similar developmental patterns seen from other users.

However, systems that don't understand causal relationships are typically *valid only in the setting to which they were exposed during their training*. If the setting changes significantly after the period in which you've trained your system, or if you're the first one to encounter a particular problem, you're in uncharted territory. The AI system can't help you much there. If a plane I'm in encounters a serious problem that has never been seen before, I much prefer a good human pilot than AI at the controls! Similarly, if you're unlucky enough to be the first patient recorded with a new kind of symptom, you're probably better off with human doctors than with AI.

NOTE   As a rule, correlation-based systems are sufficient if you don't have an ambition to change the world or if you're content with an outcome similar to something that the system has seen before. If your dream is for an innovative outcome or the ability to operate in a setting that hasn't been seen before, then knowing causal relationships is necessary.

The data scientists in the audience might mention some recent successes in the field of reinforcement learning. They'll point out that AI systems were able to play the game of *Go* better than humans [153–155], or even play complex computer games such as *StarCraft* [156] better than humans. None of these AI systems used or worried much about causation, so it's not clear that causal mechanisms are necessary to achieve better-than-human performance even on complex tasks.

Better-than-human performance of AI is certainly a trend to watch, but today, such successes with AI are rare and limited to a few domains. Being the first to achieve better-than-human performance in a completely new area, an area unlike any other in which AI has already reached superhuman performance, is difficult. It requires extremely experienced teams and large hardware budgets.

Counterfactuals require causality

Counterfactuals are scenarios in the format "If we did something else instead of what we originally did, what would have happened?" Counterfactuals are challenging to answer when causal relationships aren't known. More importantly, in the absence of defined causal relationships, explanations based on "the closest outcome when a different action was taken" could be wrong.

An example of that scenario is given by Caruana et al. [157]. When patients have pneumonia, a critical question is whether you should hospitalize them and treat the illness aggressively. Interestingly, when you look at any dataset, you'll see that having asthma predicts a less serious case of pneumonia. So, should you release asthmatic patients with pneumonia and not worry about them? Fortunately, doctors operate in the causal domain, and they're of the uniform opinion that if you have asthma, pneumonia is a more severe problem for you and has to be taken seriously.

Why did AI think asthma makes pneumonia less dangerous? Because patients who have asthma are more attuned to their breathing rhythm. They notice that something is wrong faster and seek help earlier. Their better outcome is the result of prompt treatment. An AI model that doesn't understand causality gives a dangerous answer in this case!

The reality is that most of the widely used AI methods today don't have the ability to infer (or even enforce) causal relationships in the data. The question for the future is how will AI technology evolve? One possibility is that methods capable of inferring causality will advance and gain a wider adoption. (See the sources on causality in appendix C [24–27] for an overview of the current state of causal research.) Another possibility is that further developments in the field of reinforcement learning, zero-shot learning [158], knowledge graphs [159], and maybe a combination of graphs and deep learning [160,161], might enhance AI's ability to operate in domains it wasn't exposed to during training.

NOTE   Follow these trends carefully but, for the time being, tread cautiously in any situation requiring causal reasoning. Our current tools and methods are still in their infancy.

Recent AI advances (like deep learning) have been enabled by the increase in computer processing capacity and larger training datasets [162]. We should expect AI, big data, and specialized hardware (like the use of GPUs for AI tasks) to continue to be closely intertwined.

Another area to watch closely is the field of complex systems [163], mainly because causality in complex systems is difficult to determine, not only for AI, but for humans too. Finally, if you're interested in AI, deep learning, and causality, I recommend the Marcus sources [151,164] and the Pearl and Mackenzie source [25] for further reading.

8.4   *Not all data is created equal*

Historically, AI algorithms were egalitarian with regards to the data they accepted as input. All data was considered equal, and AI algorithms typically trusted all their data equally. While that may have been a reasonable assumption at the time those algorithms were developed, that assumption didn't age well. Even now, algorithms that can operate with data sources of different veracity are rare. However, having data sources of differing veracity is the rule and not the exception in the industry. This section explains why you'll typically deal with data of variable correctness, how industry typically deals with data of different veracity, and why this area is worth watching closely.

AI and ML algorithms assume, by default, that all the data you feed them is equally trustworthy. This assumption was reasonable in an academic setting, the setting in which many ML algorithms were invented. However, in a business setting, most of the data in your pipeline isn't equally trustworthy.

Imagine that your ML pipeline is getting an input stream of your customer sentiment data, your corporation's financial statements, and your sales data. External auditors checked your financial statements, and your sales data is transactional. These are high-quality, trustworthy data sources.

In the meantime, your customer sentiment data was inferred based on transcripts of voice calls that voice-recognition AI converted to text. Afterward, NLP AI was applied to the text to extract sentiment. This data source is of limited veracity. Therefore, you need to account for this difference in the design of your AI. You must design the AI system to put more trust in the audited financial data than the inferred NLP data.

Even on the level of individual algorithms, in business and industry, it's common that datasets given to the algorithm aren't of uniform quality. For example, the quality of a GPS position varies based on how well the signal from GPS satellites can reach your phone. As a result, your phone's GPS positioning is much better in an open area under the open sky than when you're hiking in a canyon or walking between tall buildings. If you're inside a building, your position is even less precise because your GPS wasn't designed for indoor use. Yet, if you're interested in finding clusters of locations that you visit often, many of the basic clustering algorithms (such as k-means) don't account for the variable precision of GPS data. Your data scientists must account for such varying data quality.

There's plenty of literature on algorithms themselves. It's much harder to find research and guidance on how to account for the diverse quality of input data, and in practice you're often forced to use ad-hoc solutions. One such ad-hoc method is to assign more weight to the data from more trustworthy sources. Another one is to add noise to less credible data during the training. Using such ad-hoc methods in practice involves some creativity and much experimentation.

Can't we clean all the data?

If we could go through and clean all the data before it's put into the AI algorithm, the problem of variable veracity of the data wouldn't exist. Unfortunately, cleaning all the input data can be expensive and sometimes impossible. When you stand outside, your GPS position is known to within a few feet [165], while your precise position inside a building can't be recorded using only GPS, and there's no way to clean up data that doesn't exist.

More importantly, even when possible and economical, cleaning all the data doesn't solve the problem of data veracity in your ML pipeline. Even if the input data quality is perfect, the algorithms in your pipeline might themselves have a high error rate. For example, NLP is far from being able to perfectly comprehend human conversation. The output of such algorithms would reintroduce errors into the ML pipeline.

There will always be a need to improve the quality of the data that we send to AI algorithms, but I hope to see further improvement in the ability of all widely used AI methods to account for different levels of data veracity. Breakthroughs in this area could significantly facilitate operations with data sources of varying veracity.

8.5   How are AI errors different from human mistakes?

As AI is being used more and more in society, the results of its algorithmic decisions are affecting broad segments of society. As decisions that AI algorithms make are becoming more consequential, fairness and suitability for the purpose of those AI algorithms becomes the crucial consideration. It puts an onus on organizations rolling out those algorithms to consider the consequences of their use. This section talks about two underappreciated aspects of AI usage as practiced today:

- The types of errors that AI makes are fundamentally different from the mistakes humans make.
- To understand the ethical implications of the use of AI algorithms, you must focus on domain actions.

8.5.1   *The actuarial view*

The critical thing to understand is that most AI and ML algorithms have an actuarial view of the world. For example, errors in ML algorithms can be expressed as: "In $x\%$ of the cases, we make wrong decisions, but tradeoffs are made to provide the best results overall across the whole dataset." That's a direct consequence of the fact that an ML algorithm's only guarantee is to minimize the evaluation metric, as explained in section 1.5.

An actuarial view of the world suffers from the reality that AI errors are totally and fundamentally different from the errors that humans make. In extreme cases, AI errors could be so bizarre that they appear to be willfully malicious to a layperson unfamiliar with this actuarial view.

> **WARNING**   If your company creates algorithms that are perceived as malicious, don't be surprised if the public starts considering your company to be malicious!

To make things worse, if you're using one of the AI methods that are global models (mentioned in section 8.2.1), it's difficult to instruct AI to "keep everything the same, just make an exception in this one case." Finally, AI using a global model is focused solely on optimizing the evaluation metric. It doesn't have a contextual and causal understanding of the connotations and consequences of its decisions as a human would perceive them.

For example, it's easy for a university professor to mistake a student uninterested in academic accomplishments for one who is skeptical of the class's quality and structure. It's also possible for the professor to have little patience with remarks from either type of student. Ideally, we would hope that the professor could better distinguish between these two students, but we understand that the professor's lack of patience could be caused by confusing their motivations. The professor might make a mistaken assumption, but an objective observer would attribute that to a simple judgment error that anyone could make.

But what if this hypothetical class is in the late 1890s? What if it's a class in physics, and the remarks are coming from a fellow who happens to be named Albert Einstein? What if the professor is short on patience with his comments regardless? I don't know about you, but my assessment of the professor's motivation would be far less favorable. I wouldn't give the professor the benefit of the doubt that they're mistaking Albert Einstein for a student who's either skeptical of the value of physics or uninterested in academic accomplishments. At the very least, I would think that the professor has a problem distinguishing between a personality conflict they have with the student and a student who can't achieve much in physics. Once an error becomes large enough to be difficult to understand, the question of motivation emerges.

Humans are known to make mistakes caused by some amount of malice, but the knowledgeable human doesn't think that Einstein is skeptical of the value of physics. However, this is precisely the type of error that an AI algorithm might make!

Anomaly detection algorithms [166] are likely to flag Einstein being in the physics class as an anomaly. Those algorithms find rare and unusual occurrences in a population (that's what the term *anomaly* refers to in this context). In a physics program hosted by a prestigious university, people uninterested in academia or skeptical of the value of physics would be rare. Albert Einstein is certainly rare. While these two individuals look quite different to a human, algorithms don't have common sense and might declare them both to be simply *anomalous*. If your algorithm treats all anomalies as the same, a human might perceive its conclusion as a malicious treatment of Einstein.

Now, let's exit the confines of academia and enter the outside world in which AI operates today. That world uses AI in areas such as national security, medicine, autonomous vehicles, criminal justice, law enforcement, college admission, hiring, and promotion. Even if you don't care about some obscure college class, how do you feel about the extensive use of AI if AI has only an actuarial view within these domains? Imagine a situation in which a small child dressed in a bunny costume is crawling on all fours. *I certainly hope that in any decision it makes, an autonomous car will recognize that child as a human child, not as a bunny!*

Which brings us to another critical concept to understand: while AI has an actuarial view and makes actuarial errors, humans have an *instance view*. An instance view looks at the individual and tries to be *fair and to exercise the duty of care* toward that individual. Where AI might see a picture that looks like an oversized bunny moving strangely (for a rabbit), a human sees a child. AI has no common sense and often has little understanding of context and causality. AI brings an actuarial view to a problem of individual instances. Because humans think about individual cases, AI errors look like malice to most humans. Your team's job is to make AI fit for the greater context in which your system will operate.

> **WARNING** You must account for AI having an actuarial view of most problems. AI will make actuarial mistakes that an average human, uninformed about AI, will see as malicious. Juries, whether in court or in the court of public opinion, are made up of humans.

There's no way to know if AI will ever develop common sense. It may not for quite a while; maybe not even until we get strong AI/Artificial General Intelligence [76]. Accounting for AI's actuarial view is a part of your problem domain and part of why understanding your domain is crucial.

It's difficult to account for the differences between the actuarial view AI takes and human social expectations. Accounting for those differences is not an engineering problem and something that you should pass on to the engineering team to solve. It's a human problem, something that all team members—management and engineers—have a stake in solving.

> **NOTE** *You must domesticate your AI system to operate within the rules of common human decency.* Like all such problems, the responsibility for organizing the process and overseeing execution belongs to management. If you're the executive running the project, you're the one who owns this problem.

8.5.2   Domesticating AI

The first step in solving this problem is to understand the domain implications of your decisions, which starts with understanding the conclusions you can infer. You should start by analyzing the domain actions your AI will take (described in section 1.6), and then perform the appropriate safety, legal, and ethical analysis processes used for non-AI-based products in your industry.

AI engineers and safety engineers often disagree

It's common to encounter culture clashes between the AI engineering and safety engineering communities. The actuarial view inherent to AI ensures that you, on average, get the best result, but some strange decisions might be accepted if they happen in one in a million cases. The AI community has traditionally focused on the average result and on optimizing for such outcomes. As such, its focus has historically been the polar opposite of the safety community's view.

Systems engineering and safety engineering are often oriented toward generously reinforcing a system to provide a wide safety margin, and even rare failures are unacceptable. The cables holding elevators aren't merely designed to maintain the maximum weight we expect in elevators. They're designed to hold significantly more than the maximum load that's ever expected to be in that elevator.

As an executive, you should expect these cultural clashes. Authority and accountability must join forces with expertise. Experts in the area (AI or safety) should have the final call in their sphere of knowledge and must be responsible for the results of that call. Be prepared to mediate disputes and clarify policy in cases in which it's unclear which view should take priority.

Ensuring ethical outcomes goes to the core of how you run your business and live your life. You need to apply your own experience and judgment to ensure ethical outcomes—the ultimate responsibility for those outcomes is yours. Here, I'll limit myself by offering a few useful practices. These practices aren't a checklist of how to ensure an ethical result but are best used *in addition* to other policies your organization has in place. It's imperative that you, your team, and your organization do the following:

1 Understand what ethical, legal, and moral obligations you have.
2 Consider these obligations not as an engineering problem, but as a business problem. They should be primarily owned by the business side of the team.
3 Decide domain metrics to measure the ethical and legal results of your AI algorithms, just as you have business metrics measuring business outcomes. You should define these business and technical metrics and link them with each other, as presented in chapter 4.
4 Understand what the domain actions are that your AI system can take. Use the Sense/Analyze/React pattern and focus on what business actions you should take (see section 1.6) to provide a starting point for eliciting and analyzing the results of the actions of your AI system.

5 Understand whether it's important to know why your AI algorithm made a given decision. The terms *explainability and interpretability* of AI algorithms refer to the ability to identify the reasons for which algorithms have made a particular decision. Some AI methods are more straightforward to explain than others.

In some industries, such as the insurance industry, auditors and regulators will restrict you from using AI algorithms whose decisions you can't explain. The need for this explainability is also affected by recent regulations like the European General Data Protection Regulation (GDPR) [167].

If explainability of the AI algorithms is required in your domain, then your team must account for it when designing the algorithm. Some references that might help with interpretability in AI are Hall and Gill's book [168] and Ribeiro, Singh, and Guestrin's paper [169].

Today, you often end up creating *rule engines* at the end of the AI pipeline; these engines use a set of rules to guarantee that the system stays within safe parameters. If you're controlling the temperature of an environment like a conference room, you need rules to keep the room's temperature within safe parameters. If there's a particular outcome that must never happen in your system, then you need a rule to prevent the rest of the system from producing that result.

Even if you were to miss a single rule that would prevent the specific outcome, the presence of such a rule engine enables you to quickly address the problem once you become aware of it. It also shows that your team did their due diligence and at least tried to prevent such an outcome.

The ethical use of AI is a field of active research and is something you should follow. You can learn more about the current state of the research, industry practices, and discourse in several sources in the bibliography [138,170–173].

8.6 *AutoML is approaching*

AutoML is an umbrella name for the field of study that attempts to automate various aspects of the construction and building of an AI system. AutoML research covers all the specialized areas that today are associated with the technical construction of an ML pipeline. This section discusses the impact of AutoML advancement on the general field of AI.

> **NOTE** I suspect that by the time you read this book, AutoML will have advanced enough that whatever I write today won't correctly summarize the state of the field. A recent review at the time of this writing is available in papers by Zöller and Huber [174] and Zhao and Chu [175].

A significant question for this book is, "What are the implications of what we know today about AutoML?" We already know that in some areas, such as computer vision, AutoML systems can exceed the results of the deep learning networks constructed by human experts [175]. In the case of NLP, however, AutoML still lags behind human performance. However, human engineers have constructed much more impressive AI systems that exceed human performance in the game of *Go* [153–155,176], and the even more complex game of *StarCraft* [156].

Engineers are indispensable for building most state-of-the-art AI systems. Still, AutoML is making significant progress in the area of supervised learning [174], and products that offer AutoML are quickly becoming components of all big cloud platforms [177–179]. What does this mean for an AI project started in 2020? It means that you should evaluate current AutoML offerings with regards to their cost and suitability for solving your business problems. AutoML systems determine the baseline results that any AI system constructed in house must exceed.

Over time, the effect of AutoML will depend on which areas of AI system construction it can automate and how all-encompassing that automation can be. Currently, AutoML isn't able to replace data scientists or domain experts.

> **NOTE** AutoML is getting better at choosing which AI and ML models will yield the best value for the technical evaluation metric of your dataset. Simple skillsets made of rules such as "Always use method *x* with a dataset that looks like *y*" will be automated.

Regardless of how much AutoML advances, recall that currently AI is struggling with notions of context, common sense, and causality. These problems won't be solved in the near future. They'll take longer to resolve than the simpler issue of automating ML pipeline construction. Solving the problem of common sense and achieving a sophisticated understanding of context likely will require the emergence of an Artificial General Intelligence [76] that's as capable as humans.

We need humans for the foreseeable future to understand the business problems, select the right puzzles for AI to solve, and define the relationship between the business domain and a workable technical solution. The material in this book will serve you well for years to come.

Is an AI winter coming?

AI is not a new field. AI research was founded in 1956 [35]. The field of AI has a history of inflating expectations of what AI can achieve, expectations that subsequently have been unfulfilled. These failures resulted in multiple *AI winters*, during which AI businesses and AI research suffered. One reference for the history of AI is Domingo's book [105]. The Wikipedia article [35] also offers a summary of AI history.

But as of 2020, AI is riding high. However, there's always the question of, "Did we finally get it right, or is another AI winter coming?" There are many reasons why this time it will be different (see Lee's book [9] for some). There's also no question that some AI projects will fail. So, will there be more AI winters?

It depends on how many AI projects succeed and how many of them fail. Success or failure will be determined by whether AI projects deliver business value or not. This book gives you the tools your AI project needs to succeed, and perhaps that will help us to avert another AI winter!

8.7   *What you've learned isn't limited to AI*

The methods discussed in this book are presented in the context of AI projects. I designed them to remain applicable even as new and better AI algorithms advance. The application of this book's methods exceeds the narrow confines of the AI field.

First, the Sense/Analyze/React pattern (chapter 3) focuses on the question, "What does this technology do for me?" as opposed to the question, "What cool capabilities does this technology have that I can use?" This isn't to say that a *technology push* never has a place in business, but that pattern does preclude moving forward with new technologies without a solid business case.

> **WARNING**   The technology industry has a history of getting excited about the latest technologies. Sometimes, these technologies provide a significant competitive advantage to early adopters. Other times, early adopters become casualties whose purpose is to warn later users of what not to do. To avoid becoming a casualty of new technology, whatever that technology is, go back to the basics. Don't forget to ask the question, "Would I still start the same project, even if it used technology that's not in vogue?"

Sometimes, there's a reason to move to a new technology for the sake of that technology alone. Sometimes, merely learning an innovative technology will give your organization a competitive advantage. In this case, you should be able to persuade your organization of this overwhelming advantage while admitting that other business benefits are limited. You also must be able to translate the value of any technology metric that your project uses into something that has relevance in your own business domain; here, the *L*ink step of CLUE comes in handy.

We always use business metrics for all AI projects!

One of the most common objections you'll hear when you raise the issue of tying technology and business metrics is that the organization is already doing so across all its projects. I hear these objections on almost every project I'm brought in on. I've learned to be very skeptical of this statement, and you should be too.

Ask the team to construct for you a quick profit curve (or an adequate equivalent that answers the same questions) as was done in section 4.4. You'll see that, when tested, many teams don't know how to tie technical metrics and business results.

I've even seen senior technologists claiming that they "always use concrete business metrics to measure results of all our AI projects and can't imagine that there's any other way to run a project!" But later we find that some of those experts had trouble with even following a detailed description of a simple, straightforward business problem.

If your team has trouble constructing a profit curve for a simple business case, you're not in an organization used to running all its AI projects based on business metrics.

> **(continued)**
> Teams unused to thinking about business metrics can finish with technical metrics that are completely unrelated to any business outcome. When working with such a team, carefully check the relationship between their technical metrics and the business problem.

In addition to presenting the methods for linking business and technical metrics, this book has introduced MinMax analysis (chapter 6) and sensitivity analysis (chapter 7). The only real requirement for MinMax and sensitivity analyses to be applicable is that you must be able to describe your business problems as a sequence of steps. This means that if you have a pipeline, and if the time your team has to build steps in the pipeline is limited, the material you've learned in this book is applicable. The pipeline doesn't need to be an ML pipeline.

> **TIP** The methods presented in this book apply to organizations of all sizes. They apply to organizations that use waterfall processes and to organizations that use the Agile methodology. They're also applicable to organizations using the Lean Startup methodology defined in Ries's book [28]. This book's methods allow you to determine early if your AI project is on the right track to success.

The methods presented in this book have general applicability to all business processes. They can guide any pipeline. You can even apply them when the execution of a pipeline is entirely human-powered.

8.8 Guiding AI to business results

We're at the end of our journey through this book. Is this another book that provides you with a set of systems and processes that you can follow, with your brain on autopilot? Does this book finally give you the magic formula that you can apply to make money with AI, without needing to think too hard? No—this book is about the work you must do, *because AI doesn't know how to do it.*

I wrote this book to show you how to get real business results with AI. I don't promise results from buying frameworks that will solve all your problems, nor am I a believer in catalogues of case studies showing you how someone else made money using AI. If you're hoping that there are some parts of AI algorithms that you poorly understand but that will make you a ton of money, you'll be disappointed at the end of the road. I call this approach the "rainbow and unicorns approach to AI."[4] Instead of having a clear idea of where we want to take our business, we too often abdicate

---

[4] As you learned in section 2.7, there are no unicorns among data scientists and data engineers. As for the rainbow part of the "rainbow and unicorns"—there's also no pot of gold to be found if you walk to the end of the AI rainbow.

responsibility to AI and wish that some *mystic* part of AI would solve our problems. We replace initiative and understanding of the world around us with the hope that data mining with better AI algorithms will show us the way forward.

This hope is misguided—you can't get business results with AI by relinquishing control to algorithms, metrics, and AI frameworks. AI isn't a silver bullet whose application will always make you money. On the contrary, it's *much easier to use AI to lose money than to use AI to make it.* Thinking about AI as a black box that can make correct business decisions on its own is a sure way for executives and their budgets to be parted.

> **NOTE** AI can't exercise good judgment, and most common AI methods used today (such as deep learning) can't determine causal relations. AI methods are *quantitative methods* that require the right metrics to drive them. All AI algorithms know how to do is maximize a specified metric, without knowing why they're maximizing it. The context and the purpose for which AI should maximize that metric have to come from a human.

Humans alone have the capacity and skillsets to define the metrics that link business and technology. Humans must supplement AI in the areas where AI is weak. You make AI applicable to your business problem by engineering the proper link between business and technical metrics (as shown in chapter 4). Only humans can design metrics that describe a lifetime of human wisdom in a way that quantitative algorithms can understand.

On the technical side, AI solutions developed in isolation from human judgment don't work today. On a more philosophical level, there's another reason to not just follow AI blindly—we, as humans, possess *agency.* AI isn't an unstoppable force that's affecting us all, and we're not just along for the ride. The AI revolution isn't just *happening.* It's us, people like you and me, who are *creating* that revolution. We must exercise our agency. We must decide what the results of applying AI will be. In the context of a single enterprise and of individual AI projects, this book shows you how to use AI while still exercising your own agency. On the societal level, we can guide AI toward the goals we desire, instead of letting the AI revolution career toward destinations we fear.[5]

We don't know when (or if) AI will reach Artificial General Intelligence (AGI) level, in which AI matches (or exceeds) human capabilities. Until AGI arrives, we human beings need to guide business and society and to understand that AI is a tool we need to wield without being overawed by it. Companies like Google have demonstrated that you don't need AGI to build a great business, but instead a smart person who knows how to link business and technology. *AI doesn't make you money—people make you money!*

---

[5] I highly recommend O'Reilly's book [180]. It's a great discussion of the relationship between society and technology and the ability of humans to guide technology toward the goals we want to achieve.

8.9   *Exercises*

We've come to the end of the book, with this final chapter addressing the future trends you should watch. Here are a few exercises that are oriented toward tracking the effect of future trends in AI on your organization.

Question 1: Explain whether AI as practiced today is applicable to the following projects:

- **Scenario 1:** Predicting short-term retail and economic activity based on using satellite images to track the movement and number of ocean-going container ships
- **Scenario 2:** Predicting new prices of a portfolio in the case of an unexpected event that completely disrupts the foundations of the global economic system
- **Scenario 3:** Predicting the effect of genetic research on healthcare spending costs 20 years from now

Question 2: Reflect on the last three times your organization adapted a new and popular technology, after which the consensus in hindsight was that the project didn't succeed. Now, find the reasons why the project was *not* successful. By the way, saying that the wrong people were on the team or that you weren't experienced enough with technology aren't acceptable reasons.

Avoiding discussions of people and personalities makes the dialogue more palatable in a corporate setting. More importantly, after these exclusions, what remains are the inherent process weaknesses that your organization has in evaluating new technologies. The goal is to recognize those same weaknesses the next time a new technology comes in vogue. This time, the technology in vogue is AI.

Question 3: For each of the trends introduced in this chapter (as exemplified by the headings of sections 8.1 to 8.6), answer the following questions. As a reminder, those trends are listed in table 8.1.

Table 8.1   Trends introduced in this chapter. How do those trends affect you?

Section 8.1	The meaning of the term *AI* changes through time.
Section 8.2	AI use in physical systems must account for safety.
Section 8.3	AI systems today don't account for causal relationships.
Section 8.4	AI algorithms don't typically account for the variable veracity in data.
Section 8.5	AI systems' mistakes are different from human errors.
Section 8.6	AutoML is approaching.

- Does this trend affect your current project?
- Is the trend likely to affect your organization in general?
- Is the trend likely to affect your personal career?

- How do you intend to follow the trend?
- How will you know if the trend is materializing or not?

Question 4: Are there any trends of specific applications of AI in your industry that affect you but weren't enumerated in this chapter?

Summary

- AI is a rapidly evolving field. Not only are state-of-the-art AI methods changing quickly, but we're still learning what security vulnerabilities AI systems might have.
- AI systems today can't infer the causality of events. They match data about what's currently happening with outcomes that the AI system has previously encountered.
- AI systems can't reliably guide you through unknown situations. In fact, these systems fail in situations that are fundamentally different from their training.
- The errors AI makes are actuarial in nature: "Does this decision make sense when I look at the population as a whole?" Humans think in instances, in specific cases: "Is this decision reasonable?" Most people don't understand this distinction and may attribute an AI system's actuarial errors to malice.
- You can apply methods such as MinMax and sensitivity analyses to any business system that can be described as a pipeline.
- The AI revolution isn't just *happening*. We're *creating* that revolution and, therefore, must exercise our agency and think how best to use AI.

appendix A
Glossary of terms

At Manning, the publisher's policy is to help the reader by going the extra mile to make sure the terms used in our books are defined there. The reasoning is that it saves readers some time when they encounter an unfamiliar term.

As is the case for any other business book, this book's audience is diverse. Depending on your background, you'll be familiar with most of the terms used in this book but might appreciate definitions for a few of them. The terms that should be defined are different for every user. To avoid a situation in which the flow of text is broken by definitions of terms that most readers know, I've defined most of them in this glossary. To help the readers who encountered the term for the first time, I tailored the definitions toward being understandable, even if that comes at the expense of some loss of formality/precision.

- *4+1 architectural view*—A methodology that describes the software architecture based on a set of specialized views. See Krutchen's paper [85] for details, or Wikipedia [86] for a summary.
- *Accuracy*—In the context of the binary classifier, accuracy is a technical metric that measures the success of the classification algorithm. It's proportional to the data that's correctly classified. The formula for accuracy [181] is

$$Accuracy = \frac{Total\ Number\ of\ Correct\ Predictions}{Total\ Number\ of\ Predictions}$$

- *Actuary*—A business professional who uses quantitative methods to measure risk and uncertainty in business domains. Actuaries are licensed professionals who have a set of standards that guide practitioners through quantitative models that are appropriate to use in such situations. As a general rule, actuarial methods used in the insurance industry analyze the population as a whole and provide guidance on the outcomes expected for the entire population. Individual outcomes within that population can vary widely. See Wikipedia [182] for details.

- *Application programming interface (API)*—A standardized way to invoke the functionality of a software system.

- *Artificial intelligence (AI)*—For the purpose of this book, AI is defined as an area of computer science that studies how to allow computers to complete tasks that historically required human intelligence. Note that the definition of AI, as well as the relationship between AI and machine learning (ML), often depends on which source you use. Section 8.1 details some of the definitions of AI you can find in the industry today.

- *Autoregressive integrated moving average (ARIMA)*—A statistical technique for analyzing a time series and forecasting the future values of the series [109]. ARIMA is based on autoregression (regression versus previous values of the time series), differencing, and the moving average.

- *Bias-variance tradeoff*—A method for decomposing an error of some predictive algorithm in the components that could be traced to the structure of the predictive algorithm. See Wikipedia [183] for details.

- *Big data*—Data that is too big to process on a single machine. There are different definitions of big data. One of the common definitions of big data was based on *V*'s, such as Velocity (how often data changes), Volume (how big the data is), Variety (how many different data sources and data types are in the data), and Veracity (how much you can trust the data). Historically, the number of *V*'s included in a definition varied, with the early definitions based on three *V*'s: Volume, Velocity, and Variety.

- *Business vertical*—A grouping of businesses, where all businesses in that group cater to a specific customer base that shares some common characteristics, such as profession (healthcare, for example) or need (transportation, for example).

- *Classification*—In the context of ML, classification identifies to which category input data belongs. Categories in which classification would happen are predefined. Classification could be between two classes (binary classification) or across multiple classes.

- *Commercial-off-the-shelf (COTS) product*—A product that's already made and that you can purchase from someone else.

- *Cost of capital*—In the context of starting a new business project, cost of capital is the minimum rate of return that must be exceeded for the project to be worthwhile.

- *Cross industry standard process for data mining (CRISP-DM)*—A standard that defines the process for analytics and data mining. It predates the popularity of big data and AI. It's an iterative process in which you start with understanding the business, then understanding the data. Next comes preparing the data for modeling, performing the modeling, and then evaluating the results. If the results are satisfactory, you then deploy the model; otherwise, you repeat the aforementioned cycle. See Wikipedia [184] for details.

- *Customer churn*—The proportion of your recurring customers who decide to stop doing business with you.
- *Data lake*—Stores all the data available to the organization in a single repository, allowing you to reference it all during analysis. For a discussion of data lakes and the philosophy behind building them, see Gorelik's book [103] and Needham's book [185].
- *Data science*—A multidisciplinary field that uses algorithms from many different quantitative and scientific fields to extract insights from data. Similar to many other areas that have captured the popular imagination, it's not universally agreed what all the fields are that are a part of data science. Some of the fields that are often considered part of data science include statistics, programming, mathematics, machine learning, operational research, and others [66]. Closely related fields that are sometimes considered part of data science include bioinformatics and quantitative analysis. While AI and data science closely overlap, they aren't identical, because AI includes fields such as robotics, which are traditionally not considered part of data science. Harris, Murphy, and Vaisman's book [66] provides a good summary of the state of data science before the advancement of deep learning.
- *Data scientist*—A practitioner of the field of data science. Many sources (including this book) classify AI practitioners as data scientists.
- *Database administrator (DBA)*—A professional responsible for the maintenance of a database. Most commonly, a DBA would be responsible for maintaining a RDBMS-based database.
- *Deep learning*—A subfield of AI that uses artificial neural networks arranged in a significant number of layers. In the last few years, deep learning algorithms have been successful in a large number of highly visible applications, including image processing and speech and audio recognition. Deep learning also was used in AI algorithms that demonstrated a high level of performance in playing various games, such as *Go* and *StarCraft*, which exceeded the levels at which the best humans could play. See various appendix C entries [153–156,176]. Deep learning algorithms demonstrate a close-to-human (or even above human) level of performance in many of these tasks and recent newsworthy successes of AI.
- *End user license agreement (EULA)*—A legal agreement between a user and the company governing usage of the computer software.
- *Enterprise data warehouse (EDW)*—A type of database that's optimized for the reporting and analysis of enterprise data.
- *High-frequency trading (HFT)*—In the context of the financial markets, HFT is a type of trading based on the combination of computer algorithms, high volume, and low latency.
- *Internet of Things (IoT)*—A network consisting of various physical devices connected to the internet [46]. The type of physical devices varies widely, and, in principle, anything that performs any function in the physical world could be

an IoT device. Examples of IoT devices range from smart thermometers [36,37] to connected vehicles and homes.

- *K-means*—One of the original clustering algorithms, it assigns its input data to one of the K clusters, where *K* is an integer.
- *Label*—In the context of classification, a label is the name of the category that data used in training belongs to.
- *Lean startup*—A methodology for running business operations described in Reis' book [28]. Some of the principles of the lean startup methodology are to shorten the business development cycle by iterative product development and testing the product in the marketplace as soon as practical. While originally described in the context of startups, this methodology is now extensively used by organizations of all sizes. See also minimum viable product (MVP) and pivot.
- *Linear response*—A type of response in the system that's proportional to the change in input. If an input change of 1 unit results in a change of *x* output units, then 2 units of input change would result in a change of 2*x* units in the system's output.
- *Long short-term memory (LSTM)*—A type of deep learning network characterized by the particular structure of the neural network [110]. It's typically used in the prediction of future values in a time series.
- *Mindshare*—Exemplifies how well known and how often some concept, idea, or product is considered.
- *Minimum viable product (MVP)*—A product that provides enough functionality to your customers so that your organization can learn if the business direction in which your company is moving is the correct one [28].
- *Operations research (OR)*—A field of research that uses various mathematical and analytical methods to help in making better decisions. Historically, it developed as a part of applied mathematics and predates ML and AI. Today, OR is often considered one of the fields associated with data science.
- *Opportunity cost*—Suppose you have a set of actions of which you can take only one, and you chose one of the actions. The opportunity cost of the action you have taken is the value of the most valuable choice among the actions that you didn't take [186].
- *Pivot*—In the context of the lean startup methodology, a pivot is an act of structured course correction, designed to test a new hypothesis about the business or strategy [28].
- *Proportional-integral-derivative (PID) controller*—According to the Wikimedia Foundation [34]:

  A proportional-integral-derivative controller is a control loop feedback mechanism widely used in industrial control systems and a variety of other applications requiring continuously modulated control.

  PID compares errors between current values and a desired value of some process variable for the system under control and applies the correction to that process variable based on proportional, integral, and derivative terms. PID controllers are widely used in various control systems.

- *Quantitative analysis (QA)*—According to Will Kenton [187]:

  Quantitative analysis (QA) is a technique that seeks to understand behavior by using mathematical and statistical modeling, measurement, and research. Quantitative analysts aim to represent a given reality in terms of a numerical value.

- *Quantitative analyst (quant)*—A practitioner of quantitative analysis [187]. Common business verticals in which quants work are trading and other financial services.

- *Predictive analytics*—A type of analytics that uses historical data to predict future trends. It answers the question: "What would happen next?"

- *Recommendation engine*—A software system that looks at the previous choices between items that the user has made and recommends a new item that the system expects would match the user's interest. The recommendation engine can recommend many different types of items. In the case of a clothing retailer, an example of an item would be a sweater. In the case of Netflix, an example of an item would be a movie.

- *Reinforcement learning*—In the context of ML, reinforcement learning studies the design of the agents that are able to maximize a long-term reward obtained from some environment.

- *Relational database management system (RDBMS)*—A database system with a strong mathematical foundation. That foundation is known as a "relational model." RDBMSs are widely used in most of the non-big data applications and are often the default choice for data storage. RDBMSs typically use SQL as a language to query the data in the database.

- *Root mean square error (RMSE)*—A technical metric that's often used to measure the results of statistical, ML, and AI algorithms. It's used to measure the difference between the quantities that the algorithm has predicted and the actual quantities that resulted. RMSE penalizes large prediction errors more than small prediction errors [188]. RMSE is defined by the following formula:

$$RMSE = \sqrt{\frac{1}{n} \sum_{i=1}^{n} (Y_i - \hat{Y}_i)^2}$$

Where:

  - n = The number of points for which the ML algorithm has predicted the value
  - $\hat{Y}_i$ = The predicted value of point i, according to the ML algorithm
  - Y_i = The actual value of point i

- *Six Sigma*—A set of methods that help an organization improve its business processes [21,22]. While Six Sigma historically has been used to help improve the quality of many manufacturing processes, the methods and practices associated with Six Sigma have been used extensively in all fields of business. Practitioners of Six Sigma view all work as processes that are subject to never-ending improvement. Six Sigma has pioneered usage of data and statistical techniques to improve the field of business operations.

- *Smart environment*—An environment that can be computer controlled. It typically includes many IoT devices and uses a computer system and AI to control and orchestrate the behavior of those devices.

- *Streaming analytics*—A type of analytics applied to streaming data to process that data within some deadline from the moment it arrives in the system. Streaming data is data that's continuously arriving in the computer system.

- *Supervised learning*—A type of ML in which model training occurs by presenting training data for which the correct result of the application of the algorithm is known. For example, if the goal is to classify email messages in spam or not spam categories, the training set would consist of email messages that are labeled (known to be) spam messages and email messages that are known not to be spam.

- *Training*—In the context of ML algorithms, training is a necessary step in preparing the algorithm for performing its function. During training, data is presented to the model, and parameters of the model are optimized.

- *Unified modeling language (UML)*—A standard for the description of the structure and behavior of software systems using visual diagrams. See OMG's UML site [189] for details.

- *Unsupervised learning*—A type of ML in which patterns are found in the unlabeled data. One example of unsupervised learning is clustering.

- *Zero sum game*—A game in which the success of one player comes at the expense of other players. In zero sum games, my gain is your loss, and vice versa.

appendix B
Exercise solutions

This appendix provides solutions for the exercises in all of the chapters. To help you reference the questions, I repeat those questions for each chapter and then provide the answers beneath the questions.

I strongly encourage you to complete the exercises to get a better understanding of material covered in this book. This book's exercises highlight and reinforce the best practices in, and common pitfalls of, AI projects in business. If you elect to skip the exercises, I still recommend reading the answers to the questions.

The exercises may introduce some new concepts that are not discussed in the chapters but that should be already familiar to you or, if not, well within your ability to grasp. This is intentional and will help you practice the *application* of skills and concepts you learned in each chapter to new business situations.

B.1 Answers to chapter 1 exercises

This section contains answers to the questions asked in chapter 1. For ease of reference, each question is repeated with the answer below it.

B.1.1 True/False questions

Answer the following questions with True or False.

Question 1: You always need a lot of data to make significant money with AI.
Answer to question 1: *False.* Often, just a simple analysis on a small dataset can be all the analysis you'll need to make money, *if you're the first person who figured out how to link that analysis with the business actions you can take.* In the early days of what eventually became one of the biggest hedge funds in the world, Ray Dalio used a single computer much less powerful than anything you can buy today [29] for all his analyses. Such a computer would struggle to run many of the complicated models we use in AI and ML today.

Question 2: The first step when starting an AI project is to select the right technology tools to use.

Answer to question 2: *False.* No tools are *best in class* among all possible sizes of data and business applications. The first step in any AI project should always be to think about the business problem you're trying to solve.

Question 3: Sometimes, simple AI algorithms can produce large business results.

Answer to question 3: *True.* Making money is a function of the size of the business opportunity to which you apply AI, not of the technical excellence of an algorithm. A simple algorithm can make a lot of money in plenty of situations, and in plenty of situations even the best AI algorithms can't solve a problem in a way that would make for a viable business product.

Question 4: Some tools can significantly automate AI projects. Just by using those tools, you can ensure a significant and lasting advantage over your competitors.

Answer to question 4: *False.* If a tool is something anyone can buy, then that tool is a commodity and can't form the basis of a sustainable competitive advantage.

Question 5: Making money with AI requires a PhD in math, physics, or computer science.

Answer to question 5: *False.* Plenty of AI practitioners don't have PhDs.

Question 6: Every AI PhD is guaranteed to know how to make money with AI.

Answer to question 6: *True*. . . if you hire them, but at that point, they made money for themselves, not for you. Such money is called *salary*. As far as making money for *you* goes, the reality is that it isn't unheard of to find people who've earned PhDs in AI programs who have limited business understanding.

Question 7: All AI tools are created equal.

Answer to question 7: *False.* Some tools are definitely better than others in their specific areas, but that's not what's most important. I'm not claiming that tools don't matter at all, or that there aren't good business reasons to choose one tool over another. I'm just saying that a tool itself isn't what matters the most for success of an AI project.

Question 8: You're a project executive, and you leave the definition of the evaluation metrics to your data science team. Unfortunately, your data science team doesn't have strong business domain knowledge, and they provide you with a metric that you don't understand—let's call it the Gini coefficient. If they do well on that metric, the project will help your business.

Answer to question 8: *Good luck!* This is an example of using a technical metric that has an unclear relation to your business. Consequently, it's not clear what value of the Gini coefficient is "good" for your business. Now you have a technical team measuring themselves based on improving "Gini," and a business team making decisions based on some other criteria. Those two teams are disconnected, and a good dose of luck is needed for the project to succeed.

B.1.2 Longer exercises: Identify the problem

A short narrative description of a hypothetical project or actions taken during the individual projects follows. What's your opinion of the situation described?

Question 1: A friend who works in the IT department of an organization somewhat similar to yours uses tool X and approach Y with great success. Should you use that tool and approach because your friend was successful with them?

Answer to question 1: The most important question to ask yourself here is how similar are the business problem and its data to your issue and its data? If the answer is *very*, then using a similar tool is valid. The problem with mimicking your friend's approach is that you might be copying the solution to a problem that's different from yours.

Question 2: X, a Fortune 100 company, begins their AI efforts by creating an infrastructure holding petabytes of data and buying an array of tools capable of solving a broad spectrum of AI problems. They've also created a department responsible for using and maintaining all those tools. Should you buy the same set of tools?

Answer to question 2: If you're in a Fortune 100 company with the same budget and business needs, then, yes, this applies to you too. If you don't work in a Fortune 100 company, remember that, in the last few years, we've faced a market that was excited about AI and was putting less pressure on you to get demonstrable business results quickly. Is that still the case at the time you're reading this book? Overall, the problem here is that you may be copying someone who can afford what you can't.

Question 3: You want to start your AI efforts with the use cases that other people successfully employed. Can you ask consultants with AI experience for an example of AI use cases often seen in your industry?

Answer to question 3: You can, but, again, you're copying what someone else did. If they're in your industry and are making money with their approach, you're at best a follower. If they aren't in the same industry, make sure that you can monetize such an approach. The problem here is too much focus on *how* to do it and not enough focus on talking about whether you *should* do it.

Question 4: What's wrong with the following approach? You're seeing that AI is getting better in video recognition. You plan to start an AI project that would apply AI to recognizing and scoring Olympic skating. By using such an AI, you can show the viewers what the predicted scores would be as soon as the skaters are done, without needing to wait for the judges. Your AI solution must be ready before the next Olympics.

Answer to question 4: You've just set an AI goal that's limited in time and, to the best of my knowledge, beyond the scope of current AI ability. You need a new scientific discovery to have a viable business, and you have limited time. Good luck.

Question 5: Is the following a good idea? You're in a heavily regulated industry that delivers products to end consumers. You have to run all your changes by a regulator, and changes are evaluated (almost exclusively) based on legal compliance, with a typical change taking five years to be approved. You plan to use AI to understand online customer feedback and your customers' satisfaction. The technical term for this process is sentiment analysis.

Answer to question 5: How are you going to change anything based on that analysis? And, if you do, it would likely take you five years to get it approved. Would your customers still remember their feedback by then, even if you were to eventually act on it? Would they care by that time? Although the argument could be made that overwhelming customer feedback can influence eventual change in regulation or a regulator's enforcement policy, chances are that you've just chosen to use AI in a context in which the result of the analysis isn't actionable.

Question 6: What are some problems with the following proposal? We'll use this AI and feed it patterns of our customer behavior, and it will reveal to us the causes of our customers' decisions.

Answer to question 6: Although it's a common misconception that AI can find the cause of behavior, today it can't. AI can only find a correlation. Causes are something for which humans (and methods different than ones typically used in AI today [24–27,151,164]) are needed.

Question 7: You're working in a domain in which it isn't easy to define business metrics that you can use to measure the business result. Someone has proposed to use AI and make business decisions based only on technical metrics. Is this a good idea?

Answer to question 7: AI methods are quantitative methods; informally, that means that they're methods intended to operate and optimize numbers. If you really can't define a reasonable business metric, you most likely shouldn't be using quantitative methods in the first place. Fortunately, it's usually possible to define business metrics quantitatively, if not with a single number, then with some range of values representing the business value of such an outcome (for example, "This outcome would be worth between $1 million and $2 million to us").

Chapters 3 and 4 talk more about business metrics. Here, the important thing to understand is that the unwillingness to quantify business smells of a data science/AI project that's not on the right track.

B.2   *Answers to chapter 2 exercises*

This section contains answers to the questions asked in chapter 2. For ease of reference, the question is repeated with the answer below it.

B.2.1   *Short answer questions*

Please provide brief answers to the following questions:

Question 1: Think about a failed project in your enterprise. Would that project have failed in the exact same way if it also had a component based on AI?

Answer to question 1: Most likely, the answer is yes. I'm talking about a large cross-section of possible projects, but the answer given here should apply to most cases. The point is that AI projects can fail in any of the ways that other normal projects can fail, as well as in a few ways that are specific to AI projects. (I talk about this later throughout the book, for example in section 5.1.2.) Again, systems matter more than any individual component that provides AI functionality. There is no reason to hope that introducing AI to your product will somehow prevent (or resolve) problems that would cause a failure of the typical software project.

Question 2: Do you personally have enough knowledge of data science and data engineering to understand the gap between the technical skills that your team has and the skills that they need for this project?

Answer to question 2: For this one, you're the best person to answer the question as yes or no. A more important question is what will you do if the answer happens to be no? Can you ask someone else in your organization? Can you hire a consultant to help you?

Question 3: Do you have a good enough relationship with your team members that they're comfortable admitting the limitations of their skillset to you?

Answer to question 3: If the answer happens to be no, what are you going to do about it? How can you make your team members feel safe enough to disclose their perceived skill gaps? Longer term, the question is this: what should you do to improve that trust?

B.2.2 *Answers to the scenario-based questions*

Answer the following questions based on the scenario described.

Question 1: One of the important skills in applying a Sense/Analyze/React loop is to identify who will execute on the React part of the pattern. For the following scenarios, answer this question: Who or what will carry out the action and fulfill the React part of the Sense/Analyze/React loop?

- **Scenario 1:** You're making an automated car, and the AI that you're using will allow fully autonomous driving under all conditions (so-called Level 5 autonomy [38], in which there are no available controls for the driver).
- **Scenario 2:** You're writing a recommendation engine in which products are suggested to the customer.
- **Scenario 3:** You're writing an AI program to regulate a smart thermostat that controls the temperature in your home.

Answer to question 1:

- **Scenario 1:** The car itself is fulfilling the React part of the loop because AI is controlling all standard functions of the car. Some of the possible actions that the car can perform include driving within the given speed, stopping, turning, signaling, and using the horn.
- **Scenario 2:** The customer, when they make a purchase based on your recommendations.
- **Scenario 3:** In this case, it's the HVAC system.

Question 2: Use AI to create a new job. Find an example of an AI capability that would let you offer a new service that your organization doesn't yet provide. (For the job to count as a solution to this exercise, it must be a job that's so unrelated to the software development team that's building the AI that the person hired for the job is unlikely to ever meet that team.)

Answer to question 2: This is a free-form exercise, so no single answer can be provided. The "Creating new jobs with AI" sidebar in section 2.5.3 gives one such example when using AI to monitor pets while owners are at work.

Question 3: Suppose you're using an AI algorithm in the context of a medical facility—let's say a radiology department of a large hospital. You're lucky to have on the team the best AI expert in the field of image classification, who has you covered on the AI side. While you're confident that expert will be able to develop an AI algorithm to classify medical images as either normal or abnormal, that expert has never worked in a healthcare setting before. What other considerations do you need to address to develop a working AI product applicable to healthcare?

Answer to question 3: A nice thing about this question is that there are so many considerations in a project of this size that you're almost certainly able to think of at least some that are applicable. The following is an (incomplete) list of considerations on projects like this:

- What's the exact action that you should take to solve a problem? What does "problem" even mean for a medical image? Medical images of a child and an elderly person are different, and so are medical images of an athlete in top shape and someone who is living a more sedentary lifestyle. Do you provide medical analysis even for the medical images of healthy people, or is the problem you're addressing limited to finding abnormal medical conditions? Do you diagnose medical condition precisely? Do you notify a person? Which person?
- Where would you get data to train the algorithm? Is that available from the hospital? Does the data need to be labeled? Does HIPAA [72,73] apply?
- How would you get an image from a patient into your AI system? How would you interface with the hospital's system? What's the workflow?
- Is the system reliable enough for use in a clinical setting? What types of errors are permissible? Can it misclassify 10% of normal images as a problem? Can it misclassify a problem image as being normal?
- Which regulations apply to you? Do you need regulatory approvals?
- And, all other considerations that apply to any other AI project: what infrastructure do you need, where would the data be stored, what are your organizational process and standards for developing software, and so on?

Question 4: Apply the previous example from a hospital setting to a classification problem in your industry. What are the new considerations that exist in your industry as compared to the healthcare industry?

Answer to question 4: This is a free-form exercise, so no single answer can be provided.

Question 5: Provide an example of an AI that has replaced a human role but doesn't provide as good of an experience as a human would.

Answer to question 5: For me, automated voice prompts (those that are commonly encountered when you call customer support these days) are one example.

Question 6: You're a manufacturer of security cameras, and you've developed an AI algorithm that can detect a person in a picture. Regarding the taxonomy of its role in your business, how would you classify this use of AI?

Answer to question 6: This is an example of AI as a part of the larger product. Depending on how much confidence you have that you can correctly recognize a human as an intruder and the follow-up action you can take (for example, calling the police), this might also become a fully autonomous system.

Question 7: You're an insurance company, and you've developed an AI program that, based on static images from an accident site, could recognize which parts of the car are damaged in a wreck. Can this replace an insurance adjuster?

Answer to question 7: It's unlikely, if all you have to go on is images from an accident site. Insurance adjusters need to check the car itself to be able to assess the damage. As such, this isn't an example of a simple AI that can replace humans with a large cost savings, and, if used as such, it would likely fail. There's a reason why even qualified mechanics need to open the hood to see what's damaged underneath. But applied across all insurance adjusters and wrecks, this could be useful for fraud detection. For example, AI could flag for further investigation if individual adjusters often write off parts that look undamaged. As such, this type of AI can help the employees working in the fraud department (or even create new jobs in that department).

B.3   Answers to chapter 3 exercises

This section contains answers to the questions asked in chapter 3. For ease of reference, the question is repeated with the answer below it.

Question 1: Suppose you're working in the publishing industry, and you're wondering if it's better to release printed, electronic, and audiobooks at the same time or one after another. Also, if delivery is staged so that printed books are released first, how long should you wait before releasing the other formats? Within this setting, answer the following question: "What business metrics should you use?"

Answer to question 1: The appropriate business metrics to use depend on how the business of your specific organization is structured. Metrics are always *specific to your organization*. You should be suspicious of any statement of the form "Always use metric X" made *before* the person making such a statement takes a closer look at your organization.

The only correct answer to this question is, "It depends—what do you hope the book would achieve?" You should never just transplant a metric you've seen someone else use without analyzing if and why such a metric applies to you.

Maybe the total profit for the lifetime of a book would be the best metric. For some publishing organizations, and if the book's only purpose was to make a profit, it would be. However, if you're releasing a free book for a philanthropic organization, the best metric could just as well be, "The total number of new volunteers that you've recruited as a result of them reading the book."

Question 2: If you're a business leader, define a business question and an appropriate metric to measure it. Think about some hypothetical scenarios not directly applicable to your organization (for example, some scenarios related to philanthropy). Think about actions that you can take while running a nonprofit. Use the techniques introduced in chapter 3 to select your first hypothetical business question, as well as the metrics you'd use to measure success.

Answer to question 2: This is a free-form exercise.

Question 3: Once you've identified your business question from the previous exercise, take your senior AI expert to lunch and talk about the business problem. Ask them how they'd formulate a research question. Use the process described in chapter 3 to check whether or not the answer supports the business action you intend to take. And, while you're having that lunch, talk about how you'd find a dataset to answer such a research question. Do you think you can acquire that dataset?

Answer to question 3:

- For a research question, this is a free-form exercise.
- Finding a dataset for your research question clearly depends on the problem you're trying to address, but it's not uncommon that the answer to the question "Is it possible to acquire a dataset?" is no. Often, obtaining labeled data is the real obstacle to an application of AI.
- Also, if during this hypothetical conversation, neither of you thought about which data science/AI/ML methods you could use on the dataset, chances are, you might have missed some of the needed data. Remember that needed data and its quantity depend on the AI methods you use (and vice versa).

B.4   *Answers to chapter 4 exercises*

This section contains answers to the questions asked in chapter 4. For ease of reference, the question is repeated with the answer below it.

Question 1: If your organization has run AI projects before, look at some progress reports and the metrics used in those reports. Answer the following:

- If we release software today, in its current state, how much money will we make/lose?

- If we can't release today, how much better do our results need to be before we can release?
- Is it worth investing $100 K extra in getting 5% better results than we have today?

Answer to question 1: The answers for this exercise, of course, depend on the project. But, after completing this exercise, you already have the answers to whether your historical projects used metrics that business decisions could be based on.

Question 2: Based on the answers to the previous questions, do you feel that your organization is making decisions in its AI projects based on the data, or is it possible that in some cases you had to make important decisions based on intuition?

Answer to question 2: Most organizations today have some ways to go before making the most of management decisions on AI projects based strictly on data. Don't feel bad if your organization is in the same position. While transforming organizational mindsets is always a job that must be customized, I hope that the material in chapter 4 gives you some starting points. You might also want to review Osherove's book [82] and Kotter International's website [190] for a larger discussion on techniques for organizational transformation.

Question 3: Suppose the cost to start a project is $100 K, and the policy of your organization is that no project that can't create a 10% return on investment is worth doing. If your business metric is profit, what would be your value threshold for the project?

Answer to question 3: A minimum value threshold would be $100 K + 10%, or $110 K. However, in practice, you're unlikely to be certain that the cost of the project is really going to be $100 K, so add whatever safety factor you think you should to $110 K. This is a simplified example in which the only consideration is ROI. In many organizations, you would also need to account for the cost of capital/how long you would need to earn those $10 K.

Question 4: Go back to the bike rental example from this chapter. Suppose the estimated cost to assign a data scientist to the project is $10 K, and each extra bike costs $1 K. How much should you expect to improve the peak hour's RMSE to make it worthwhile to assign a data scientist to the project?

Answer to question 4: If an extra bike costs $1 K, then you'd need to believe that you can improve the peak hour's RMSE for at least $10 K/$1 K = 10 for it to be worthwhile to assign a data scientist to the project.

B.5   Answers to chapter 5 exercises

This section contains answers to the questions asked in chapter 5. For ease of reference, the question is repeated with the answer below it.

Question 1: Construct an ML pipeline for this AI project: the project takes feedback from your customers and analyzes it. If a customer appears unhappy, an alert is issued so that you can contact the customer and try to appease them before they decide to leave. (That part of AI which determines whether a customer is happy or not is technically called *sentiment analysis*.) You already have an AI software library that performs sentiment analysis. The data is in your customer support system, which is a web application.

Answer to question 1:

- More than one result is an acceptable answer to this question; after all, there's no universal ML pipeline that works the best in all cases!
- Figure B.1 shows one ML pipeline I'd start with.

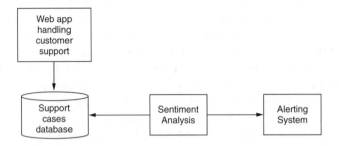

Figure B.1   ML pipeline for sentiment analysis of the customer feedback

Question 2: Suppose you implement the ML pipeline from the previous example in your organization. Which departments would be responsible for the implementation of which parts of the pipeline?

Answer to question 2: The answer depends on your organization. The goal of this question is to get you thinking about your organization and visualizing people who would be involved.

Question 3: What business metric would you use to measure the success of the ML pipeline from question 1?

Answer to question 3:

- It depends on what you're trying to achieve. As mentioned in chapter 3, you shouldn't just blindly transplant metrics from other organizations to your project, even the metrics that happened to be suggested by me in the answers to the exercises in this book.
- Suppose that what you're trying to achieve is the reduction of total customer turnover (churn). Clearly, reduction in churn is one such business metric.
- What if you're trying to maximize profit from future business with customers? There are some questions as to how you'd exactly measure it, but let's suppose that, for the sake of argument, you'd assume that past recurring business is a good predictor of future recurring business. Then the metric would be profit per customer saved, which in itself is different from revenue per customer saved. Moreover, as not all of the customers are of the same value (which is a common situation in many businesses), the result you'd get from this metric is *very different* from the result you'd get from churn reduction.

Question 4: What is the history of the coordination between departments from question 2 in past projects that they've participated in? Were projects on which those teams worked successful?

Answer to question 4:

- The history, of course, would depend on your organization. What matters for the hypothetical project (and any new project) is to ask, "Which of the historical patterns you've seen are likely to repeat on the new project?"

- What has worked well? What didn't work well? Can you fix issues that historically didn't work well before they create a problem on the new project?

- How would you assess the risk that your organizational structure and way of working pose to the hypothetical project?

NOTE The next questions (5 and 6) are targeted toward data scientists. You can skip them if you don't have data science expertise.

Question 5: As a part of the installation of an AI security product, you're offering a 30-day, money-back guarantee. Your customers have taken a survey about their satisfaction with the product, which they completed as soon as the product was installed. You're interested in predicting if your customers would return the product. During discussions, the team has mentioned that this problem could be solved using either an SVM, a decision tree, logistic regression, or a deep learning-based classification. Should you use deep learning? After all, it's an exceedingly popular technology, has a substantial mindshare, and could solve the problem. Or should you use one of the other suggested options?

Answer to question 5:

- You can use a deep learning-based classifier, but I typically wouldn't try it as my first (or even second) choice. Unless your survey is a monster with a thousand questions, it's unclear that you'll be able to train a large deep learning network at all.

- I'm not persuaded that for the typical survey of only a few questions, more complicated methods are going to produce better results. It is possible to analyze whether you need to apply a more complicated AI method to the problem (such as variance-bias tradeoff analysis [183]). However, in practice, I would start with a simple method such as logistic regression, a decision tree, or an SVM classifier. I would also try gradient boosting machines (GBMs) prior to trying deep learning; in most cases, they work better on tabular data anyway.

Question 6: You answered question 5 using an algorithm of your choice. Suppose the algorithm you chose didn't provide a good enough prediction of a customer returning the product. Should you use a better ML algorithm? Is it now time to use the latest and greatest from the field of deep learning?

Answer to question 6:

- Your data may not be related to the problem you're trying to solve (a customer returning your security product)! Remember, the survey result is completed as a mandatory step immediately after installation of the AI security system. Does the customer know enough at that time to know if they like the system as it is when they're using it?

- Can you collect data about what the system was doing between installation and the moment a customer returned it? Is that data a better predictor of whether the customer will return the system? For that matter, can you survey customers when they're returning the system?

- And a larger topic you should remember for practical AI projects is that, unlike an academic or Kaggle competition [191], you control which data you can collect! Don't just take data you have as a given and assume you must use better ML algorithms.

B.6   *Answers to chapter 6 exercises*

This section contains answers to the questions asked in chapter 6. For ease of reference, the question is repeated with the answer below it. To help you look at the questions and solutions all in one place, in addition to the text of the questions, I'm also repeating the figure that the exercises refer to.

Figure B.2   An example ML pipeline. This figure is a repeat of figure 6.10.

You'll also need to refer to table 6.1 (which is repeated here for your convenience as table B.1).

Table B.1   Summary of the possible results of MinMax analysis

Min result/Max result	Max passed	Max failed
Min passed	The ML pipeline is business-viable.	This combination can't happen.
Min failed	The ML pipeline needs improvement to be business-viable.	The current ML pipeline is not suitable for solving the business problem.

Remember that because analyzing the ML pipeline is a technical and business skill, it is hoped that you were able to form a team consisting of a business specialist and an engineer and that your team does some of these exercises together.

Question 1: Note that in table B.1, you don't have any guidance for the situation in which the Min part of the MinMax has passed, but the Max part of the MinMax failed. Explain why this is the case.

Answer to question 1: The Min part of the MinMax analysis returns what the ML pipeline you have today can achieve. The Max part shows you the best that can be achieved. By definition, "the best you can do" can't be worse than what you've already done.

Question 2: For the ML pipeline in figure B.2, assume that the value threshold at which the project becomes business-viable is $1 million. Determine whether the pipeline is worth pursuing if the results of the MinMax analysis are as follows:

- **Scenario 1:** The Min part is $2.3 million, and the Max part is $23 million.
- **Scenario 2:** The Min part is $500 K, and the Max part is $1 million.
- **Scenario 3:** The Min part is $500 K, and the Max part is $2 million.
- **Scenario 4:** The Min part is $1.1 million, and the Max part is $900 K.
- **Scenario 5:** The Min part is $500 K, and the Max part is $900 K.

Answers to question 2:

- **Scenario 1:** The Min part is above the value threshold; you already have a business-viable ML pipeline.
- **Scenario 2:** I would say that you need a new pipeline. Your Max analysis barely reaches the value threshold. I'm typically skeptical of the possibility that business and industry teams will be able to reach or exceed the best currently published result. I'm also skeptical that any value threshold's estimate is entirely on target. There should be some safety factor here, and I'd assume that this isn't a viable business pipeline.
- **Scenario 3:** In this case, I'd assume that the Min pipeline isn't good enough, but (unless I have a reason for a safety factor above 2) I'm working with an ML pipeline that could be made business-viable. I'd perform a sensitivity analysis and see what happens.
- **Scenario 4:** Excuse me, how did this situation happen? Find a way to (politely) ask your engineering team to repeat the complete analysis. See the answer to this chapter's question 1 for details.
- **Scenario 5:** Your ML pipeline isn't business-viable. I wouldn't attempt to pursue it unless I had one of the world's leading teams in that particular area of AI, and I'd also be conscious of the possibility that the project might fail. Even if I had such an all-star team, I'd first check if I'd be able to construct a better pipeline.

Question 3: If you're a data scientist or technical manager, take a technical problem of your choice and construct an ML pipeline for it. Perform the Max part of the MinMax analysis for it.

Answers to question 3: This is a free-form exercise, and the goal is to begin to get you comfortable with thinking about which tools you'd use for the MinMax analysis:

- Are you familiar with the academic literature in the area and comfortable following it? Would you instead ask an expert? Who are the experts who could help you?

- What would be a good proxy problem for your ML pipeline?
- How much of a safety factor should there be? For that matter, do you feel that in your organization the safety factor should be based primarily on a technical opinion or primarily on a risk management (how much am I afraid of being wrong) decision?

Question 4: If you're a data scientist or technical manager, look at the examples given in section 6.4.1 and perform a MinMax analysis as described in that section. Determine where the dollar amount given in that section comes from. Hint: a profit curve was constructed from the confusion matrix of the classifier.

Answers to question 4:

- Because the city is hedging you 50 parking overstays a year, your worst-case scenario is 51 illegal parking overstays per year. At that point, you still need to make a profit.
- I used the following formula to calculate the result:

$$(Accuracy * Profit\_when\_right - (1 - Accuracy) * Loss\_when\_wrong) * 51$$

Question 5: How would you classify the use of AI in the context of saving litigation costs during the e-discovery process described in section 6.5.5? Use the taxonomy of AI uses introduced in section 2.5. It's shown in figure 2.5, duplicated here as figure B.3, which summarizes the taxonomies discussed in that section.

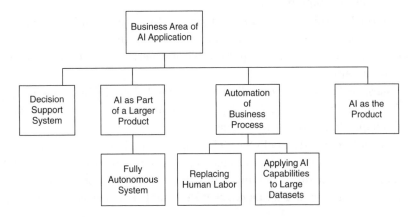

Figure B.3 An AI taxonomy based on the high-level role it plays in business. You could use this taxonomy to guide you in eliciting available business actions you can help with AI. This figure is a repeat of figure 2.5.

Answers to question 5:

- In the problem formulation presented in section 6.5.5, the role of AI is limited to just rejecting the document, as in, "For sure not related to litigation." You are automating a step in the business process, and therefore such a use of AI would best fit under the category of automation of the business process.

- Note that if we were to extend the use of AI to help the attorney with all aspects of the e-discovery, then it would be better classified as a decision support system.

B.7   *Answers to chapter 7 exercises*

This section contains answers to the questions asked in chapter 7. For ease of reference, the question is repeated with the answer below it. To help you look at the questions and solutions all in one place, in addition to the text of the questions, I'm also repeating the figure that the exercises refer to.

Figure B.4   An example ML pipeline. We use this pipeline as a motivating example for sensitivity analysis. This is a repeat of figure 6.10 for the reader's convenience.

Question 1: This question gives you the results of the sensitivity analysis for the pipeline in figure B.4. Assume that the business metric is profit and the value threshold is $2 million/year. The results of your MinMax analysis are the Min part being $1.9 million/year and the Max part being $3 million/year. You decide to perform a sensitivity analysis. Why is it necessary to perform the sensitivity analysis? You've worked on all the stages for a while, and you've reached a point where it's more and more challenging to improve any of the stages. Determine in which stage of the pipeline you should invest if the results of the sensitivity analysis are as follows:

- Stage A would require 6 months to improve by 1%. When you improve stage A, the overall improvement in the ML pipeline will be $10 K/%.
- Stage B would require 2 months to improve by 1%. When you improve stage B, the overall improvement in the ML pipeline will be $200 K/%.
- Stage C would require 1 year to improve by 1%. When you improve stage C, the overall improvement in the ML pipeline will be $800 K/%.
- The ML pipeline doesn't show any appreciable improvement in results when stages D and E are improved. When does such a situation occur in practice?

Answer to question 1:

- You needed to perform sensitivity analysis because your Min analysis failed and your Max analysis passed. Your ML pipeline isn't business-viable as-is but hopefully can be made so.
- I'd personally try to improve stage B first or, if I had the resources, work on improving stages B and C in parallel. You're reasonably close to business viability, and improvement in stage B is much faster to develop than in stage C. A lot can happen in a year, so try to make your AI pipeline business-viable soon.
- It's not atypical for some of the stages in the ML pipeline (such as stages D and E in this pipeline) to contribute little to the quality of its overall result. The data

those stages are producing may be unimportant for the ML pipeline as a whole. As an example, holiday sales data may have only minimal value for predicting customers' ultimate satisfaction with the product—the person making a holiday purchase may not be the same person who would be using the product in the end. In that case, improving the quality of that data might not do much for the ML pipeline when predicting future customer satisfaction.

Question 2: This question gives you the results of the sensitivity analysis for the pipeline in figure B.4. Assume that the business metric is profit and the value threshold is $2 million/year. The results of your MinMax analysis are the Min part being $1.9 million/year and the Max part being $3 million/year. You decide to perform a sensitivity analysis. You haven't constructed any prototype or tried to clean the data. Determine in which stage of the pipeline you should invest if the results of the sensitivity analysis are as follows:

- Stage A would require 3 months to improve by 2%. When you improve stage A, the overall improvement in the ML pipeline will be $200 K/%.
- Stage B would require 2 months to improve by 1%. When you improve stage B, the overall improvement in the ML pipeline will be $100 K/%.
- Stage C would require 1 year to improve by 1%. When you improve stage C, the overall improvement in the ML pipeline will be $800 K/%.
- The ML pipeline doesn't show any appreciable improvement in results when stages D and E are improved.

Answer to question 2:

- If you haven't constructed any implementation of even a minimal ML pipeline, you have no reason to believe that only small, incremental improvements are possible in your system. After all, it's not like you tried hard to improve and are facing diminishing returns in every stage.
- Consequently, I don't believe that assuming a linear response in the ML pipeline to the analysis is reasonable. I would recommend performing a full range sensitivity analysis of this pipeline.
- If I was facing a rare case in which linearization of this pipeline would be a reasonable assumption (for example, I didn't try to improve it, but many other people tried and failed), I'd probably choose to upgrade stage A or stage B, based on how critical it was to deliver this ML pipeline quickly.
- Without a prototype, how was your Min analysis completed—is it only an estimate, or did you use commercial-off-the-shelf (COTS) products? If you used COTS, why can't you use that COTS to build a Proof of Concept (POC) of your pipeline? Is that COTS appropriate for performing Min analysis (as opposed to Max analysis)? Similarly, how did you perform a sensitivity analysis?

  There are situations in which you will have a Min analysis completed without any POC. However, in the absence of POC, the questions above should be asked, as they would influence safety factors and the confidence you have in the results.

Question 3: Your AI project is investigating if, by installing an IoT sensor to monitor a vehicle's sound, you'd be able to determine what kinds of changes in tone would indicate a mechanical problem in the vehicle. You've deployed a sensor in 150 vehicles and waited for a month. Only a single vehicle had a mechanical problem. After the month-long investigation, your data scientists tell you that from the data collected, they can't predict breakage of the vehicles, and that a single broken vehicle is an insufficiently small dataset. Does this mean you can't make an AI that can predict vehicle breakage?

Answer to question 3:

- No, it doesn't mean that you can't make an AI that can predict vehicle breakage! There's only a single breakage, and your team already hinted that they don't think they got enough data to train AI algorithms.
- With more data, they might be able to succeed. However, with the current rate of breakage, it might take you many years to get enough data.
- This project should be classified as "We need more data to know the answer," not as "AI prediction of breakages was tried and is impossible." However, you should pause the project and try a different and easier one.

Question 4: Suppose you have two ML pipelines. Your business metric is revenue. The value threshold is constant at $10 million/year. You have two parallel teams that could work on both ML pipelines. Pipeline 1 would deliver $20 million/year, and pipeline 2 would provide $30 million/year. The cost of the team to develop the pipeline is small compared to the lifetime profit expected from the AI project. Your organization can implement pipeline 1 in 4 months and pipeline 2 in 1 year. Determine which of the two pipelines you should release, and when. Also, draw a timing diagram showing these two pipelines.

Answer to question 4:

- You should release both pipelines, as they both exceed the value threshold, and the cost of the team is small compared to the lifetime value of the pipeline.
- Figure B.5 shows the timing diagram.

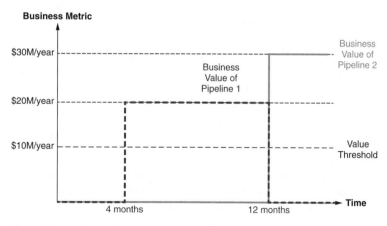

Figure B.5   A timing diagram that answers question 4 of chapter 7's exercises

B.8   *Answers to chapter 8 exercises*

This section contains answers to the questions asked in chapter 8. For ease of reference, the question is repeated with the answer below it.

Question 1: Explain whether AI as practiced today is applicable to the following projects:

- **Scenario 1:** Predicting short-term retail and economic activity based on using satellite images to track the movement and number of ocean-going container ships
- **Scenario 2:** Predicting new prices of a portfolio in the case of an unexpected event that completely disrupts the foundations of the global economic system
- **Scenario 3:** Predicting the effect of genetic research on healthcare spending costs 20 years from now

Answers to question 1:

- **Scenario 1:** AI is definitely applicable to this problem. You can recognize a container ship on a satellite picture. The picture can also recognize the approximate size of the ship and direction of travel. That allows you to know the amount of goods that are being transported. There's a clear relationship between transportation and sale of goods, and in the globalized economy, transportation of goods comes before retail activity.
- **Scenario 2:** AI is likely hopeless on this problem because it doesn't account for a causal relationship. Remember, correlation-based AI is valid only in the world that looks like the one in which it's trained. This question doesn't describe such a world.
- **Scenario 3:** Not likely. We certainly don't have data about such a world. It's not clear that we can predict what genetic research will come up with or how that would be applicable to healthcare. It also isn't clear that we even understand what causal relationships exist between genetic data and future healthcare costs. Any model trying to extrapolate that far out is probably extrapolating well beyond the breaking point.

Question 2: Reflect on the last three times your organization adapted a new and popular technology, after which the consensus in hindsight was that the project didn't succeed. Now, find the reasons why the project was *not* successful. By the way, saying that the wrong people were on the team or that you weren't experienced enough with technology aren't acceptable reasons.

Avoiding discussions of people and personalities makes the dialogue more palatable in a corporate setting. More importantly, after these exclusions, what remains are the inherent process weaknesses that your organization has in evaluating new technologies. The goal is to recognize those same weaknesses the next time a new technology comes in vogue. This time, the technology in vogue is AI.

Answers to question 2:

- The answers for each organization are going to be specific. The goal of this question is for you to concentrate on the system your organization uses, not on the personalities or one-time events. Chances are, you'd see problems that are produced by the weaknesses of the system even after employees changed.
- For extra credit, you can apply counterfactual analysis on the characteristics of your organization that you've identified. Has your organization made any recent changes that are likely to result in a different outcome than the ones that have happened historically?

Question 3: For each of the trends introduced in this chapter (as exemplified by the headings of sections 8.1 to 8.6), answer the following questions. As a reminder, those trends are listed in table 8.1 (which is repeated here for your convenience as table B.2).

Table B.2   Trends introduced in this chapter. How do those trends affect you?

Section 8.1	The meaning of the term *AI* changes through time.
Section 8.2	AI use in physical systems must account for safety.
Section 8.3	AI systems today don't account for causal relationships.
Section 8.4	AI algorithms don't typically account for the variable veracity in data.
Section 8.5	AI systems' mistakes are different from human errors.
Section 8.6	AutoML is approaching.

- Does this trend affect your current project?
- Is the trend likely to affect your organization in general?
- Is the trend likely to affect your personal career?
- How do you intend to follow the trend?
- How will you know if the trend is materializing or not?

Answer to question 3: Every organization will have specific answers to these questions.

Question 4: Are there any trends of specific applications of AI in your industry that affect you but weren't enumerated in this chapter?

Answer to question 4: Almost certainly there are some, because AI use is still in its infancy and is not widely adopted across many different industries today. Chances are, if you performed a serious and complete analysis and still have trouble identifying an AI trend that affects your industry, you've just discovered a business opportunity. You might be among the first people who seriously thought about the best ways to use AI in your industry!

appendix C
Bibliography

1 Luftig JT, Ouellette SM, editors. Business performance excellence. Bloomsbury Academic; 2012.

2 Luftig JT. TOTAL asset utilization. Measuring Business Excellence. 1999 Jan;3(1):20–25.

3 Luftig JT. EMEN 5041 CU Boulder Fall 2011 class and post-class conversations. CU Boulder, Boulder, CO, USA; 2011 Fall.

4 Drucker P. Managing for business effectiveness. Harvard Business Review. 1963 May:53–60.

5 Strickland E. IBM Watson, heal thyself. IEEE Spectrum. 2019 Aug:24–31.

6 Zumel N, Mount J. Practical data science with R. Shelter Island, NY: Manning Publications Co; 2014.

7 Chollet F. Deep Learning with Python. Shelter Island, NY: Manning Publications; 2017.

8 Chollet F, Allaire JJ. Deep learning with R. Shelter Island, NY: Manning Publications Co; 2018.

9 Lee K-F. AI superpowers: China, Silicon Valley, and the new world order. Boston: Houghton Mifflin Harcourt; 2018.

10 Peng T. Andrew Ng says enough papers, let's build AI now! Synced. 2017 Nov 4 [cited 2019 Feb 15]. Available from: https://syncedreview.com/2017/11/04/andrew-ng-says-enough-papers-lets-build-ai-now/

11 Amazon.com, Inc. Amazon Web Services. [Cited 2019 Jul 19.] Available from: https://aws.amazon.com

12 Google, Inc. Build. Modernize. Scale. [Cited 2019 Jul 19.] Available from: https://cloud.google.com

13 Microsoft Corporation. Microsoft Azure. [Cited 2019 Jul 19.] Available from: https://azure.microsoft.com/en-us/

14 Apache Software Foundation. Apache Spark™—Unified analytics engine for big data. [Cited 2018 Jul 4.] Available from: https://spark.apache.org/

15 Apache Software Foundation. Welcome to Apache™ Hadoop®! [Cited 2018 Jul 4.] Available from: http://hadoop.apache.org/

16 Apache Software Foundation. Apache Flink®—Stateful computations over data streams. [Cited 2019 Jul 19.] Available from: https://flink.apache.org

17 Wikimedia Foundation. Machine Learning. Wikipedia. [Cited 2019 Jul 12.] Available from: https://en.wikipedia.org/wiki/Machine_learning

18 Techopedia. Artificial intelligence (AI). Technopedia. [Cited 2019 Jun 2.] Available from: https://www.techopedia.com/definition/190/artificial-intelligence-ai

19 Domingos P. A few useful things to know about machine learning. Communications of the ACM. 2012; 55(10):78–87.

20 Apollo 17 crew. *The blue marble.* 1972. Available from: https://en.wikipedia.org/w/index.php?title=The_Blue_Marble&oldid=846541979

21 ASQ. Six Sigma belts, executives and champions—What does it all mean? [Cited 2018 Jul 5.] Available from: http://asq.org/learn-about-quality/six-sigma/overview/belts-executives-champions.html

22 ASQ. Six Sigma definition—What is lean Six Sigma? [Cited 2018 Jul 5.] Available from: http://asq.org/learn-about-quality/six-sigma/overview/overview.html

23 Whitehorn M. The parable of the beer and diapers. 2006 Aug 15 [cited 2018 Jul 5]. Available from: https://www.theregister.co.uk/2006/08/15/beer_diapers/

24 ASQ. What is design of experiments (DOE)? [Cited 2018 Jul 7.] Available from: http://asq.org/learn-about-quality/data-collection-analysis-tools/overview/design-of-experiments.html

25 Pearl J, Mackenzie D. The book of why: The new science of cause and effect. New York: Basic Books; 2018.

26 Kleinberg S. Why: A guide to finding and using causes. Beijing; Boston: O'Reilly Media; 2015.

27 Pearl J. Causality: Models, reasoning and inference. 2nd ed. Cambridge, UK; New York: Cambridge University Press; 2009.

28 Ries E. The lean startup: How today's entrepreneurs use continuous innovation to create radically successful businesses. New York: Currency; 2011.

29 Dalio R. Principles. New York: Simon and Schuster; 2018.

30 Prahalad CK, Hamel G. The core competence of the corporation. Harvard Business Review. 1990 May–Jun.

31 Richard B. Closing the strategy gap. CFO. 1996 Oct.

32 Magretta J. The most common strategy mistakes. HBS Working Knowledge. 2011 Dec 21 [cited 2019 Dec 11]. Available from: http://hbswk.hbs.edu/item/the-most-common-strategy-mistakes

33 Lee RG, Dale BG. Policy deployment: An examination of the theory. International Journal of Quality & Reliability Management. 1998;15(5):520–540.

34 Wikimedia Foundation. PID controller. Wikipedia. [Cited 2017 Mar 12.] Available from: https://en.wikipedia.org/wiki/PID_controller

35 Wikimedia Foundation. History of artificial intelligence. Wikipedia. [Cited 2019 Jun 28.] Available from: https://en.wikipedia.org/wiki/History_of_artificial _intelligence

36 Nest. Create a connected home. Nest. [Cited 2018 Jul 2.] Available from: https://www.nest.com/

37 ecobee. ecobee3. [Cited 2018 Jul 2.] Available from: https://www.ecobee.com/ecobee3/

38 Wikimedia Foundation. Autonomous car. Wikipedia. [Cited 2018 Jun 30.] Available from: https://en.wikipedia.org/w/index.php?title=Autonomous_car&oldid =848201994

39 ASQ. What is the plan-do-check-act (PDCA) cycle? ASQ. [Cited 04-Jul-2018.] Available from: http://asq.org/learn-about-quality/project-planning-tools/overview/pdca-cycle.html

40 Wikimedia Foundation. PDCA. Wikipedia. [Cited 2018 Jun 26.] Available from: https://en.wikipedia.org/w/index.php?title=PDCA

41 Wikimedia Foundation. OODA loop. Wikipedia. [Cited 2019 Jun 10.] Available from: https://en.wikipedia.org/w/index.php?title=OODA_loop

42 Ullman D. 'OO-OO-OO!' The sound of a broken OODA loop. 2007 Apr 1 [cited 2017 Jun 25]. Available from: https://www.researchgate.net/publication/268415631_OO-OO-OO_The_sound_of_a_broken_OODA_loop

43 Wikimedia Foundation. Cross-industry standard process for data mining. Wikipedia. [Cited 2019 Jul 12]. Available from: https://en.wikipedia.org/w/index.php?title=Cross-industry_standard_process_for_data_mining

44 Godfrey-Smith P. Other minds: The octopus, the sea, and the deep origins of consciousness. New York: Farrar, Straus and Giroux; 2016.

45 Brockman J. Know this: Today's most interesting and important scientific ideas, discoveries, and developments. New York, NY: Harper Perennial; 2017.

46 Wikimedia Foundation. Internet of things. Wikipedia. [Cited 2018 Jul 2]. Available from: https://en.wikipedia.org/wiki/Internet_of_things

47 Wikimedia Foundation. Nicolas-Joseph Cugnot. [Cited 2019 Jul 15]. Available from: https://en.wikipedia.org/wiki/Nicolas-Joseph_Cugnot

48 Wikimedia Foundation. History of the automobile. [Cited 2019 Jul 15]. Available from: https://en.wikipedia.org/wiki/History_of_the_automobile

49 Gulshan V, et al. Development and validation of a deep learning algorithm for detection of diabetic retinopathy in retinal fundus photographs. JAMA. 2016 Dec;316(22):2402.

50 Apple, Inc. Siri. Apple. [Cited 2019 Jul 15]. Available from: https://www.apple .com/siri/

51 Ackerman E, Guizzo E. iRobot brings visual mapping and navigation to the Roomba 980. IEEE Spectrum. 2015 Sep 16 [cited 2019 Jul 15]. Available from: https://spectrum.ieee.org/automaton/robotics/home-robots/irobot-brings-visual -mapping-and-navigation-to-the-roomba-980

52 Amazon.com, Inc. Amazon Echo & Alexa Devices. [Cited 2019 Jul 22.] Available from: https://www.amazon.com/Amazon-Echo-And-Alexa-Devices/b?node=9818 047011

53 Google, Inc. Google Home. [Cited 2019 Jul 22.] Available from: https://store .google.com/product/google_home

54 Google, Inc. Google Assistant is ready and built-in to specific speakers. Assistant. [Cited 2019 Sep 19.] Available from: https://assistant.google.com/platforms/ speakers/

55 Apple, Inc. The new sound of home. [Cited 2019 Jul 22.] Available from: https:// www.apple.com/homepod/

56 SAS Institute. Analytics, artificial intelligence and data management. [Cited 2019 Sep 19.] Available from: https://www.sas.com/en_us/home.html

57 International Business Machines Corporation. SPSS Software. [Cited 2019 Sep 19.] Available from: https://www.ibm.com/analytics/spss-statistics-software

58 Schmarzo B. Big data: Understanding how data powers big business. Indianapolis, IN: Wiley; 2013.

59 Schmarzo B. Big data MBA: Driving business strategies with data science. Indianapolis, IN: Wiley; 2015.

60 Wikimedia Foundation. Gradient boosting. Wikipedia. [Cited 2020 Jan 13.] Available from: https://en.wikipedia.org/wiki/Gradient_boosting.

61 Gorman B. Kaggle master explains gradient boosting. Kaggle.com. 2017 Jan 23 [cited 2017 Jun 30]. Available from: http://blog.kaggle.com/2017/01/23/a-kaggle-master-explains-gradient-boosting/

62 He K, Zhang X, Ren S, Sun J. Deep residual learning for image recognition. arXiv. 2015 Dec;arXiv:1512.03385 [cs.CV].

63 Szegedy C, et al. Going deeper with convolutions. arXiv. 2014 Sep;arXiv:1409.4842 [cs.CV].

64 Suzuki K. Overview of deep learning in medical imaging. Radiological Physics and Technology. 2017 Sep;10(3):257–273.

65 Liu Y, et al. A deep learning system for differential diagnosis of skin diseases. arXiv. 2019 Sep;arXiv:1909.05382 [eess.IV].

66 Harris HD, Murphy SP, Vaisman M. Analyzing the analyzers: An introspective survey of data scientists and their work. Beijing: O'Reilly; 2013.

67 Wikimedia Foundation. No free lunch theorem. Wikipedia. [Cited 2016 Apr 2.] Available from: https://en.wikipedia.org/wiki/No_free_lunch_theorem

68 Cloudera, Inc. Hortonworks data platform for HDInsight: Component versions. [Cited 2019 Nov 24.] Available from: https://docs.cloudera.com/HDP Documents/HDPforCloud/HDPforCloud-2.6.5/hdp-release-notes/content/hdp _comp_versions.html

69 Wikimedia Foundation. Gap analysis. Wikipedia. [Cited 2019 Jul 10.] Available from: https://en.wikipedia.org/wiki/Gap_analysis

70 Tolstoy L; Pevear R, Volokhonsky L, translators. Anna Karenina. New York: Penguin Books; 2004.

71 Wikimedia Foundation. General Data Protection Regulation. Wikipedia. [Cited 2019 Jul 21.] Available from: https://en.wikipedia.org/wiki/General_Data _Protection_Regulation

72 Wikimedia Foundation. Health Insurance Portability and Accountability Act. Wikipedia. [Cited 2019 Jul 21.] Available from: https://en.wikipedia.org/wiki/ Health_Insurance_Portability_and_Accountability_Act

73 U.S. Department of Health & Human Services. Summary of the HIPAA Security Rule. HHS.gov. [Cited 2019 Jul 21.] Available from: https://www.hhs.gov/hipaa/ for-professionals/security/laws-regulations/index.html

74 June Life, Inc. The do-it-all oven. [Cited 2019 Jul 15.] Available from: https:// juneoven.com/

75 Hubbard DW. How to measure anything: Finding the value of intangibles in business. 2nd ed. Hoboken, NJ: Wiley; 2010.

76 Wikimedia Foundation. Artificial general intelligence. Wikipedia. [Cited 2018 Jun 13.] Available from: https://en.wikipedia.org/w/index.php?title=Artificial _general_intelligence

77 Shani G, Gunawardana A. Evaluating recommendation systems. In: Ricci F, Rokach L, Shapira B, Kantor PB, editors. Recommender systems handbook. New York: Springer; 2011. p. 257–297.

78 Konstan JA, McNee SM, Ziegler , Torres R, Kapoor N, Riedl JT. Lessons on applying automated recommender systems to information-seeking tasks. Proceedings of the Twenty-First National Conference on Artificial Intelligence; 2006.

79 Wikimedia Foundation. Expected value of perfect information. Wikipedia. [Cited 2019 Aug 9.] Available from: https://en.wikipedia.org/wiki/Expected_value _of_perfect_information

80 ACM. SIGKDD—KDD Cup. [Cited 2018 Jul 2.] Available from: http://www .kdd.org/kdd-cup

81 Provost F, Fawcett T. Data science for business: What you need to know about data mining and data-analytic thinking. 1st ed., 2nd release. Beijing: O'Reilly; 2013.

82 Osherove R. Elastic leadership: growing self-organizing teams. Shelter Island, NY: Manning; 2017.

83 Bostrom N. Superintelligence: Paths, dangers, strategies. Oxford: Oxford University Press; 2014.

84 Bird S, Klein E, Loper E. Natural language processing with Python: Analyzing text with the natural language toolkit. Beijing; Cambridge MA: O'Reilly Media; 2009.

85 Kruchten PB. The 4+1 view model of architecture. IEEE Software. 1995 Nov; 12(6):42–50.

86 Wikimedia Foundation. 4+1 architectural view model. Wikipedia. [Cited 2017 Mar 25.] Available from: https://en.wikipedia.org/w/index.php?title=4%2B1 _architectural_view_model&oldid=772138375

87 Sculley D, et al. Machine learning: The high interest credit card of technical debt. Google AI. 2014 [cited 02-Jul-2018]. Available from: https://ai.google/research/ pubs/pub43146

88 Conway M. Conway's law. Datamation. 1968 Apr.

89 Wikimedia Foundation. Conway's law. Wikipedia. [Cited 2018 May 6.] Available from: https://en.wikipedia.org/w/index.php?title=Conway%27s_law&oldid=839 894590

90 Dahl G. Starting simple and machine learning in meds. [Cited 2018 Jul 2.] Available from: https://soundcloud.com/talkingmachines/episode-nine-starting-simple -and-machine-learning-in-meds

91 TensorFlow. An end-to-end open source machine learning platform. TensorFlow. [Cited 2019 Jul 24.] Available from: https://www.tensorflow.org/

92 image-net.org. ImageNet. ImageNet. [Cited 2019 Jul 24.] Available from: http:// www.image-net.org/

93 Apple, Inc. iOS 12. Apple. [Cited 2019 Jul 25.] Available from: https://www .apple.com/ios/ios-12/

94 Google, Inc. Android: The world's most popular mobile platform. Android. [Cited 2019 Jul 25.] Available from: https://www.android.com/

95 Fowler M. Who needs an architect? IEEE Spectrum. 2003 Oct;20(5).

96 Bass L, Clements P, Kazman R Software architecture in practice. Reading, MA: Addison-Wesley; 1998.

97 Wikimedia Foundation. Architecture tradeoff analysis method. Wikipedia. [Cited 2019 Aug 12.] Available from: https://en.wikipedia.org/w/index.php?title =Architecture_tradeoff_analysis_method&oldid=909460419

98 Poppendieck M, Poppendieck T. Lean software development: An Agile toolkit. Boston: Addison-Wesley Professional; 2003.

99 Kuhn M. The caret package. [Cited 2018 Jul 2.] Available from: http://topepo .github.io/caret/index.html

100 Meng X, Bradley J, Sparks E, Venkataraman S. ML pipelines: A new high-level API for MLlib. Databricks. 2015 Jan 7 [cited 2019 Jul 26]. Available from: https:// databricks.com/blog/2015/01/07/ml-pipelines-a-new-high-level-api-for-mllib.html

101 Google, Inc. TensorFlow Extended (TFX) is an end-to-end platform for deploying production ML pipelines. TensorFlow. [Cited 2019 Jul 26.] Available from: https:// www.tensorflow.org/tfx

102   LeCun Y, Cortes C, Burges C. MNIST handwritten digit database. [Cited 2019 Jul 24.] Available from: http://yann.lecun.com/exdb/mnist/

103   Krunic V. What should your analytics organization focus on? In: Gorelik A. The enterprise big data lake: Delivering the promise of big data and data science. Sebastopol, CA: O'Reilly Media; 2019. p. 56–59.

104   Benenson R. What is the class of this image? Discover the current state of the art in objects classification. 2016 Feb 22 [cited 2017 Apr 21]. Available from: https://rodrigob.github.io/are_we_there_yet/build/classification_datasets_results

105   Domingos P. The master algorithm: How the quest for the ultimate learning machine will remake our world. New York: Basic Books; 2015.

106   Goodfellow I, Yoshua B, and Aaron C. Deep learning. Cambridge, MA: MIT Press; 2017.

107   Cortes C, Vapnik V. Support-vector networks. Machine Learning. 1995 Sep;20(3): 273–297.

108   Wikimedia Foundation. Support-vector machine. Wikipedia. [Cited 2019 Jul 26.] Available from: https://en.wikipedia.org/w/index.php?title=Support-vector_machine&oldid=906858102

109   Wikimedia Foundation. Autoregressive integrated moving average. Wikipedia. [Cited 2019 Aug 9.] Available from: https://en.wikipedia.org/w/index.php?title=Autoregressive_integrated_moving_average&oldid=908993535

110   Wikimedia Foundation. Long short-term memory. Wikipedia. [Cited 2019 Aug 9.] Available from: https://en.wikipedia.org/w/index.php?title=Long_short-term_memory&oldid=909220363

111   Bischl, B. Machine learning in R. [Cited 2019 Nov 16.] Available from: https://mlr-org.com/

112   Kuhn M, Johnson, K. Applied predictive modeling. New York: Springer; 2013.

113   Keras documentation. [Cited 2018 Jul 2.] Available from: https://keras.io/

114   Wikimedia Foundation. Minimax. Wikipedia. [Cited 2019 July 29.] Available from: https://en.wikipedia.org/wiki/Minimax

115   Wikimedia Foundation. Sensitivity analysis. Wikipedia. [Cited 2019 Jun 20.] Available from: https://en.wikipedia.org/w/index.php?title=Sensitivity_analysis&oldid=846760482

116   Loucks DP, van Beek E. Water resource systems planning and management: An introduction to methods, models, and applications. New York: Springer; 2017.

117   Saltelli A, et al. Global sensitivity analysis: The primer. Chichester, UK: John Wiley & Sons, Ltd.; 2007.

118   Agile Alliance. What is Agile software development? Agile Alliance. [Cited 2015 Jun 29.] Available from: https://www.agilealliance.org/agile101/

119   Wikimedia Foundation. Agile software development. Wikipedia. [Cited 2017 Jul 3.] Available from: https://en.wikipedia.org/w/index.php?title=Agile_software_development

120 Tucker FG, Zivan SM, Camp RC. How to measure yourself against the best. Harvard Business Review. 1987 Jan 1 [cited 2018 Jul 7]. Available from: https://hbr.org/1987/01/how-to-measure-yourself-against-the-best

121 Hu B, Chen Y, Keogh E. Time series classification under more realistic assumptions. Proceedings of the 2013 SIAM International Conference on Data Mining. 2013:578–586.

122 Wikimedia Foundation. Uncanny valley. Wikipedia. [Cited 2019 Dec 9.] Available from: https://en.wikipedia.org/wiki/Uncanny_valley

123 St. George D. Automation dependency: 'Children of the magenta'. Aviation Ideas and Discussion! [Cited 2019 Dec 9.] Available from: https://safeblog.org/2016/01/14/automation-dependency-children-of-the-magenta/

124 Derczynski L. Complementarity, F-score, and NLP evaluation. Proceedings of the Tenth International Conference on Language Resources and Evaluation (LREC'16), Portorož, Slovenia. 2016:261–266.

125 Taleb NN, Douady R. Mathematical definition, mapping, and detection of (anti)fragility. arXiv. 2012 Aug;arXiv:1208.1189 [q-fin.RM].

126 Taleb NN, Canetti E, Kinda T, Loukoianova E, Schmieder C. A new heuristic measure of fragility and tail risks: Application to stress testing. IMF Working Papers. 2012 Aug;12.

127 Taleb NN. The black swan: the impact of the highly improbable. 2nd ed. New York: Random House Trade Paperbacks; 2010.

128 Johnson K. Nvidia trains world's largest Transformer-based language model. VentureBeat. [Cited 2019 Aug 19.] Available from: https://venturebeat.com/2019/08/13/nvidia-trains-worlds-largest-transformer-based-language-model/

129 Halevy A, Norvig P, Pereira F. The unreasonable effectiveness of data. IEEE Intelligent Systems. 2009 Mar;24(2):8–12.

130 MMC Ventures. The state of AI: Divergence. 2019 [cited 2020 Jan 13]. Available from: https://www.stateofai2019.com/

131 Wikimedia Foundation. Artificial intelligence: Definitions. [Cited 2019 May 22.] Available from: https://en.wikipedia.org/wiki/Artificial_intelligence#Definitions

132 Poole DL, Mackworth AK, Goebel R. Computational intelligence: A logical approach. New York: Oxford University Press; 1998.

133 Kaplan A, Haenlein M. Siri, Siri, in my hand: Who's the fairest in the land? On the interpretations, illustrations, and implications of artificial intelligence. Business Horizons. 2019 Jan;62(1):15–25.

134 Wikimedia Foundation. AI effect. Wikipedia. [Cited 2019 Sep 10.] Available from: https://en.wikipedia.org/w/index.php?title=AI_effect&oldid=915081794

135 Wikimedia Foundation. Deep Blue (chess computer). Wikipedia. [Cited 2019 Sep 10.] Available from: https://en.wikipedia.org/wiki/Deep_Blue_(chess_computer)

136   Techopedia. Artificial intelligence. Techopedia.com. [Cited 2019 Sep 10.] Available from: https://www.techopedia.com/definition/190/artificial-intelligence-ai

137   Mnih V, et al. Playing Atari with deep reinforcement learning. arXiv. 2013 Dec; arXiv:1312.5602 [cs.LG].

138   Simonite T. When it comes to gorillas, Google Photos remains blind. WIRED. 2018 Jan 11 [cited 2018 Jul 2]. Available from: https://www.wired.com/story/when-it-comes-to-gorillas-google-photos-remains-blind/

139   Gallagher S. UK, Australia, others also ground Boeing 737 MAX after crash [Updated]. Ars Technica. 2019 Mar 12 [cited 2020 Jan 8]. Available from: https://arstechnica.com/information-technology/2019/03/another-737-max-jet-crash-prompts-groundings-by-china-indonesia-ethiopia/

140   Wikimedia Foundation. Maneuvering Characteristics Augmentation System. Wikipedia. [Cited 2019 Sep 10.] Available from: https://en.wikipedia.org/w/index.php?title=Maneuvering_Characteristics_Augmentation_System&oldid=9148 99059

141   Leggett T. What went wrong inside Boeing's cockpit? BBC News. [Cited 2020 Jan 8.] Available from: https://www.bbc.co.uk/news/resources/idt-sh/boeing_two _deadly_crashes

142   Wikimedia Foundation. Boeing 737 MAX groundings. Wikipedia. [Cited 2020 Jan 8.] Available from: https://en.wikipedia.org/w/index.php?title=Boeing_737 _MAX_groundings&oldid=934819447

143   Wikimedia Foundation. Smart city. Wikipedia. [Cited 2019 Sep 10.] Available from: https://en.wikipedia.org/wiki/Smart_city

144   Tesla Autopilot—Review including full self-driving for 2019. AutoPilot Review. 2019 Apr 23 [cited 2019 Sep 7]. Available from: https://www.autopilotreview .com/tesla-autopilot-features-review/

145   Papernot N, McDaniel P, Goodfellow I, Jha S, Celik ZB, Swami A. Practical black-box attacks against machine learning. arXiv. 2016 Feb;arXiv:1602.02697 [cs.CR].

146   Goodfellow I, et al. Generative adversarial networks. arXiv. 2014 Jun;arXiv: 1406.2661 [stat.ML].

147   Eykholt K, et al. Robust physical-world attacks on deep learning models. arXiv. 2017 Jul;arXiv:1707.08945 [cs.CR].

148   Lei Q, Wu L, Chen P-Y, Dimakis AG, Dhillon IS, and Witbrock M. Discrete adversarial attacks and submodular optimization with applications to text classification. arXiv. 2018 Dec;arXiv:1812.00151 [cs.LG].

149   Shokri R, Stronati M, Song C, Shmatikov V. Membership inference attacks against machine learning models. arXiv. 2016 Oct;arXiv:1610.05820 [cs.CR].

150   Tramèr F, Zhang F, Juels A, Reiter MK, Ristenpart T. Stealing machine learning models via prediction APIs. arXiv. 2016 Sep;arXiv:1609.02943 [cs.CR].

151   Marcus G. Deep learning: A critical appraisal. arXiv. 2018 Jan;arXiv:1801.00631 [cs.AI].

152 Anderson C. The end of theory: The data deluge makes the scientific method obsolete. WIRED. 2008 Jun 23 [cited 2018 Jul 2]. Available from: https://www.wired.com/2008/06/pb-theory/

153 Wikimedia Foundation. AlphaGo versus Lee Sedol. Wikipedia. [Cited 2018 Jun 21.] Available from: https://en.wikipedia.org/w/index.php?title=AlphaGo_versus_Lee_Sedol&oldid=846917953

154 DeepMind. AlphaGo. DeepMind. [Cited 2018 Jul 2.] Available from: https://deepmind.com/research/alphago/

155 Wikimedia Foundation. AlphaGo. Wikipedia. [Cited 2019 Jul 10.] Available from: https://en.wikipedia.org/w/index.php?title=AlphaGo

156 The AlphaStar Team. AlphaStar: Mastering the real-time strategy game StarCraft II. DeepMind. [Cited 2019 Sep 9.] Available from: https://deepmind.com/blog/article/alphastar-mastering-real-time-strategy-game-starcraft-ii

157 Caruana R, Simard P, Weinberger K, LeCun Y. The great AI debate—NIPS2017. 2017.

158 Xian Y, Schiele B, Akata Z. Zero-shot learning—The good, the bad and the ugly. arXiv. 2017 Mar;arXiv:1703.04394 [cs.CV].

159 Wikimedia Foundation. Knowledge graph. Wikipedia. [Cited 2019 Sep 10.] Available from: https://en.wikipedia.org/wiki/Knowledge_Graph

160 Zhou J, et al. Graph neural networks: A review of methods and applications. arXiv. 2018 Dec;arXiv:1812.08434 [cs.LG].

161 Zhang Z, Cui P, Zhu W. Deep learning on graphs: A survey. arXiv. 2018 Dec; arXiv:1812.04202 [cs.LG].

162 Sutton R. The bitter lesson. Incomplete Ideas. 2019 Mar 13 [cited 2019 Apr 8]. Available from: http://www.incompleteideas.net/IncIdeas/BitterLesson.html

163 Wikimedia Foundation. Complex system. Wikipedia. [Cited 2018 Jul 1.] Available from: https://en.wikipedia.org/w/index.php?title=Complex_system&oldid=848412761

164 Marcus GT, Davis E. Rebooting AI: Building artificial intelligence we can trust. New York: Pantheon Books; 2019.

165 GPS.gov. GPS accuracy. NOAA. [Cited 2019 Sep 7] Available from: https://www.gps.gov/systems/gps/performance/accuracy/

166 Wikimedia Foundation. Anomaly detection. Wikipedia. [Cited 2018 May 16.] Available from: https://en.wikipedia.org/w/index.php?title=Anomaly_detection&oldid=841569898

167 Burt A. Is there a 'right to explanation' for machine learning in the GDPR? [Cited 2019 Sep 9.] Available from: https://iapp.org/news/a/is-there-a-right-to-explanation-for-machine-learning-in-the-gdpr/

168 Hall P, Gill N. An introduction to machine learning interpretability. Sebastopol, CA: O'Reilly Media, Inc.; 2018.

169 Ribeiro MT, Singh S, Guestrin C. 'Why should I trust you?': Explaining the predictions of any classifier. arXiv. 2016 Feb;arXiv:1602.04938 [cs.LG].

170 Microsoft Corporation. FATE: Fairness, accountability, transparency, and ethics in AI. *Microsoft Research.* [Cited 2019 Sep 9.] Available from: https://www.microsoft .com/en-us/research/group/fate/

171 Pichai S. AI at Google: Our principles. Google. 2018 Jun 7 [cited 2018 Jun 30]. Available from: https://www.blog.google/technology/ai/ai-principles/

172 O'Neil C. Weapons of math destruction: How big data increases inequality and threatens democracy. New York: Crown; 2016.

173 Corbett-Davies S, Goel S. The measure and mismeasure of fairness: A critical review of fair machine learning. arXiv. 2018 Jul;arXiv:1808.00023 [cs.CY].

174 Zöller M-A, Huber MF. Benchmark and survey of automated machine learning frameworks. arXiv. 2019 Apr;arXiv:1904.12054 [cs.LG].

175 He X, Zhao K, Chu X. AutoML: A survey of the state-of-the-art. arXiv. 2019 Aug; arXiv:1908.00709 [cs.LG].

176 Silver D, et al. Mastering the game of Go with deep neural networks and tree search. Nature. 2016 Jan;529(7587):484–489.

177 Google, Inc. Cloud AutoML. Google Cloud. [Cited 2019 Sep 9.] Available from: https://cloud.google.com/automl/docs/

178 Microsoft Corporation. What is automated machine learning? Microsoft Azure. [Cited 2019 Sep 9.] Available from: https://docs.microsoft.com/en-us/azure/ machine-learning/service/concept-automated-ml

179 Amazon.com, Inc. H2O.ai H2O-3 Automl Algorithm. AWS Marketplace. [Cited 2019 Sep 9.] Available from: https://aws.amazon.com/marketplace/pp/H2Oai-H2Oai-H2O-3-Automl-Algorithm/prodview-vbm2cls5zcnky

180 O'Reilly T. WTF: What's the future and why it's up to us. New York: Harper Business, an imprint of HarperCollins Publishers; 2017.

181 Google, Inc. Classification: Accuracy. Machine Learning Crash Course. Google Developers. [Cited 2019 Sep 29.] Available from: https://developers.google.com/ machine-learning/crash-course/classification/accuracy

182 Wikimedia Foundation. Actuary. Wikipedia. [Cited 2019 Sep 12.] Available from: https://en.wikipedia.org/w/index.php?title=Actuary&oldid=914560578

183 Wikimedia Foundation. Bias–variance tradeoff. Wikipedia. [Cited 2019 Jul 25.] Available from: https://en.wikipedia.org/w/index.php?title=Bias%E2%80%93 variance_tradeoff&oldid=904412736

184 Wikimedia Foundation. Cross-industry standard process for data mining. Wikipedia. [Cited 2019 Jul 12.] https://en.wikipedia.org/w/index.php?title=Cross-industry_standard_process_for_data_mining

185 Needham J. Disruptive possibilities: How big data changes everything. Beijing: O'Reilly; 2013.

186 Wikimedia Foundation. Opportunity cost. Wikipedia. [Cited 2019 Oct 7.] Available from: https://en.wikipedia.org/w/index.php?title=Opportunity_cost &oldid =916733399

187 Kenton W. Quantitative Analysis (QA) Definition. Investopedia. [Cited 2019 Oct 10.] Available from: https://www.investopedia.com/terms/q/quantitative-analysis.asp

188 Wikimedia Foundation. Mean squared error. Wikipedia. [Cited 2019 Sep 29.] Available from: https://en.wikipedia.org/wiki/Mean_squared_error

189 Object Management Group, Inc. What is UML. [Cited 2019 Sep 11]. Available from: http://uml.org/what-is-uml.htm

190 Kotter International. 8-step process. [Cited 2019 Jul 15.] Available from: https://www.kotterinc.com/8-steps-process-for-leading-change/

191 Kaggle, Inc. Kaggle: Your home for data science. Kaggle. [Cited 2018 Jul 2.] Available from: https://www.kaggle.com/

index